The Modern Spanish Economy

The Modern Spanish Economy

Transformation and Integration into Europe

by

Keith G. Salmon

Pinter Publishers
London and New York

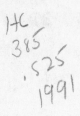

First published in Great Britain in 1991 by
Pinter Publishers Limited
25 Floral Street, London WC2E 9DS

British Library Cataloguing in Publication Data

A CIP catalogue record for this book is available from the
British Library
ISBN 0 86187 132 4

For enquiries in North America please contact PO Box 197, Irvington, NY 10533

Library of Congress Cataloging-in-Publication Data

Salmon, Keith G., 1947-
    The modern Spanish economy : transformation and integration into Europe / by Keith G. Salmon.
      p. cm.
    Includes bibliographical references and index.
    ISBN 0-86187-132-4
    1. Spain–Economic–conditions–1975- 2. Spain–Economic policy.
3. European Economic Community–Spain. I. Title.
HC385.S25 1991   90-22281
338.946–dc20   CIP

Typeset by Communitype Communications Ltd
Printed and bound in Great Britain by Biddles Ltd

Contents

List of figures

List of tables

Notes

One billion is used throughout the book to refer to one thousand million

—   In the tables this symbol refers to 'no data available'

Te recuerdo como eras en el último otoño.
Eras la boina gris y el corazón en calma.
En tus ojos peleaban las llamas del crepúsculo.
Y las hojas caían en el agua de tu alma.
Pablo Neruda

Where three roads joined it was green and fair,
And over a gate was the sun-glazed sea,
And life laughed sweet when I halted there;
Yet there I never again would be.
Thomas Hardy

To all those who have sacrificed their time and provided invaluable encouragement and assistance in the production of this book; especially Jenny, Alfonso Pajuelo, Rogelio Velasco, Francisco Mochón, Francisco Zambrana, Vicente Granados, Joaquin Aurioles, Damian López Cano and many others at the University of Málaga, as well as my parents and many friends.

Keith G. Salmon
July 1990

ISLAS CANARIAS

Te   La

0   Km   50

PROVINCES
Al   Alicante
Av   Avila
Ba   Barcelona
Ca   Cástellon
Gu   Guipúzcoa
La   Las Palmas
Pa   Palencia
Po   Pontevedra
Ta   Tarragona
Te   S.C. Tenerife
Vi   Vizcaya

REGIONS
CA   CANTABRIA
NA   NAVARRA
PV   PAIS VASCO

Provinces and regions in Spain

◆ Chapter 1 ◆

Evolution and structure of the Spanish economy

1.1 Evolution of the Spanish economy

The contemporary structure of the Spanish economy reflects its own peculiar evolution perhaps more than that of other western economies, in part a result of previous isolation from the global economy and from modern western currents of social change. The roots of this individualism can be traced to the Reconquest and the formation of the Spanish state in the Middle Ages. Wealth and power were polarised as a land-tenure system emerged that left central and southern Spain dominated by large estates. This power base was then protected through successive centuries by the Church, the large landowners, the army and the central government (composed largely of the same élite group of people). Between them these groups suffocated innovation and social mobility, preventing the emergence of a significant group of urban industrial capitalists who might have challenged the system, and maintaining the elements of a traditional society into the mid twentieth century: 'If the process of economic modernization is characterized by a systematic effort to implement more efficient ways of production and distribution, then Spain did not start modernizing until the early 1960s' (Lieberman, 1982; pp.7–8). There was no Spanish Renaissance in the sixteenth century, no social revolution as in France in the eighteenth century or social evolution as in England, neither was there any agricultural or industrial revolution.

While a sense of history is important in understanding contemporary economic development, it is equally important that images of the past do not obscure current reality. This is especially true where economic change has been rapid and past images have been very strong, as in Spain. Thus an analysis of the contemporary economy must incorporate history in so far as it explains current processes, but it must simultaneously extricate itself from past perceptions.

1.2 The Francoist economy: autarchy 1939–59

In the decade or so after the the Nationalist victory in the Civil War, the system of intervention and protection that had been built up in the early twentieth century was reinforced around the political dictatorship of General Franco. The semi-fascist Falange provided the dominant ideology, the Movimiento (Falangists and

Carlists) providing most of the ministers and high functionaries of the major government economic departments. Clearly rejecting *laissez-faire* principles, in retreat since 1891, the huge interventionist apparatus was aimed at establishing complete control over the economy. Controls covered wages, prices, agricultural output, trade (through quantitative restrictions on imports, foreign exchange and investment controls) and direct state participation in the economy. The latter was most clearly demonstrated in the formation of a series of state companies (for example in energy, Endesa, and in transport equipment, EN Bazan, Enasa and Seat), mostly under the umbrella of the state holding company, the National Industry Institute (Instituto Nacional de Industria (INI)). Alongside this restrictive economic regime was a repressive political system that denied civil liberties and quashed initiative. Free trade unions were banned, and they were replaced by 'sindicatos' that represented both employers and employees in a given field of economic activity and operated in effect as organs of the government, principally serving the interests of the state. The highest development priority was given to the quest for self-sufficiency, promoted through such legislation as the Law of Protection and Development of National Industry (Ley de Protección y Fomento de la Industria Nacional) (1939): 'During the period 1939–59, Spain presents the historian with an almost unique study in autarchic development' (Lieberman, 1982).

Autarchic development was centred around a policy of rapid industrialisation based on import substitution and guided by the desire for self-sufficiency. Public enterprises were set up to achieve this objective. The policy also meant a decoupling of Spain from the international economy. Thus in 1950 trade represented only five per cent of the gross national product (GNP). However, this extreme level of isolation was not only the outcome of internal policy but resulted too from decisions taken by the international community, as illustrated by the United Nations decision to institute an economic boycott of Spain (taken in 1946 and not rescinded until 1953) and by the exclusion of Spain from the European Recovery Programme (Marshall Aid, 1948).

Reconstruction of the Spanish economy after the Civil War was long drawn out both because of the damage wrought by the Civil War itself and because of the international environment faced by the country in the 1940s and early 1950s. The Civil War brought immense human loss in terms of the dead and injured (perhaps one million dead during and immediately after the Civil War), losses through emigration and a bitter human legacy. There was also widespread damage to physical structures. Following the Civil War there was a severe shortage of materials occasioned first by the Second World War and then by the international isolation of Spain. Not until 1950 did the index of industrial production rise above its level in 1929, and in agriculture regeneration was even more tardy, remaining below its late 1920s level of production until 1958 (Carreras, 1989).

During the 1940s and 1950s the Spanish economy struggled to survive, isolated from the mainstream of development building in the western economies. In 1950 manufacturing industry still represented only a small part of the economy (about eighteen per cent of the economically active population), while almost fifty per cent of the economically active population remained in agriculture. The population was essentially poor, with real incomes per capita only about one third of those in 1980 (Carreras, 1989). This small domestic market (28 million people in 1950), energy and raw material shortages as well as poor communications combined to frustrate autarchic development. Costly industrialisation and agricultural policies created consumer goods shortages and inflation (rising to 15.5 per cent in 1957). The balance of trade recorded a series of deficits (Tena, 1989), running down foreign exchange reserves and reflecting an overvalued currency. By the late 1950s these problems had reached crisis proportions. There was a high level of inflation, the value of the peseta was in decline outside of Spain, and balance-of-payments deficits, coupled with the lack of foreign-exchange reserves, threatened to bankrupt the country.

1.3 The Francoist economy: economic miracle 1959–73

The keys to the 'economic miracle', which propelled Spain from the ranks of the less developed countries to an industrialised country, were changes in the political outlook of those controlling the economy and the desire by Spaniards for modernisation (Fuentes Quintana, 1988), together with a break in the extreme isolation and autarchy of the early 1950s. An initial break in isolation came in 1953 with a defence agreement enabling United States military bases to be established in Spain. In return Spain received substantial economic aid (estimated at $625 million between 1951 and 1957). Cabinet changes in 1957 brought to prominence a new group of technocrats (associated with the Opus Dei) less wedded to autarchic policies than their predecessors. In 1958 Spain became a member of the World Bank and in 1959 a member of the International Monetary Fund (IMF), and subsequently part of the Organisation for European Economic Cooperation (OEEC).

The prelude to economic growth in the 1960s and early 1970s was thus set in changing internal economic perspectives and increased international recognition of the Spanish regime: changes that were marked by the adoption of the Stabilisation Plan of 1959 (Plan Nacional de Estabilización Económica), which heralded a significant change in Spanish economic policy and the end of autarchy. The Plan emerged following visits and recommendations from the OEEC and the International Bank for Reconstruction and Development. The Plan (underwritten by foreign aid) was characterised by deflationary and tight monetary policies embracing: i) a reduction in public expenditure and lending to the public sector; ii) restrictions on lending to the private sector; iii) increased prices for public services; iv) higher interest rates; v) devaluation of the peseta exchange rate within Spain and an end to multiple exchange rates and vi) measures to liberalise foreign investment and trade. The immediate impact of the Plan was an improvement in the balance of payments coupled with a severe recession (increased unemployment and reduced demand).

The fact that measures taken under the Stabilisation Plan did not trigger a long drawn out recession but were followed by an 'economic miracle' was due to favourable external factors. The international economy (especially that of north-west Europe) was growing, providing a market for Spanish goods and direct employment for substantial numbers of Spanish migrants (remitting equally substantial sums of money back to Spain). Tourism was emerging as a leading sector, generating considerable direct employment and income together with important multiplier effects in related industries such as transport and construction. In addition, foreign investment had returned. Thus a Plan that was designed to promote stability in the economy actually contributed to a period of rapid growth (Fuentes Quintana, 1988)!

Despite the pronouncements made in the Stabilisation Plan to liberalise the economy and some moves in this direction, in practice protectionism remained alongside new forms of intervention. For example, 'acción concertada' involved joint action between the private sector and the government, which gave discretionary assistance. Government assistance was also given, especially to the traditional sectors of shipbuilding and steel. The involvement of INI in the economy expanded, for example in the Asturian steel complex Uninsa and the coal mining group Hunosa. Nationalisation of the Bank of Spain in 1962 provided increased government control over the banking system. In trade the tariff structure was carefully graded to give most protection to consumer goods with lower tariffs for intermediate goods and the lowest tariffs for capital goods. There were also incentives to export, including tax rebates, official credit and insurance. This continuing excessive protectionism distorted the market and stored up problems for the future.

Indicative national planning (through a series of National Development Plans (Planes de Desarrollo Nacional)) and regional planning were embraced by the government in the 1960s. Planning was not very successful, partly due to a weak technical base and the existence of a large, inefficient public sector. Indeed it may have been detrimental in that it directed attention away from fundamental institutional reform and a more efficient allocation of resources. An enormous apparatus of complex discretionary grants and loans was set up favouring those within the privileged circle (circuitos privilegiados de crédito). Public investment in the 1960s was directed particularly at those sectors suffering problems of adaption to the changing economic climate or at basic industry: for example, chemicals, steel, shipbuilding and transport equipment, which were often not very technologically advanced but were experiencing rapid economic growth. Thus while development was stimulated by the Stabilisation Plan, it was hindered by the National Development Plans (Fuentes Quintana, 1988)!

The Spanish 'economic miracle' of the 1960s is clearly documented by both the growth and changing composition of the gross domestic product (GDP). Between 1959 and 1971 the average annual growth of GDP was about seven per cent, surpassed at the time only by Japan. GDP doubled in real terms during the 1960s, narrowing the development gap with other countries; thus in 1953 GDP was fourteen per cent that of France and twenty-two per cent that of Italy, in 1965 it was twenty-two per cent that of France and thirty-nine per cent that of Italy, and in 1974 it was twenty-three per cent that of France and forty per cent that of Italy. The growth of gross domestic industrial product (value added by the industrial sector) was even more rapid, growing in real terms at an annual average rate of 9.4 per cent between 1960 and 1973.

Growth was matched by structural and spatial change in the economy. The proportion of the labour force employed in agriculture declined sharply, while that in services grew. Energy consumption switched decisively from coal to oil and increasing use was made of capital in place of labour. In industry, synthetic materials replaced many traditional products and the composition of production changed towards the greater importance of capital goods industries: metallurgy, construction materials, chemicals and transport equipment. Spatially, a new prosperity began to emerge around the coast, led by tourism but also including new agricultural and industrial developments. These patterns of economic change were accompanied by rural out migration and depopulation of the interior, urbanisation and the growth of coastal populations. However, broad expanses of industry (including steel and textiles) remained technologically backward, small in size and protected by high tariffs. There was excessive geographical concentration of growth, which was at the root of wide spatial variations in per-capita incomes. Unemployment was contained only by mass emigration (a process sponsored by an active government emigration policy).

Increased foreign trade and foreign investment were important features of economic growth: 'The rapid growth of foreign trade and of foreign investment constituted the most salient features of the evolution of the Spanish economy in the 1960s' (Lieberman, 1982). Imports rose from seven per cent of GNP in 1960 to seventeen per cent in 1970, and exports from ten to fifteen per cent of GNP. The growth of imports was associated with rapid industrialisation and rising incomes: thus industrial raw materials, semi-finished and finished goods increased in importance to represent seventy-five per cent of total imports in 1970. Exports of manufactured goods increased, with industrial equipment and consumer goods becoming more important relative to raw materials and agricultural products. The massive growth of imports and deficits on the balance of trade were largely financed by tourism earnings, migrant remittances and foreign investment, which ensured that the balance of payments current account was generally in surplus.

Foreign investment (especially by US, West German and Swiss firms) was generally directed towards high-technology industry and services, and was spatially concentrated in Madrid, Cataluña and País Vasco. Investment was attracted by labour-force considerations (abundant labour derived both from the agricultural sector and from increased female participation in the labour force, low labour costs and weak union organisation) and the protected and expanding market (for example, in the motor-vehicle industry, authorisation for foreign investment was given only on condition that the domestic market would be protected). Other multinationals were established in sectors with low import duties and where products could not be produced by Spanish companies.

Rapid economic growth in the 1960s masked problems embedded in both the organisation and structure of the economy. The Stabilisation Plan had not led to a market economy; rather there had been a further evolution of corporate capitalism permeated by state intervention. Factor markets, especially the labour market, were inflexible. The taxation system was poorly developed (resulting in a noticeable lack of public goods, contributing to private affluence amidst public squalor) and many institutions (for example accountancy and insurance) were antiquated. Problems in the industrial structure were fundamentally those of small scale and the prevalence of traditional industries using traditional technologies. Hence the character of Spanish industry was midway between that of a newly industrialising country and an advanced industrial one, with competitive advantage often based on relatively low labour costs in traditional industries.

Public policy measures, developed within the context of the rapid economic growth of the 1960s, further emphasised the concentration on traditional industries through investment in increasing their capacity, while giving little attention to stimulating innovation and technological development. An example of the lack of attention given to promoting a climate of technological change was that associated with the law governing patents. Until 1985 patents were covered by the Industrial Property Law (Estatuto de la Propriedad Industrial (1929)), which provided inadequate protection for the inventors of new products.

1.4 Economic crisis, political transition and preparation for membership of the European Community (1974–85)

International recession was triggered by oil price rises commencing in 1973. Between January 1973 and January 1974 the Organisation of Petroleum Exporting Countries (OPEC) succeeded in raising the price of crude oil by almost 500 per cent. At that time crude oil constituted fifty-five per cent of Organisation for Economic Co-operation and Development (OECD) energy sources, of which about seventy-five per cent was imported. The shock to the international economic system of these sharp price increases was to reverberate through the following decade, spawning a reappraisal of production processes that led to de-industrialisation in traditional manufacturing areas, shifts in the international division of labour and a reorganisation of energy use; in OECD countries unemployment increased and the phenomenon of stagflation (stagnation in growth accompanied by inflation) appeared.

In Spain the economic miracle ground to a halt. Growth of the industrial product, which had been running at an annual average rate of 10.2 per cent between 1960 and 1973, fell to an average annual rate of 0.8 per cent between 1975 and 1983 (Pérez Simarro, 1987). Recession was broken by signs of recovery in 1978 (helped by a twenty per cent devaluation), renewed growth in tourism and increased foreign investment. But this recovery was strangled by further steep oil price rises at the turn of the decade that threw the economy into a severe crisis.

The particular path of the economic crisis in Spain was determined by the special characteristics of the Spanish political economy. The dominant factor was the transition from dictatorship to democracy following the death of General Franco in 1975. It was inevitable that in the late 1970s economic problems would be subordinated to political considerations as the political system moved cautiously towards democracy (the peaceful achievement of this political transition was thrown into sharp relief by the political changes sweeping through eastern Europe in 1989). Policy measures were also increasingly overlaid by preparations for entry into the European Community (EC) in 1986 and the adoption of a liberal and more open economy.

Lack of domestic energy resources and consequent dependence on imported energy left the Spanish economy particularly vulnerable to increased oil prices. In 1973 oil accounted for 68.3 per cent of Spain's energy requirements. Increased energy costs thus affected both production costs and the balance of payments. Industrial expansion in the 1960s and early 1970s had relied heavily on cheap oil. Consumption of energy increased by 170 per cent between 1961 and 1974 . Hence the vulnerability of the Spanish economy to oil price rises. Yet while in other OECD countries the consumption of primary energy per unit of GDP decreased from 1973, in Spain it continued to increase until the end of the 1970s. By 1978, 72.6 per cent of all energy requirements were based on oil, almost all of which was imported (Harrison, 1985). Energy imports as a proportion of the total import bill increased from twelve per cent in 1973 to twenty-four per cent in 1975 (Table 1.1). In 1978 the cost of Spanish energy imports was equivalent to forty-one per cent of the value of merchandise exports (Lieberman, 1982). After the second oil shock in 1979 the costs of imported energy rose even higher. By 1981 Spain spent pta. 1,253 billion on energy imports, equivalent to 43.9 per cent of the total merchandise trade import bill and 66.7 per cent of the total value of merchandise exports (Banco de Bilbao, 1982).

Table 1.1 Evolution of energy imports, 1973–89

Year	Total (pta. billion)	Energy (pta. billion)	Total ($ million)	Energy ($ million)	Percentage (energy/total)
1973	—	73	8,948	1,096	12.2
1975	—	241	15,193	3,662	24.1
1980	—	943	32,386	12,199	37.7
1981	—	1,253	31,186	13,682	43.9
1982	3,466	1,376	31,465	12,475	39.7
1985	5,115	1,835	29,963	10,665	35.9
1987	6,051	978	49,112	7,985	16.2
1988	6,989	790	54,428	6,369	11.3
1989	8,458	993	71,469	8,449	11.8

Sources: 1973 to 1981 from Mochón *et al.*, 1988; 1982 onwards from Banco de España, (1990)

Inflation accompanied economic stagnation in the 1970s (Table 1.2), reaching an annualised rate of thirty-seven per cent in the summer of 1977. High inflation resulted from the sustained increase in oil prices, huge public sector deficits, a permissive monetary policy and social peace bought at the cost of large rises in monetary wages in advance of increased productivity. Real wages in industry increased by 130 per cent between 1970 and 1982, more than in any other European country, while productivity increased by only forty-two per cent. Simultaneously, negative real rates of interest (with inflation higher than interest rates) contributed to increased borrowing and higher levels of company debt, which would result later in crippling financial burdens.

Unemployment increased sharply to become the most pressing political problem. This sharp increase resulted from domestic recession, technological change, an expanding population of working age, a continued increase in female labour participation rates and the curtailment of emigration coupled with the return of many former migrants (following growing employment problems in north west Europe). Agriculture and industry each shed over one million jobs between 1974 and 1982 (Harrison, 1985).

The extent to which the economy was 'managed' by the government and the

Table 1.2 Evolution of the economy, 1961–90

Year	GDP Growth* (%)	Inflation† (%)	Current-account balance	
			$ million	pta. billion
1973	8.5	11.8	557	35.1
1974	5.4	15.7	−3,245	−179.8
1975	1.1	17.0	−3,487	−177.9
1976	2.9	17.7	−4,294	−284.8
1977	2.6	24.5	−2,164	−161.6
1978	1.5	16.6	1,633	113.7
1979	−0.1	15.5	1,126	61.3
1980	1.2	15.2	−5,188	−365.5
1981	−0.2	14.4	−4,981	−459.7
1982	1.2	14.0	−4,102	−489.8
1983	1.8	12.2	−2,679	−340.2
1984	1.8	9.0	1,980	349.5
1985	2.3	8.1	2,654	449.3
1986	3.3	8.3	4,131	594.1
1987	5.5	4.6	1,233	98.8
1988	5.2	5.8	−3,098	−348.8
1989	4.9	6.9	−11,600	−1367.6
1990‡	4.1	6.5	−16,000	

‡ Figures for 1990 are forecasts

* GDP growth at constant market prices

† Inflation figure based on retail price index (Indice de Precios al Consumo), December to December)

Sources: Banco Bilbao Vizcaya, 1988; Banco de España (1990); *Carreras*, 1989; *El País*, 20 August 1989; *El País*, 1990; Mochón *et al.* 1988

rigidity of institutions and factor markets impeded automatic market responses and placed particular importance on government policy. In 1974 there was a climate of uncertainty following the assassination of Carrero Blanco and the illness of General Franco. Hence the policy response was to buy time by attempting to isolate the economy from the international recession (*política compensatoria*, abandoned in 1975). There was also a vain hope that recession would be short lived. Measures were implemented to stimulate internal demand and prevent domestic oil prices from rising. The immediate impact was a sharp deterioration in the balance of payments, exacerbated by a continued increase in oil consumption. Following the death of General Franco in November 1975 the political situation became even more delicate, haunted by the spectre of the previous attempt at democracy in a similarly adverse economic climate in the 1930s. Thus a highly permissive economic policy was adopted (*política permisiva*, 1976 to 1977) clearly linked to securing the transition to democracy. Wages were allowed to rise ahead of inflation, monetary policy was lax and the peseta was devalued by twenty per cent in 1977, with no attempt to reduce domestic demand

(Fuentes Quintana, 1988).

The first democratic elections in 1977 finally brought measures to adjust the economy to the recession and begin the difficult process of economic liberalisation. The policy of adjustment began with the Moncloa Pacts (Los Pactos de la Moncloa), agreed between all political parties, employers and trade unions: agreements that above all represented a commitment to democracy. The Moncloa Pacts also announced the broad direction of economic policy that was to continue through the years of crisis: a policy that allowed for the continued macro-economic management of a protected economy within the context of an overall commitment to a more freely working market economy, and international integration oriented especially towards eventual membership of the European Community. Policy was designed primarily to fight inflation and to create an economic environment in which the economy could grow and unemployment could be reduced. Strategy combined measures to control the money supply (monetary policy), measures to control government expenditure and reduce the public sector borrowing requirement (budgetary policy), and measures to control wages (incomes policy). In addition, steps were taken to improve the competitiveness of Spanish industry, to reform economic institutions and to increase the flexibility of factor markets. All this implied continued government intervention.

Continued government intervention was deemed necessary to dismantle the existing system of widespread regulation (required for entry to the European Community), to increase the flexibility of institutions and factor markets, to introduce the reforms necessary to harmonise economic practices in Spain with those in other western industrialised countries (especially those in the European Community), and above all to secure an orderly economic restructuring process in the face of the increased competition occasioned by a more open economy. A large slice of the Spanish economy remained uncompetitive and, without continued government intervention, much of this industry may have been lost. There were also other arguments in favour of government intervention, including the promotion of new industry and new labour-force skills. In practice, political necessities ensured that the main emphasis was actually on cushioning the effects of the restructuring process on traditional industries (although unemployment continued to rise from 8.8 per cent in 1979 to twenty-two per cent in 1985) and attracting foreign investment.

Following the election to government of the Socialist Party (PSOE) in 1982, a new urgency crept into economic policy, prompted by the imminence of entry into the European Community. Industrial reconversion plans were strengthened (while providing safeguards for the social costs involved). Measures to liberalise the economy, increase flexibility (especially in the labour market) and adopt international economic practices were accelerated. The general objective was to restructure the sectors in crisis and channel resources into new, more profitable, sectors. Liberalisation of the economy was to be achieved through a thorough overhaul of economic institutions.

The economic crisis brought a change in the comparative advantage of Spanish industry, as both energy and labour costs increased (Maravall, 1987 and Perez Simarro, 1986) and as Newly Industrialised Countries (NICs) emerged. Thus the economic crisis of the late 1970s and early 1980s was centred on those industries in which Spain had specialised in the 1960s, such as steel, shipbuilding, textiles and heavy chemicals.

1.5 The contemporary political economy

At the beginning of the 1990s the Spanish economy can be described as of medium size in relation to the economies of other European Community countries (GDP measured at current market prices of pta. 44,985 billion in 1989). It is less wealthy than its Community partners, with GDP per head greater only than that of Ireland, Greece and Portugal; GDP per head at purchasing power parities only seventy-five per cent that of the EC (Banco Bilbao Vizcaya, 1989). It is also an open economy, increasingly integrated into the European Community and the corporate space of multinational companies.

The economic crisis of the early 1980s was followed by rapid growth in the late 1980s, during which time the Spanish economy was the most dynamic in Europe, growing at an annual rate of between four and five per cent in the four years 1987 to 1990 (inclusive). Growth was driven by domestic demand, which grew at an annual average rate of 4.2 per cent between 1984 and 1989 (seven to eight per cent in 1989). Domestic demand benefited from real increases in incomes, greater employment and increased consumer credit (which grew by twenty per cent in 1989). Public consumption grew even more quickly, at 5.6 per cent a year. Gross capital formation grew at 11.2 per cent a year, such that in 1989 seventy per cent more was invested than in 1984. Similar pictures of growth were recorded in company investment, industrial production and corporate profits. Unfortunately, more rapid growth than in other OECD countries has resulted in symptoms of overheating, notably inflation and grave balance-of-payments problems. Rapidly rising consumer credit also contains the seeds of a private-debt crisis.

Further structural change has characterised contemporary economic development to leave an economy dominated by the service sector, which contributes over sixty per cent of the gross domestic product compared with less than fifty per cent in the early 1970s (Banco Bilbao Vizcaya, 1989). Expansion of employment in services has been dramatic (Table 1.3). In 1960 only twenty-seven per cent (3.1 million) of the occupied population were in services: by 1990 this figure had grown to fifty-four per cent (6.8 million). Tourism-related activities have been a particular focus of growth in services. By contrast, the importance of the agriculture sector has dwindled to between five and eight per cent of gross domestic product from around twelve per cent in the early 1970s. Employment in agriculture has displayed both a continued absolute and relative decline, although the sector remains large by north-west-European standards. In 1960 forty-two per cent of the occupied population (4.9 million people) were engaged in agriculture, a figure which had been reduced to thirteen per cent (1.6 million people) by 1990. The contribution of industry (including mining, gas, electricity and water) to the gross domestic product has fallen slightly since the early 1970s, from a little above to a little below thirty per cent. Industrial employment has declined to about twenty-four per cent of the occupied population, although in absolute terms employment is similar to that in 1960 (at 2.9 million). Finally, the

Spanish economy has retained a large construction industry, representing between seven and ten per cent of the occupied population (1.2 million people in 1990) and a similar percentage of the gross domestic product.

Table 1.3 Evolution of the labour force, 1960–90

	Occupied population					
	1960	%	1970	%	1975	%
Agriculture	4,855,800	41.7	3,662,300	29.2	2,751,100	21.7
Industry	2,874,400	24.7	3,583,100	28.6	3,599,000	28.4
Construction	797,000	6.8	1,042,000	8.3	1,238,600	9.8
Services	3,113,700	26.7	4,251,900	33.9	5,084,300	40.0
Total	11,640,900	100.0	12,539,300	100.0	12,673,000	100.0
	Occupied population					
	1980	%	1985	%	1990	%
Agriculture	2,253,600	19.1	2,023,300	19.0	1,574,600	12.6
Industry	3,188,400	27.1	2,612,500	24.6	2,981,400	23.9
Construction	1,050,700	8.9	744,100	7.0	1,174,200	9.4
Services	5,284,300	44.9	5,257,200	49.4	6,751,800	54.1
Total	11,777,000	100.0	10,637,100	100.0	12,481,900	100.0
	Economically active population					
	1980	%	1985	%	1990	%
Agriculture	2,362,700	17.8	2,242,500	16.5	1,766,400	11.8
Industry	3,429,800	25.9	3,135,300	23.0	3,273,400	21.8
Construction	1,359,000	10.2	1,208,500	8.9	1,398,000	9.3
Services	5,571,600	42.0	5,908,300	43.3	7,409,300	49.4
Unclassified	540,700	4.1	1,135,600	8.3	1,145,200	7.6
Total	13,263,800	100.0	13,630,200	100.0	14,922,400	100.0

Note: Figures refer to the first quarter of each year, except 1960

Source: INE, *Encuesta de la Población Activa*

The broad thrust of government policy in the late 1980s was to repudiate the dirigist and massively interventionist policies of the 'old regime', introducing instead market oriented reforms (involving liberalisation and increased flexibility of the economy), thereby aligning Spain with economic policies elsewhere in western Europe (Vickers and Wright, 1988). This alignment was emphasised by membership of the Exchange Rate Mechanism (ERM) of the European Monetary System (EMS) in June 1989 (within the wide band of + or − six per cent), a move that sacrificed a further degree of national control over the economy.

Restraining demand and containing inflation have been key policy objectives, pursued through the application of a tight monetary policy, associated with reducing the public-sector deficit, moderating salary increases and achieving greater productivity. Membership of the ERM particularly was hoped to provide a monetary discipline inside which inflation could be contained. After a year of membership inflation had been held at about seven per cent (the year-on-year rate having actually fallen from 7.1 per cent in June 1989 to 6.8 per cent in May 1990), although this may have been achieved more through the policy of high interest rates (in June 1990 the interbank rate stood at fifteen per cent) and bank lending restrictions than through the ERM. In this indirect way the government has sought to tackle the principal economic problem for society, that of the exceptionally high rate of unemployment (sixteen per cent at the beginning of 1990). Such a policy orientation has brought the government directly into confrontation with the unions, which have argued for more state promotion of employment. But even the General Strike in 1988 failed to shift the government's position.

1.5.1 Human Resources

The human resources of a country represent its most important asset, providing the drive and vitality on which economic change is based. From the population emerge the entrepreneurs to lead development, the administrators and the managers, the engineers and the designers. A successful economy and a healthy society must make adequate provision for developing the potential of its population to fulfil these roles and to contribute fully to society. In this respect a comprehensive system of education and training is essential, linked to a democratic meritocracy. From the population too springs the demand for goods and services, the magnitude of which is determined by the size of the population and per-capita incomes, while changing patterns of consumer preferences are bound up with cultural change.

The resident population of Spain in 1990 was estimated at a little over 39 million, which when set against the geographical area of the country (504,750 sq. km) yields one of the lowest population densities in western Europe (seventy-seven persons per square kilometre). The actual market, however, is much larger than that for the resident population alone, as to it must be added some 50 million visitors a year, adding several million to the population in the summer months.

The distribution of population is very uneven, concentrated around the coast and in dispersed population clusters in the interior, notably in the capital city of Madrid and in the other provincial capitals. Provinces with a coastline account for fifty-six per cent of the normally resident population (on thirty-one per cent of the area); the majority of these people are crowded along the coastal littoral. In practice the actual population around the coast is over sixty per cent, swollen in summer by foreign and Spanish tourists. Two of the three provinces with population densities in excess of 500 persons per square kilometre are found along the coast: Barcelona (595 per sq. km), and Vizcaya (532 per sq. km). The third, Madrid (592 per sq. km), accounts for 12.4 per cent of the total population (INE, 1986). These three provinces alone, covering just 3.6 per cent of the area of Spain, contain 27.5 per cent of the national population. The choice of Madrid as the national capital, located at the geographical heart of Spain, has served to retain a major population cluster in the interior. Outside of Madrid the interior is characterised by provinces in which population densities are less than half the

progressive accumulation of employment in the service sector of the economy and a continued decline of the proportion in the primary and secondary sectors. Between 1975 and 1985 agriculture shed some three quarters of a million jobs and industry almost one million, while there was a net gain of a quarter of a million jobs in services. Between 1985 and 1990 the most remarkable feature was the explosion of employment in services, adding one and a half million to the employment total. In industry employment stabilised but there was a continued substantial decrease in the occupied population in agriculture. Outside of these sectors a notable characteristic of the employment structure is the large proportion classified to construction, a group particularly vulnerable to cyclical changes in the economy. While there is still some scope for further labour shedding from agriculture, this labour reservoir will gradually diminish (although the submerged economy and higher female participation rates will provide additional sources of labour).

Rigidity has been a particular feature of the labour market, maintaining uneconomic overstaffing and discouraging employment creation. There has been a long tradition of job security. Dismissals necessitated large redundancy payments (often much in excess of that stipulated by labour legislation), which tended to strengthen workers' bargaining power in collective wage negotiations. Moreover, the very limited possibility up until the mid 1980s for employers to use part-time or fixed-term contracts tended to increase average labour costs through overtime payments to existing workers. In the late 1970s and early 1980s successive governments were unable to break away from this tradition, needing to retain the support of the new trade unions. Rent controls, inadequate training facilities and strong regional attachments further hindered labour mobility. Thus rigidity was supported by the legal framework of employment and by labour-market practices.

Official statistics are unable to embrace an important part of the Spanish economy, that part described as the submerged economy (*la economía sumergida*; Benito, 1987). Although by definition the magnitude and importance of this sector are unknown, it is generally recognised to be substantial (possibly employing two million people). It is of particular importance in the service industry, in construction and in those manufacturing industries (for example in textiles, toys and food) where entry is easy; significant submerged employment is therefore likely to exist for example in the shoe and toy industries of Alicante and Valencia and in the textile industry of Cataluña. Its existence is deeply embedded in social attitudes to the payment of taxes, in informal working arrangements and in the widespread existence of small family firms. Many people work in the visible economy for long enough to gain entitlement to unemployment benefit, then seek work in the submerged economy where they are exempt from taxation. Simultaneously employers avoid both having to make social security payments and the difficulties of complying with employment legislation, allowing them to cut labour when necessary. Thus the submerged economy has long provided a flexible employment system.

1.5.3 Unemployment

The number of people registered as unemployed increased from the early 1970s through to the mid 1980s, peaking at the exceptionally high level of twenty-two per cent in 1985 (covering about three million people; Table 1.4). This rise in registered unemployment occurred against a background of economic recession and structural change, an increase in the population of working age, an increase in economic-activity participation rates, the existence of widespread multiple employment (*pluriempleo*) and overtime working, the end of large-scale emigration and the appearance of return migration, and high social-security payments that discouraged employers from taking on more employees.

Table 1.4 Evolution of unemployment, 1973–90

Year	Unemployment (million)	Percentage of labour force	Year	Unemployment (million)	Percentage of labour force
1973	0.4	3.2	1983	2.4	17.7
1975	0.6	4.7	1984	2.8	20.6
1976	0.7	5.0	1985	3.0	21.9
1977	0.7	5.3	1986	3.0	21.5
1978	0.9	7.1	1987	2.9	20.6
1979	1.1	8.7	1988†	2.9	20.2
1980	1.5	11.5	1989	2.7	18.4
1981	1.9	14.4	1990	2.5	16.7
1982	2.1	16.2			

* Unemployment rate as a percentage of the economically active population according to official definitions

† 1988 to 1990 figures are for the first quarter

Source: *Encuesta de la Población Activa*

Particular characteristics of unemployment have been the high proportion of youth unemployment, the concentration of unemployment among the less skilled, the higher rates of unemployment among women than among men (for example among women aged fifteen to twenty-four the rate has been almost fifty per cent) and the high levels of long-term unemployment. Significant spatial variations in unemployment have been present for a long time, reflecting historical and structural factors, the composition of output, the level of economic development, the mobility of labour and social characteristics. Thus in 1976 the national unemployment rate was 4.5 per cent, ranging from only 1.75 per cent in Galicia and Rioja to 10 per cent in Andalucía. This differential was magnified in 1985 to 13 per cent in Galicia and 30 per cent in Andalucía (around a national average of 21.9 per cent; Banco de Bilbao, 1988).

Unemployment stabilised in the mid 1980s, then from 1986 it began to fall, reaching less than 2.5 million (seventeen per cent of the economically active population) in August 1989, of whom over half were female. Unemployment rates however are likely to be resistant to much downward movement as a result of the low economic-activity rates, pools of underemployed labour and economic policies designed to curb demand.

1.5.4 Flexibility in the economy

Flexibility in the economy has been sought by both the government and the private sector as one means of achieving greater competitiveness. Flexibility has been sought in the factor markets of land, labour and capital, in the institutions regulating the economy and in flexible production techniques (such as the 'just-in-time delivery system').

The labour market has been one area into which the government has been keen to inject flexibility as a means of stimulating employment creation and increasing competitiveness. Employment legislation has also been required to bring Spain into line with other European Community countries. Greater flexibility covers increased occupational and geographical labour mobility, more flexibility in the pattern of work and reduction in labour costs (not just in moderating wage settlements but also reducing social payments on new employment). Thus new measures have included the introduction of fixed-term contracts under which unemployed people can be taken on for a limited period (for example six months), the encouragement of part-time employment, employment of young people under twenty-five and people over forty-five, the promotion of training schemes and provisions for early retirement.

There have also been special employment programmes such as Community and Rural Employment Programmes (Plan de Empleo Rural), and schemes to promote small industry and self-employment. Included in these schemes have been employment and training grants, relief from social-security contributions, fiscal measures and soft loans. There have also been grants to assist geographical mobility. Employment assistance has been further bolstered by resources available through the regional governments and through the European Social Fund (ESF) (for example assistance from the ESF was taken into account in the setting up of the National Training Programme (Plan Nacional de Formación e Inserción Profesional) in 1986, under which attention was directed at those industries where there were skill shortages, at promoting the introduction of new technologies and at expanding professional and management training. Coupled with these measures have been others designed to improve working practices, including attempts to reduce absenteeism, to eliminate '*pluriempleo*' from the Civil Service and to reduce social-security fraud.

1.5.5 Internationalisation of the economy

The most important structural change in the Spanish economy during the 1980s was the further opening of the economy to international trade and the avalanche of foreign inward investment occasioned by new legislation and membership of the European Community.

Opening the economy has led to a flood of imports, creating a serious deficit on the current account of the balance of payments. Imports rose at an average rate of fifteen per cent per year in the late 1980s (twenty per cent in 1989), rising on the back of higher domestic demand coupled to an increasing propensity to import (associated with lower tariff barriers and thus more competitive imports). Simultaneously the entry of foreign capital has maintained a strong peseta, reducing the international competitiveness of exports (which have grown more slowly than imports in the late 1980s; by twelve per cent in 1989). The resulting current-account deficit would have occurred earlier and been even larger had it not been for the decline in oil prices and devaluation of the peseta at the end of 1982.

In the 1970s and early 1980s deficits in merchandise trade were generally compensated for by surpluses on the invisible account in services and transfers: specifically the substantial surpluses on the tourism account and in the net inflow of foreign investment (Table 1.5). Then from a position of surplus in the mid 1980s (assisted by the fall in oil prices that reduced the cost of energy imports), the current account moved sharply into the red from 1987, producing a deficit of around pta. 1,368 billion ($11,600 million) (some three per cent of GDP) in 1989 and a forecast further deterioration in 1990. This situation has been produced by the growing merchandise trade deficit and a deterioration on the invisible account as tourism revenues have stagnated while tourism expenditure has increased.

Table 1.5 Balance-of-payments current account, 1985 and 1989 (pta. billion)

	1985			1989		
	Income	Payment	Balance	Income	Payment	Balance*
Balance of trade	4,005	4,717	−712	4,868	7,770	−2,902
Travel and tourism	1,375	170	1,205	1,924	365	1,559
Investment income	288	596	−307	745	1,109	−364
Balance of services	2,515	1,523	992	3,629	2,615	1,014
Balance of transfers	302	115	187	1,206	685	521
Current-account balance	6,823	6,356	467	9,702	11,069	−1,368

* 1989 balances in dollars: trade $26,800 million, services $8,445 million and current account −$11,642 million

Sources: Banco de Bilbao, 1988; Informe Economico 1987

Several factors are of particular concern in relation to the balance of payments. A deficit on the capital account may simply reflect substantial capital investment that will enable Spanish industry to be more competitive in the future. In addition, foreign-exchange reserves swollen by inward investment were considerable in the late 1980s ($45 billion in mid 1990). However, the tourism sector now looks vulnerable in relation to further net income growth and many elements of continued foreign investment are unreliable. Any further upsurge in speculative capital inflow after 1992 will put further upward pressure on the exchange rate, so reducing the competitiveness of exports and worsening the balance-of-trade position. Possibly of greatest significance is the potential damage that would result from any significant upward movements in oil prices (oil prices have already strengthened and contributed to the growing merchandise trade deficit). Dependence on imported oil remains a latent threat to the Spanish economy.

Apart from the growing current account deficit and structural features of trade, the other characteristic of trade has been the increasing orientation towards the European Community as trade barriers have progressively been dismantled (for example import duties on Spanish manufactured goods entering the EC and European Free Trade Association (EFTA) were reduced to zero from 1 July 1989). Hence the proportion of imports arising in EC countries has increased from thirty-seven per cent in 1985 to about fifty-seven per cent in 1989, while in the same period the proportion of exports destined for EC countries has increased from fifty-two per cent to over sixty-six per cent (Table 1.6). Included in the above figures is a substantial increase in trade with Portugal, exports having increased from pta. 91 billion in 1985 to pta. 328 billion in 1989 and imports from pta. 40 billion to pta. 197 billion.

Table 1.6 The direction of trade, 1982 – 9

	Total (pta. billion)	OECD		EC	
		pta. billion	%	pta. billion	%
Imports					
1982	3,466	1,884	54	1,100	32
1985	5,115	2,890	57	1,870	37
1987	6,051	4,471	74	3,300	55
1988	6,989	5,418	78	3,969	57
1989	8,458	6,574	78	4,828	57
Exports					
1982	2,258	1,391	62	1,098	49
1985	4,109	2,872	70	2,139	52
1987	4,212	3,338	79	2,681	64
1988	4,659	3,770	81	3,056	66
1989*	5,258	4,277	81	3,510	67

* 1989 figures are provisional

Source: Banco de España, 1990

Substantial foreign investment has been the second element associated with the creation of a more international economy. Legislation to liberalise foreign investment began in the 1970s and was notably enhanced in 1986 when Spanish regulations were brought into line with other countries in the European Community, enabling the transfer abroad of unlimited amounts of capital, profits and dividends. The only sectors where formal restrictions are due to persist are defence industries and certain services (sectors with their own regulations are established in articles 56.1 and 223.1 of the Treaty of Rome: gambling, national defence – including telecommunications and mining for minerals – television and radio, air transport). The government may also intervene where the national interest is at risk.

Although foreign inward investment has not been an entirely new phenomenon, echoing the substantial foreign investment in the mid nineteenth century, it has been a new feature of the contemporary economy. In comparison with other OECD countries, foreign investment was almost non existent in the 1950s and very small in the 1960s, increasing during the 1970s and early 1980s. A sharp rise occurred in 1986, when net foreign inward investment increased by seventy-five per cent on the previous year (Table 1.7), amounting to a sum greater than for the whole ten years 1970 to 1979. After 1986 net foreign inward investment continued to rise rapidly, reaching a record level in 1989 (inflows being $32.85 billion and net investment $16.6 billion, the latter equivalent to about three per cent of GDP; Alcaide, 1990). The rise was due to the internal strength of the Spanish economy (to the attractions of low labour costs, regional, financial and fiscal incentives and a large and growing domestic market), political stability, membership of the European Community (and harmonisation of working practices to those in the EC), links with Latin America, and finally to the strong peseta.

Table 1.7 Net foreign investment in Spain, 1982–9 (pta. billion)

Year	Total	Direct	Portfolio	Property	Other
1982	199	106	1	73	19
1983	243	117	7	114	6
1984	322	156	37	138	−9
1985	413	164	82	159	7
1986	717	284	235	191	7
1987	997	322	435	221	19
1988	1,064	521	246	267	29
1989	1,730	667	733	303	27

Note: Total net balance in dollars in 1989 was $16.6 billion, total foreign inward investment was $32.85 billion

Sources: Alonso, 1988; Banco de España, 1990; 1989 dollar figures from Alcaide, 1990

Until 1986 the largest component of gross inward investment was made up of direct investment (defined by the Bank of Spain as acquisitions of twenty per cent or more of Spanish companies). However, portfolio investment took off in 1984, doubled in 1985 and quadrupled in 1986 to become the dominant component of gross inward investment in that year, a situation that continued in the three years 1987 to 1989 (inclusive). This component of foreign investment must be seen as being highly volatile (for example foreign funds in mid 1989 were going into Treasury Bills issued by the government, to take advantage of high interest rates coupled to the strong peseta). Property investment has been the least volatile, showing steady growth from the beginning of the 1980s.

Direct foreign investment is the most important component of foreign investment in terms of the future growth of the economy. Stable long-term inflows of productive investment could enable Spain to maintain a higher growth rate than other OECD countries. However, when deductions are made for the purchase of existing companies and other non-productive investment, direct investment in new productive assets may represent only about fifty per cent of total direct investment (Leal, 1990). Furthermore, income from the purchase of Spanish assets has been directed into the property market, fuelling a land-and-property price spiral.

Penetration of inward foreign investment has varied between sectors. In the late 1970s and early 1980s the major destination of direct foreign investment was industry, notably transport equipment where examples included General Motors' new car-assembly plant in Zaragoza and the acquisition by Volkswagen of Seat. However, the service sector, especially financial services, became the most important focus of foreign investment in the late 1980s (accounting for thirty-nine per cent of the pta. 466 billion foreign investment in 1989).

The ultimate geographical destination of foreign investment is difficult to identify as it is often channelled through national headquarters of companies in Madrid. Hence by region most foreign investment has been made in Madrid and Cataluña, attracting between forty and sixty per cent of inward investment between 1985 and 1987 inclusive. This concentration of foreign investment in Madrid and Cataluña has underpinned the dynamism of these two areas, but not that of the third major industrial region, País Vasco. Cataluña has been a particular focus of Japanese investment (attracting for example Nissan, Suzuki and Sanyo).

The majority of foreign direct investment in the late 1980s had its origin in the European Community, especially in West Germany, the Netherlands, France and the United Kingdom. This contrasts with the position in the 1960s and early 1970s when the United States tended to dominate inward direct investment (for example with investment by Ford and ATT). In 1989 West Germany had the largest industrial presence in Spain but the UK was the largest single source of direct investment. The United States continues to be a source of investment in large projects (for example investment by Ford and General Motors) but its proportion of total direct investment is generally small compared with that from European Community countries – a characteristic also shared by Japanese investment.

Outward foreign investment also grew rapidly in the 1980s from an almost non-existent base, with relatively small volumes of investment associated primarily with the creation in Europe of commercial networks (for example banks and hotels). Between 1982 and 1984 gross outflows exceeded those for the whole period 1960 to 1981, with the total gross direct investment reaching pta. 65 billion in 1982. However, the real upsurge in Spanish foreign investment only materialised after 1986, when gross foreign investment was estimated at pta 185 billion (portfolio investment accounted for over two thirds, followed by direct investment amounting to some pta. 67 billion; total net investment was estimated at pta. 131 billion) compared with pta. 131 billion in 1985. In 1987 gross foreign investment rose to pta. 155 billion, surpassed by gross direct investment alone in 1989 of pta. 280 billion. The bulk of this foreign investment has been concentrated in the European Community and the United States. By sector it has continued to be directed into financial services, commerce, hotels and restaurants, although industrial investment has been slowly developing.

In general, increased foreign investment has been accepted as an integral part of the process of modernisation, liberalisation and integration into the world economy. Until the mid 1980s it was also relatively moderate (although in 1984 it was estimated that multinationals represented twenty-four per cent of sales and twenty-three per cent of employment and were dominant in twenty-seven per cent of industries in Spain; Ruiz and Fernandez, 1986). Thus an analysis of the period 1974 to 1984 concluded that: 'El grado de penetración extranjera en nuestra economía por empresas con capital mayoritariamente extranjero no es todavía excesivamente elevado' (Ruiz and Fernandez, 1986). Issues such as the loss of sovereignty and control over national resources, the risks of a branch plant economy, the long-term outflow of capital and the impact of a cessation of inward investment (portfolio investment being particularly volatile) have appeared academic alongside the immediate benefits of increased investment and employment, technological transfer, access to international distribution networks and general access to the resources of multinational companies. Thus in 1981 Tsoukalis stated that the opening of the Spanish economy to foreign investment had played a crucial role in terms of the balance of payments, its contribution to fixed capital formation and employment as well as the transfer of technology (Tsoukalis, 1981).

1.6 Restructuring of the Spanish economy

Restructuring is a continuous process as economic structures evolve to accommodate technological developments and changes in the political economy. For the most part this process only becomes visible and dramatic when precipitated by a revolution in technology or a marked swing in the political economy. In Spain the political and economic transformation since the mid 1970s from dictatorship to democracy, from centralism to regionalism, from protectionism to liberalism and from isolation to internationalism has been nothing short of revolutionary, compounding the changes induced by technological developments and precipitating restructuring throughout the economy. This process is documented sector by sector in the following chapters.

At the heart of the restructuring process has been the transformation from a rural, then industrial, economy to a post-industrial one dominated by the service sector and especially reliant on tourism. In 1950 Spain displayed many features akin to those of a less-developed country. Half the labour force were in agriculture, forestry and fishing, and the infant mortality rate was over sixty per thousand. Autarchic policies in the first half of the twentieth century had fashioned the economy into one lacking competitiveness and dominated by small businesses, using cheap labour and traditional technologies. Relaxation of these policies at the end of the 1950s contributed to the 'economic miracle', characterised by rapid economic growth and industrialisation based on cheap energy. But inefficient production structures were sustained by protectionism, while innovation continued to be repressed by extensive government intervention. The long period of suffocating political inertia under the Franco regime was finally broken in the mid 1970s, political metamorphosis coinciding with worldwide economic reorganisation to accommodate the escalation in oil prices. The extent and profound nature of these changes were then magnified by measures to liberalise the Spanish economy and integrate it into the European Community. As the Spanish economy moves towards full integration into the European Community there remains considerable further potential for growth. Simultaneously restructuring continues, characterised by the decline of the traditional economy and of traditional industrial areas, the emergence of new commercial activities and new economic growth zones (especially around the Mediterreanean, widespread penetration by international capital and a greater international orientation of production.

The pace of change has left great contrasts between different economic sectors, geographical areas, communities and people, setting up tensions in society that will challenge government policy. Modern electronics factories contrast with cottage textile plants, intensive horticulture with extensive cereal and olive cultivation, cosmopolitan 'urbanisations' around the coast with abandoned rural settlements in the interior. The poverty of the unemployed contrasts with a new affluence, especially amongst urban professionals. Male peasant farmers in Andalucía continue to bring home their produce on mules and their wives to wash by hand in streams, while female executives travel to meetings in Barcelona using the commuter aircraft from Madrid.

The success or otherwise of the Spanish economy in a competitive international setting will rest in part on the quality of its human resources, on its ability to deal with economic disequilibria and the poor image of many of its products and services. Attitudinal changes will be necessary to free management from the mould of working within a protected economy, and significant improvements will have to be made in education and training, especially in technological areas. Unemployment persists at an exceptionally high level, presenting a serious social problem. Inflation and a current account deficit continue to threaten economic growth, while reliance on imported energy and the vagaries of inward foreign investment overhang economic stability.

But internal change will be overshadowed by strong currents of international restructuring, especially within the context of a Single European Market, that will remodel the pattern of economic activity, consolidating decision making, research and development, and many high value added activities in existing core areas of north-west Europe, from south-east England through Amsterdam, Brussels, Paris and Luxembourg to Frankfurt, while permitting a scatter of new centres (for example, in southern Germany, southern France and Cataluña). Furthermore, a unified Germany and the emergence of market economies in eastern Europe open up an eastward dimension to future European development. In this context the position of Spain looks peripheral, lacking significant economic control functions and a supplier of low-value added products and services with a low-cost labour content. It will be a magnificent sunny property on the edge of the European Community: 'España es un magnífico solar [soleado] al lado del Mercado Común Europeo.' (Fuentes Quintana, 1988; p.68), more reminiscent of Florida than California.

References and Bibliography

Alcaide, C. (1990) 'La balanza de pagos en 1989', *El País*, 11 January, p.13

Alcaide Guindo, C. and J. Alcaide Inchausti (1989) 'The Spanish economy in 1989', *Situacion* No. 18., pp.33–59

Alonso, J. (1988) 'El sector exterior', in J. García Delgado (ed.) *España: Tomo II, Economía*, pp.273–365. Madrid: Espasa-Calpe SA

Anon (1989) 'Las inversiones españolas directas e immobiliarias en el exterior durante 1988', *Boletín ICE*, No 2, 172, pp.869–79

Banco Bilbao Vizcaya (1988) 'Población', *Situación*. Bilbao

Banco Bilbao Vizcaya (1989) 'The Spanish economy in 1988 and 1989', *Situacion*. Bilbao

Banco de Bilbao (1982) *Informe económico*. Bilbao

Banco de Bilbao (1988) *Renta nacional de España*, 1985. Bilbao

Banco de España (1990) *Boletín Estadístico*, April

Benito, S. (1987) 'La economía sumergida en España', *Revista del Instituto de Estudios Económicos* 1, pp.254–88

Bradshaw, R. (1972) 'Internal migration in Spain', *Iberian Studies*, No.2., pp.68–75

Campo, S. Del (1979) 'Spain' in R. Krane (ed.), International labour migration in Europe, pp.156–63, New York; Praeger Publishers

Carr, R. and J. Fusi (2nd ed. 1981) *Spain: dictatorship to democracy*. London: Unwin Hyman

Carreras, A. (1988) 'La industrialización española en el marco de la historia económica europea', in J. García Delgado (ed.), *España: Tomo II, Economía*, pp.79–118. Madrid: Espasa-Calpe *SA*

Carreras, A. (ed.) (1989a) *Estadísticas historicas de España: Siglos XIX–XX*. Madrid: Fundación Banco Exterior

Carreras, A. (1989b) 'La renta y la riqueza', in A. Carreras (ed.) *Estadísticas historicas de España: Siglos XIX–XX*, Chapter 13. Madrid: Fundación Banco Exterior

Clark, R. and M. Haltzel, (eds) (1987) *Spain in the 1980s: the democratic transition and a new international role*. Cambridge, Mass.: Ballinger Publishing Company

Donges, J. (1974) *La industrialización en España*. Barcelona: Oikos-Tau

El País (1990) *Anuario El País*, 1990. Madrid

Fontana, J. and J. Nadal (1976) 'Spain 1914–1970', in C. Cipolla (ed.), *The Fontana economic history of Europe, Vol.6, Pt.ii.* pp.460–529 London: Collins

Fontana, J. (ed.) (1986) *España bajo el franquismo*. Barcelona: Crítica

Fuentes Quintana, E. (1988) 'Tres decenios de la economía española en perspectiva', in J. García Delgado (ed.), *España: Tomo II, Economía*, pp.1–75. Madrid: Espasa-Calpe SA

García Delgado, J. (ed.) (1988) *España: Tomo II, Economía*. Madrid: Espasa-Calpe SA

Información Comercial de Española (1990) 50 años de economía española 1939-1989, 2 volumes Nos. 676 and 677, diciembra 1989-Enero 1990. Madrid: Ministerio de Economía y Hacienda

Gilmour, D. (1985) *The transformation of Spain*. London: Quartet Books

Harrison, J. (1985) *The Spanish economy in the twentieth century*. London: Croom Helm

Instituto Nacional de Estadística (INE) (1986) *El Padron, 1986*. Madrid

Leal, J. (1990) 'Las inversiones extranjeras en España', *El País*, 15 April, Sección Negocios p2

Lieberman, S. (1982) *The contemporary Spanish economy*. London: George Allen and Unwin

Maravall, F. (ed.) (1987) *Economía y política industrial en España*. Madrid: Ediciones Pirámide, SA

Martinez-Serrano, J. *et al.* (1983) *Economía española: 1960–1980*. Madrid: H. Blume Ediciones

Mochón, F. *et al.* (1988) *Economía española 1964–1987: introducción al análisis económico*. Madrid: McGraw-Hill

Nadal, J. (1970) *La economía española (1829–1931)*, Vol. 4, in Banco de España, *Una historia económica*, pp.317–417. Madrid: Banco de España

Nadal, J. (1973) 'The failure of the industrial revolution in Spain', 1830–1914, in C. Cipolla (ed.), *The Fontana economic history of Europe Vol.4, Pt.ii.* pp.532–626. London: Collins

Nadal, J. (1975) *El fracaso de la revolución industrial en España, 1814–1913*. Barcelona: Editorial Ariel SA

Nadal, J. (4th ed. 1976) *La población española (siglos XVI a XX)*. Barcelona: Editorial Ariel SA

Nadal, J., A. Carreras, and C. Sudria (eds) (1987) *La economía española en el siglo XX: Una perspectiva histórica*. Barcelona: Editorial Ariel SA

OECD (1986) *Spain, economic survey*. Paris

Pérez Simarro, R. (1986) 'Situación comparativa de la industria española', *Economía Industrial* No.246, p.21–31

Roman, M. (1971) *The limits of economic growth in Spain*. New York: Praeger Publishers

Ruiz, M. and F. Fernandez, (1986) 'Estudio de la evolución del grado de penetración de las empresas de capital mayoritariamente extrangero en España durante la crisis 1974–1984', ETS (Vigo) Mimeo. Santiago: University of Santiago

Tamames, R. (1986) *The Spanish economy*. London: C. Hurst and Company

Tamames, R. (18th ed. 1989) *Estructura económica de España*. Madrid: Alianza Editorial

Tena, A. (1989) 'Comercio exterior', pp.327–62, in A. Carreras (ed.), *Estadísticas historicas de España: Siglos XIX-XX*, Chapter 8. Madrid: Fundación Banco Exterior

Tsoukalis, L (1981) *The European Community and its Mediterranean enlargement*. London: George Allen and Unwin

Velasco Barroetabeña, R. and R. Alvarez Llano (1988) 'La inversión en España: un intento de visión global', *Situación* 1, pp.5–64

Vicens Vives, J. (1969) *An economic history of Spain*. Princeton: Princeton University Press

Vickers, J. and V. Wright (1988) 'The politics of industrial privatisation in western Europe: an overview', *Western European Politics* 11, No.4, pp.1–30

Vilar, P. (2nd ed. 1977) *Spain: a brief history*. Oxford: Pergamon Press

Wright, A. (1977) *The Spanish economy 1959–1976*. London: Macmillan

♦ Chapter 2 ♦

The public sector

2.1 The public sector

The Spanish economy has been characterised by an extensive web of state intervention during the twentieth century, in which the magnitude of public expenditure and public enterprises only partially disclosed the extent to which public sector institutions regulated the economy. In 1964 public expenditure was only nineteen per cent of gross domestic product (Mochón *et al.*, 1988) and public enterprises contributed less than ten per cent of gross domestic product. These were small figures in comparison with Britain and France. However, all aspects of the political economy, including administration and a wide range of prices, wages and trade, were highly centralised and closely controlled from Madrid.

During the 1970s and early 1980s the size of the public sector increased, such that public expenditure (embracing responsibilities for administration, the legal system, social security and public enterprises, Figure 2.1) as a percentage of gross domestic product reached forty-two per cent in 1986 (inflated especially by higher social-security payments and larger local-authority spending bills, but roughly in line with other OECD countries). Meanwhile public enterprises were swollen by the acquisition of many failing industries, to leave a public-enterprise sector contributing about ten per cent of the gross domestic product (though it remained far smaller than in France, where nationalised industry accounted for about thirty per cent of gross national product in 1989; Guy de Jonquiéres, 1990).

Reorientation of public-sector activity was the dominant trend in the late 1980s and remains so at the beginning of the 1990s, reflecting a tendency throughout western Europe for governments to retrace their role in the economy, withdrawing from many traditional forms of intervention (especially from direct participation through public enterprises; Guy de Jonquiéres, 1990; Vickers and Wright, 1988), while expenditure on administration and services continues to rise. Thus public expenditure as a percentage of gross domestic product in Spain has stabilised at around forty per cent, numerous public enterprises have been privatised and many forms of state regulation have been dismantled. Simultaneously new systems of intervention have been emerging both at the supra-national (European Community) level and at the sub-national (regional) level. For example, the national system of agricultural price support in Spain has been replaced by that operating under the Common Agricultural Policy and responsibility for planning development control is now largely devolved to the regions and local authorities. Less direct state participation in economies has allowed the advance of capitalism and further integration into the international economic system. A corollary of this change has been the retreat of socialism, not just in western Europe, but also in eastern Europe and the Soviet Union.

Figure 2.1 The structure of the public sector

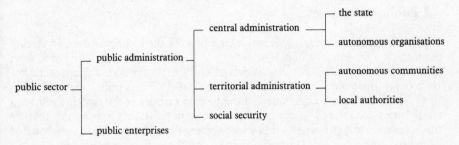

Source: Adapted from Mochón *et al.*, 1988

The broad shift towards market capitalism has followed from disillusion in certain circles with earlier economic policies to deal with the economic crisis of the 1970s, coupled with a reassertion of individual freedom over the state. Disenchantment with *dirigisme* and Keynesianism was bound up in ideological and economic arguments, which embraced the perceived bureaucratic inefficiency of the public sector, the appearance of stagflation, the strains of higher public debt, a reaction against the high levels of taxation needed to support weighty public sectors and the political risks associated with managing a large public-sector labour force. In relation to nationalised industries, these were left in a weaker position by more international forms of production, marketing and finance. The private firm operating within a market economy was held to be the means of achieving wealth creation. Thus policies emerged to secure changes in the economic environment: more restrictive budgetary macro-economic policy, tighter control on public expenditure, attacks on regional policy, tax reforms, labour market policies designed to increase flexibility, and reductions in the size of public administrations and subsidies to 'lame duck' industries.

European Community initiatives, especially competition policy and progress towards the 'Single European Market', have heightened the pace of public-sector decline. These initiatives have required the removal of barriers to trade and competition within the Community, necessitating measures to increase competitiveness within member countries. In some countries, notably Britain under successive Thatcher governments, this emphasis on reduced state involvement has been underpinned by a clearly stated ideological position. It is not surprising therefore that Britain has witnessed the most radical revision of the public sector (with the public-sector borrowing requirement being transformed into a public-sector surplus and all saleable public enterprises, including public utilities and defence industries, being privatised). In other countries, including Spain, the process of change has been more a pragmatic response to circumstances. Once Spain opted to join the European Community (as much for political as for economic reasons), there was little choice but to adopt the reforms necessary to participate (and survive) within the new economic environment; the march of international capitalism was irresistible.

2.2 Public enterprises

Public enterprises are an important component of the public sector and among the most visible elements of it. They are none the less difficult to define precisely, having evolved through the acquisition of enterprises for various reasons rather than being the product of a single coherent policy. Thus public enterprises in Spain have not been concentrated in the field of utilities and strategic industries (sometimes considered as areas of natural state monopoly where the market mechanism is inappropriate). They have emerged across the whole spectrum of economic activity, their composition changing through time as companies have passed to and from the private sector.

The limits of the public sector are drawn according to the extent of public ownership in companies (from one to 100 per cent) and the extent of control (from minority participation to full control). A rough guide to the definition of a public enterprise is an organisation whose main purpose is to produce goods and services for the market and in which there is more than fifty per cent ownership by the public administration, or where the public administration has a significant role in the management (as in Telefónica, where the state has only a thirty-two per cent holding; Myro, 1988). These companies are listed by the government in official statistics (a listing produced by the Intervención General de la Administración del Estado (State Administration Supervisory Office)). However, many companies in which the state has some influence are excluded from this list, as are the enterprises that have been transferred to lower tiers of government.

Once enterprises that belong to the public sector have been defined, there is then the problem of their classification. Initially this may be based on the tier of government within which they are located: within the central, regional or local administration. Then, for those companies dependent on the central administration, further classification can be made according to: i) whether they fall into one of the major state holding companies (Instituto de Crédito Oficial (ICO); Dirección General del Patrimonio del Estado (DGPE); Instituto Nacional de Hidrocarburos (INH) and Instituto Nacional de Industria (INI)) or depend directly on one of the ministries, and ii) the type of activity undertaken. On this basis, public enterprises can be divided into: i) Commercial services: Currently only the Postal and Telecommunication service (Dirección General de Correos y Telecomunicaciones); ii) Autonomous organisations: In the Law of the 1989 Budget (Ley de Presupuestos Generales del Estado, 1989) sixty-five enterprises were included in this group, which can be subdivided into a) non-financial organisations such as the water authorities (confederaciones hidrográficas), seaport authorities (juntas de puertos), the Official Bulletin of State (Boletín Oficial del Estado), the National State Lottery Organisation (Organismo Nacional de

Loterías y Apuestas del Estado), the National Airports Authority (Aeropuertos Nacionales), agricultural organisations such as ICONA, SENPA, FROM, etc.; and b) financial organisations such as the Postal Savings Bank (Caja Postal de Ahorros) and the insurance group Consorcio de Compensación de Seguros: iii) State enterprises (trading organisations): Within which four types of company can be distinguished: a) non-financial trading companies including all the companies with majority participation by the three state holding companies DGPE, INH and INI, b) non-financial trading entities including the industrial companies INH and INI, and the railway company RENFE, c) financial trading companies covering the state banks (Banco de Crédito Agrícola, Exterior, Hipotecario, Industrial and Local), and the public insurance companies which are the Compañía Española de Seguros de Crédito y Caución and la Mutualidad de Seguros of the INI, and d) financial trading entities such as the Instituto de Crédito Oficial.

2.3 Public enterprises in the Spanish economy

Public enterprises have operated throughout the Spanish economy, but they have been particularly prominent in coal mining, mercury, oil and gas, electricity and water, iron and steel, aluminium, tobacco, shipbuilding, transport materials, transport and communications. In 1986 there were 180 companies in which the state had a direct majority holding, together with 300 subsidiaries and more than 500 minority holdings (Fernández Rodriguez, 1989). It is estimated that between 1980 and 1986 state public enterprises were responsible for eight to ten per cent of the total value of production of goods and services (gross value added), and ten to sixteen per cent of the gross capital formation in Spain (Ortiz Junquera and Gómez Rodrigo, 1989). In terms of employment they accounted for about five per cent of the labour force. In the industrial sector they represented about sixteen per cent of the gross value added and nine per cent of the industrial labour force (Fariñas el al., 1989; these magnitudes have since been reduced by company disposals). Of those public enterprises dependent on the state, the three state holdings INI, INH and DGPE represented about sixty-nine per cent of the gross value added of all state public-sector enterprises in 1984 (Myro, 1988). The largest group by employment, value of sales, social capital and number of companies is INI, followed by the DGPE and INH (Table 2.1).

2.4 Major non-financial public enterprise groups

The National Industry Institute (Instituto Nacional de Industria, INI) is the holding company that provides the main focus for public involvement in manufacturing. It operates within the legal framework of a public company (within the Ministry of Industry and Energy) subject to private company law (this legal status was adopted in 1989 under the Ley de Presupuestos del Estado, para. 1989, artículo 123, which transformed the company into 'una entidad de derecho público sometida al ordenamiento privado'). This status allows INI to operate like a private company, simultaneously obliging it to take more account of profit and efficiency in its allocation of resources, thereby placing more emphasis on entrepreneurial activity than in a traditional public enterprise. Along with other public enterprise trading companies, under European Community regulations it must abandon its dependence on state funds from 1993.

Table 2.1 The state holding companies, 1988

State holding company	Sales (pta. million)	Gross value added (pta. million)	Labour force
DGPE*	1,246,903	766,552	94,926
Telefónica	612,536	627,127	66,062
Tabacalera	443,443	50,462	8,492
INH (Repsol/Enagas)	990,844	196,202	19,594
Repsol	926,283	187,026	18,716
INI †	1,714,395	—	155,945
Endesa Group	457,502	181,790	15,709
Iberia	334,806	144,718	28,003
Ensidesa	153,321	60,550	16,351
Enasa*	116,281	29,058	5,930
Inespal	119,613	46,697	6,102
Casa	73,212	45,065	10,370
Bazán	52,565	28,427	10,908
Hunosa	39,472	—	19,307
Aesa	31,434	—	9,623
RENFE	159,678	206,578	52,910
Correos	—	—	—

* Excludes the Banco Exterior and those companies in which the DGPE has small holdings.

† Only those companies are included with sales of over pta. 50 billion or employment of over 5,000

Source: Anuario *El País*, 1990

INI has been involved in almost all areas of the economy, participating directly in over fifty companies in 1988, nine of which accounted for about three quarters of the labour force, social capital and value of sales of the INI group. Despite diversification and the turnover of companies, the group's main industrial products continue to reflect its early ancestry and its core structure of heavy industries. Major products include coal, aluminium, steel and electricity, as well as ships and aircraft. At the world level INI is among the top 100 major industrial groups by sales (sixty-first in 1988) and in Europe it is among the top fifty (twenty-fifth in 1988). In Spain it is the country's largest industrial group (employing 155,945 people at the end of 1988 (*El País*, 1990), and accounting for about five per cent of the gross domestic industrial product) and a leading exporter.

The National Hydrocarbon Institute (Instituto Nacional de Hidrocarburos, INH) controls the hydrocarbon group Repsol SA and the natural-gas company

Enagas (Table 2.2). INH was formed in 1981 under the Ministry of Industry and Energy to co-ordinate the dispersed interests of the state in the hydrocarbon industry. Prior to its formation, state control was exercised in a variety of companies through both the Ministry of Economy and Finance (especially through Campsa), and the Ministry of Industry and Energy (especially through INI). Co-ordination of the public-sector interests in hydrocarbons facilitated a policy of restructuring, reducing costs, investment in distribution networks (for example the modernisation of petrol stations) and improving the image of the constituent companies through advertising campaigns. The process of internal restructuring began in 1983 and was completed with the formation of Repsol in 1987, the latter representing over ninety-five per cent of group sales and employment in 1988.

Table 2.2 INH Group, 1989

Companies	% participation	Formally	Employment (1987)	Sales (pta. million) (1987)
Repsol Exploración	100.0	Hispanoil	717	100,887
Repsol Petróleo	99.9	EMP	5,348	563,051
Repsol Butano	100.0	Gas Butano, SA	3,031	111,116
Repsol Química	100.0	Alcudia	1,956	95,420
Campsa	70.0		7,806	115,148
Total Repsol group			18,858	985,622
Enagas	100.0		740	54,932
Total INH			19,598	1,040,554

Source: El País (1989) Anuario *El País* 1989. Madrid.

The State Assets Office (Dirección General del Patrimonio del Estado, DGPE) supervises a loose grouping of companies (regulated by the Ley Patrimonio del Estado 1964 (States Assets Law 1964) and the Ley General del Presupuestaria 1977 (the General Budget Law 1977)) within the Ministry of Economy and Finance. Shares in its constituent holding companies are held directly by the state, allowing the State Budget Office (Dirección General de Presupuestos) close financial control. Outside of budget control considerable freedom has been granted to management. Traditionally the DGPE has been responsible for those companies yielding important tax revenues (for example the tobacco company Tabacalera) or during the economic recession for those companies that required rapid financial restructuring prior to being reprivatised (for example the Rumasa group). At the beginning of 1989 the DGPE participated directly in twenty-six companies (together with investments in other companies through these twenty-six), holding 100 per cent of the capital in thirteen and more than fifty per cent of the capital in a further nine. While the grouping is very diverse both in activities and in size of companies, it is dominated by Telefónica and Tabacalera (Table 2.3). At the end of 1987 the DGPE had over 94,000 employees (about one third of employment in public companies) and about one third of public enterprise sales.

Table 2.3 Main companies in the Dirección General del Patrimonio del Estado, 1988

Company	Activity	Holding	Sales (pta. million)	Employment
Agencia Efe	Information	98.1	5,361	728
Aldeasa	Duty-free shops	100.0	14,444	516
Banco Exterior	Banking	51.4	—	8,572
Emausa	Roads	100.0	4,246	447
Hytasa	Textiles	100.0	4,655	1,047
Imepiel	Shoes	99.9	6,518	1,450
Intelhorce*	Textiles	100.0	6,684	1,685
Mercasa	Food marketing	44.3	2,444	102
Mercosa	Food marketing	72.4	44,056	1,235
Minas de Almadén	Mercury mining	100.0	3,322	876
Salinas Torrevieja	Salt mining	38.5	1,919	411
Telefónica (CTNE)	Telecommunications	32.4	612,536	66,062
Tabacalera	Tobacco	52.4	443,443	8,492
Tragsa	Infrastructure	20.0	43,336	1,294
Trasmediterránea	Shipping	95.2	29,756	3,333

* Now privatised

Source: El País, 1990

2.5 Evolution of the public-enterprise sector

INI was set up by the government in 1941 as a holding company with 'the objective of strengthening defence industries and promoting self-sufficiency in areas where private resources were insufficient' (Tsoukalis, 1981), the only existing state grouping being the DGPE (established in 1874). In the aftermath of the Civil War it was considered essential for the state to provide the substantial investment necessary to underpin private initiative and promote economic take-off. Thus the INI became particularly active in the basic manufacturing area (especially coal, iron and steel, electricity, shipbuilding, vehicles and transport), helping to lay the foundations for Spain's industrialisation. By the end of the 1950s public enterprises had become a sizeable element in the Spanish economy. In transport, communications and credit there were important nationalisations. In energy, water and manufacturing new companies were created.

Justification for intervention varied between sectors. Air and rail transport were nationalised for strategic reasons, to co-ordinate the different means of transport, to promote development, and to offset decapitalisation; in communications the objective was to reduce the control of foreign capital; while in credit there was a desire to offer privileged facilities to promote development. Intervention in energy was focused on the need to substitute imports of energy and primary products and promote the use of national resources. Similarly in manufactured goods there was a desire to become more self-sufficient. Thus public enterprises performed a clear, if questionable, role.

The growth of public enterprise in the GDP continued during the period

1959–74, along with some diversification both into expanding industries (such as transport materials) and into industries in crisis. Optimism associated with rapid national economic growth led to heavy investment in the early 1970s, consolidating the basic structure of the group but also contributing to the problems of overcapacity in the recession that followed. Public enterprises thereby assumed a more ambiguous role, not only promoting national economic growth but also protecting the industrial and employment base: a role that became much more pronounced in the late 1970s and early 1980s.

Economic recession between 1974 and 1984 coincided with political transition from dictatorship to democracy, leaving government concerned more with political rather than business strategy. The public sector became a hospital for sick industries (including Astilleros Españoles, Babcock Wilcox, Viajes Marsans and the largest acquisition, Seat, in 1980), developing a deeper involvement in iron and steel, railway materials, shipbuilding and capital goods, while spreading out into a wide range of manufacturing industries, including ceramics, food, shoes and textiles. These acquisitions significantly diversified the portfolio of companies and increased the labour force. From 1976 the financial position of INI and the other state holdings deteriorated. Management problems were increased by the diversity of the group. Excess capacity developed in the heavy industries of steel, shipbuilding and chemicals, and there was generally a low level of productivity. By the early 1980s public enterprises faced mounting debt and it was clearly necessary to clarify their objectives. The most important change in government policy during the latter part of this period was the move away from the nationalisation of companies in crisis at the turn of the decade towards the development of reconversion plans put forward by the private sector and supported by state assistance (García Fernández, 1989).

The evolution of public-sector enterprises in the mid 1980s occurred within the context of a more secure democratic government, an improving international economic climate and the integration of Spain into the European Community. Also, the important political process of devolution continued, resulting in the increased importance of public enterprises operating at the regional and local level. This was reflected in higher levels of assistance from the territorial administrations, which between 1979 and 1986 increased their proportion of total public sector operating assistance from eleven to twenty-six per cent. In capital transfers their proportion increased from 0.1 to 11 per cent (Ruiz Cañete, 1989; p.86).

The election to government of the PSOE in 1982 heralded a period of greater political stability than before. The government felt able to adopt a more pragmatic approach to industrial policy and to tackle the very serious problems that existed. Set alongside entry into the European Community, the twin policy guidelines became: i) profitability, giving greater emphasis to the balance sheet of public enterprises and reinforcing reconversion programmes (for example in iron and steel, aluminium, fertilizers and railway equipment), and ii) liberalisation, which not only reduced the level of direct government intervention, but also overturned the traditional goal of a solid 'national' industrial base to look benignly on multinationalisation.

Reconversion and restructuring were assisted by improvements in the international economic environment (many public enterprises being particularly dependent on international trade and thus influenced by the international market situation; Fariñas et al., 1989). In the energy sector, improvements came as crude-oil prices fell, helped by the depreciation of the dollar against the peseta (the cost of obtaining crude oil in Spain fell by sixty per cent between 1985 and 1986; Fariñas et al., 1989), while the government maintained the level of final-energy prices. In the manufacturing sector, improvements came with lower financial costs and increasing consumption. Losses became concentrated in specific sectors, notably minerals, shipbuilding and defence (although these sectors embraced a large proportion of the workforce of INI).

Hence, as a result of both the improved economic environment and government measures, public enterprises reduced their losses in the mid 1980s. For example, losses in the INI group fell from a record pta. 204 billion in 1982 to pta. 42 billion in 1987, the group returning to profit in 1988 for the first time since 1975. As part of this economic regeneration, INI has been shedding its socio-political roles of dustbin for unprofitable industry, adapting sectors in difficulty and cushioning the effects of industrial rationalisation, to leave a more efficient organisation acting as a catalyst for industrial development.

Measures taken by the government during the mid 1980s (particularly after 1984) involved a strategy of financial improvements and rationalisation to increase efficiency. Improvements to the financial position of companies included tighter financial controls and financial restructuring along with measures to reduce costs, for example through energy savings and employment reduction. From 1984 to 1986 the government reduced levels of operating assistance, although capital transfers continued to increase. The main beneficiaries of state assistance were the non financial public enterprises, with especially large transfers being made to the state railway company RENFE, the coal-mining company Hunosa and the agricultural fund FORPPA. There were reductions in employment in public enterprises (probably greater than 40,000 between 1984 and 1986, excluding losses through privatisations that would take the total up to about 70,000), reductions that were concentrated in the manufacturing sector (especially in iron, steel and shipbuilding) and largely compensated by the Fondos de Promoción de Empleo (Fariñas et al., 1989).

Rationalisation embraced: i) disinvestment through a) the liquidation of companies that were not viable (for example Viajes Ita (DGPE), Aplesa (INH), Potasas de Navarra (INI)), b) the closure of excess capacity (as with the reduction of 45,000 tonnes of aluminium capacity achieved through the closure of plant at Valladolid and part of the aluminium capacity at Avilés; also the closure of the blast furnace at Sagunto and the Enfersa fertilizer plant at Puentes de García Rodriguez) and c) privatisation; ii) the restructuring of whole industrial sectors (for example in hydrocarbons with the formation of INH in 1981 and Repsol in 1987; iii) the internal restructuring of public enterprises into sub-holdings (in INI for example with Inespal in electronics and defence equipment in the company Santa Barbara; Figure 2.2); iv) company mergers (for example in aluminium between Alugasa and Endasa); v) the interchange of holdings between companies in the public sector (for example the sale in 1988 of four food companies of INI to Tabacalera; and in electricity where Endesa for example acquired a further holding in Eléctricas Reunidas de Zaragoza (ERZ) in 1986); vi) selective investment (for example the fertilizer company Enfersa converted its ammonia plant in Sagunto to natural gas and added a new nitrates plant); vii) the reorientation of production in some companies and viii) other measures to increase efficiency including adoption of new technology, improvements in management organisation and better quality of products.

Figure 2.2 Organisation of INI, 1990

Electrical energy	—— Endesa Group (Endesa, Enher, Unelco, Gesa, *ERZ*, Encasur) —— Enusa			
Minerals	—— Hunosa —— Figaredo			
Iron and steel	—— Ensidesa —— Sidmed —— Foarsa —— Presur			
Aluminium	—— Inespal Group (Aluminio Español, Alúmina Española)			
Shipbuilding	—— Aesa —— Astano —— Astican —— Barreras			
Defence	—— Casa —— Bazán —— Santa Barbara			
Machinery	—— FSC —— BWE —— Ensa			
Engineering and construction	—— Initec —— Auxini —— Enadimsa			
Electronics	—— Inisel Group (Enosa, Eria, Pesa)			
Paper	—— Ence			
Craft industry	—— Artespaña —— Gea			
Air transport	—— Iberia —— Aviaco			
Sea transport	—— Elcano —— CTE			
International trade	— Iniexport —— Carboex —— Infoleasing —— Musini			
Industrial development	— Sociedades Desarrollo Industrial ———— Enisa			

Source: Adapted from MINE, 1989

The process effectively brought to an end the incorporation of industries in crisis. There were no new public enterprises formed, except for Redesa and ERZ (both the result of rationalisation in the electricity sector) and the brief nationalisation of the Rumasa companies.

2.6 Privatisation

Privatisation has been defined as 'that wide range of policies designed to reduce the scope, limit the functions and generally weaken the influence of the public sector' (Vickers and Wright, 1988). It embraces wider participation by the private sector in areas previously reserved for the public sector, selling land and publicly owned housing stock as well as industrial privatisation. In Spain the policy of industrial disinvestment followed by the state has been attributed more to considerations of industrial rationale than to any political belief in privatisation (Aranzadi, 1989). There has been no full privatisation policy underpinned by an explicit market-centred ideology as in Britain (Fernández Rodriguez, 1989). Nevertheless, privatisation did gain momentum during the 1980s.

Until 1988 privatisation had not substantially altered the sectoral composition of the public sector, except in transport materials and, apart from the cases of SKF and Seat, had involved the disposal of companies of relatively little significance (in food and textiles) or those in deficit (Table 2.4). Privatisations simplified the portfolio of companies held by the state and improved the efficiency of control. There were also relatively few sales given the number of public enterprises. However, the partial privatisation of the hydrocarbon group Repsol in 1989, the sale of the fertilizer group Enfersa to the Ercros group and the planned sale of the national airline Iberia suggest a viewpoint on public enterprises that has become more firmly market oriented.

Table 2.4 Examples of privatisations of INI companies, 1984 – 90

Enterprise	Sector	Buyer	Year	% privatised
Textile Tarazona	Textiles	Cima Eursa	1984	70
Secoinsa	Electronics	Fujitsu CTNE	1985	69
SKF Española	Ball bearings	Aktiebolaget SKF	1985	99
Viajes Marsans	Travel	Trapsa	1985	100
Motores MDB	Veh. engineering	Klockner Humboldt	1986	60
Olcesa	Food	Mercosa	1986	51
Seat	Vehicles	Volkswagen	1986	75
Dessa	Shipbuilding	Forestal del Atlántico	1987	80
Purolator	Vehicles	Knecht Filterwerke	1987	95
Carcesa	Food	Tabacalera	1988	100
Lesa	Food	Tabacalera	1988	100
Astican	Shipbuilding	Italmar	1989	91
Ateinsa	Engineering	GEC–Alsthom	1989	85
Enfersa	Fertilizers	Ercros	1989	80
MTM	Engineering	GEC–Alsthom	1989	85
Oesa	Food	Grupo Ferruzzi	1989	100
Pesa	Electronics	Amper, SA	1989	97
Enasa	Vehicles	Fiat	1990	60

Source: Adapted from Angel Noceda, 1990

Privatisation has involved the direct sale of companies to the private sector and the flotation of companies on the Stock Exchange. Companies sold wholly or in part directly to private companies have included those sold as part of the process of financial rehabilitation of the banks in crisis and the expropriation of Rumasa, the sale in 1985 of the ball-bearing manufacturer SKF to Asea Brown Boveri and the electronics company Secoinsa to Fujitsu, in 1986 the motor-vehicle manufacturer Seat to Volkswagen, in 1989 the fertilizer company Enfersa to Ercros and the electrical-engineering companies Ateinsa and MTM to GEC-Alsthom and in 1990 the motor-vehicle manufacturer Enasa to Fiat (leaving INI as a minority shareholder).

Apart from the banks and the special case of Rumasa, sales have been prompted by the opportunity of gaining access to technological, logistical or commercial expertise and facilities (for example developed networks of international distribution), economies of scale and industrial synergy. These opportunities are considered to offer companies a more secure future, although some of them have been gained simply through co-operation between companies, for example between Enasa and DAF, Casa and Airbus, Iberia and Lufthansa. Overwhelmingly sales have been to multinational companies. The privatisation of Seat in 1986 has been the most important example of a direct sale to the private sector, illustrating the logic of disinvestment. It gave to Seat the advantages of scale economies, access to new technology and marketing outlets that INI could not provide.

The other form of privatisation has involved flotation of companies on the Stock Exchange. In most cases these have been only partial privatisations, broadening the capital base while leaving control in the hands of the state; for example, a thirty-eight per cent holding in the electricity utility Gesa was sold in 1986, 39.8 per cent in the cellulose manufacturer Ence and twenty per cent of the electricity utility Endesa in 1988, followed in 1989 by the largest flotation, that of thirty per cent of Repsol. The objectives have been to diversify the sources of finance, broaden the base of shareholding and introduce the discipline of the market into management.

Privatisation, while raising public revenue at the time of sale, has usually only been achieved following considerable public investment in companies to secure their sale (through debt write-offs and cash injections, etc.), although the process cuts future government spending on public enterprises. For example, between 1983 and 1988 INI invested pta. 1,800 billion in its subsidiaries (of which pta. 1,350 billion was provided directly by the state, the rest – some pta. 500 billion – was raised by INI through sales of companies; Tizón, 1989). At the turn of the decade INI was continuing to invest to consolidate the process of reconversion, including the completion of the reconversion programme for shipbuilding. In the one case of MTM and Ateinsa, INI invested pta. 20 billion (£100 million) to enable it to be sold to the GEC-Alsthom group (although similar investment in debt write-offs and cash injections have been made by other governments: in 1989 the British government allocated £6 billion to the water authorities prior to their privatisation, and the Italian government wrote off most of the £4 billion debt of the public-sector steel group Finsider).

2.7 Deregulation

Deregulation and liberalisation have been spreading through the Spanish economy to affect all public enterprises. The process has been hastened by the need to comply with European Community requirements. As a result, national market restrictions are being eliminated, state monopolies broken up, and the whole economy exposed to much more intense competition than before. Trade barriers to European Community imports have largely disappeared. In the financial sector, deregulation is moving forwards in banking (for example with the removal of the geographical restrictions on savings banks) and reform of the Stock Exchange (finalised in July 1989). Entry to the European Community has been directly responsible for the break-up of numerous state monopolies, forcing the public enterprises concerned to adopt new strategies. For example, the long-established monopolies of Campsa and Tabacalera have both been broken up, land transport was reformed by the transport law of 1987 (Ley de Ordenación de los Transportes Terrestres, LOTT) and the new law of telecommunications has broken the monopoly of Telefónica (Ley de Ordenación de las Telecomunicaciones, LOT, 1987).

2.8 Restructuring in the public sector

While public enterprises have been used to illustrate tendencies in the broader public sector, it is important not to equate the pace of privatisation with any denial of the importance of state intervention in the modern Spanish economy. 'The State continues to be a provider, regulator, entrepreneur, purchaser and umpire in industrial affairs' (Vickers and Wright, 1988).

The role of public enterprises in Spain remains unclear in the absence of a specific public-enterprise policy ('no existe una política específica de empresa pública'; García Fernández, 1989; p.224). The stated position is that privatisations are not founded on any government strategy of denationalisation ('En España, no ha existido hasta 1988 una verdadera estrategia gobernamental de desnacionalización de empresas públicas 'Myro, 1988; p.496), nor on political ideology, but on the industrial logic of securing an efficient public sector ('Las decisiones de desinversión del INI no responden a imperativos de carácter político o ideológico, sino a criterios de racionalidad industrial y financiera ligados, en última instancia, al cumplimiento del objectivo prioritario del INI: la maximización del Patrimonio del Grupo' (Aranzadi, 1989; p.258). In practice, as companies become profitable they become candidates for privatisation.

Without state subsidies, economic efficiency will be essential if public enterprises are to survive. More-efficient operation is seen to come at least in part from exposure to market disciplines. Thus both INI and INH have shed their previous close ministerial control and now operate under statutes similar to those of private companies. However, many public enterprises will continue to find it difficult to achieve efficiency where they are unable to take advantage of economies of scale and need to cut excess labour in strong union environments such as steel and shipbuilding.

The case for a smaller public-enterprise sector is readily made by reference to its poor record, both operationally and in implementing government policies. Governments have used the INI to implement such policies as guaranteeing the supply of basic products, preventing the formation of private monopolies, contributing to regional development and salvaging loss-making companies. In terms of the supply of basic products, Spain remains critically dependent on foreign supplies, especially of energy. In preventing monopolies 'the INI never applied any prices lower than those set by private enterprise; in fact it joined forces with private companies in a series of mixed public and private ventures of dubious general interest' (Tamames, 1986). In regional policy, public enterprises have played a relatively minor role and the state regional-development associations (SODI) have been overshadowed by their regional-government counterparts. As for the role of the public sector in salvaging loss-making companies, the policy substantially increased the burden on public finance and may be seen in retrospect to have diverted public funds away from technological development towards redundant technologies. However, operational inefficiency was at least in part a reflection of the broader inefficiency of government in the past, and in many cases losses were inherited from the private sector. Moreover, as the public sector is slimmed down, so an important axis of control over the economy is lost to the government, and lost largely to foreign multinationals.

The rising tide of foreign penetration in the Spanish economy is closely linked to privatisation, as companies have frequently been sold to foreign owners. The government has actively sought out and encouraged foreign investors. Despite attempts by the government to promote the formation of larger Spanish companies able to compete effectively against foreign multinationals, the prospect of losing national control over large segments of the economy has been viewed as the inevitable price of securing employment and industrial and economic development.

Thus the government has played an active role in promoting restructuring in the economy through the radical surgery it has applied to public enterprises in an attempt to meet the competitive conditions of an international market-place. Outside of public enterprises the future role of the public sector in Spain, as elsewhere in western Europe, is less clear. Ideologies change, and disillusion with the market mechanism, especially to deliver an acceptable society as opposed to an efficient economy, may bring a return to increased state participation and more of a social market economy. 'At the beginning of the 1990s, attention is switching back to the public sector. This is less a reflection of a desire to expand the sphere of government than a belated recognition that ... the performance of the public sector is a crucial determinant of the quality of our lives' (Prowse, 1990).

References and Bibliography

Angel Noceda, M. (1990) 'El INI sin lastre', 'La marcha hasta los beneficios', 'Reconversión con nombres propios', El País 18 March, pp.3–5

Aranzadi, C. (1989) 'La política de desinversiones en el INI', Papeles de Economía Española 38, pp.258–61

Arriaga Fano, J. and L. Lerena Guinea (1989) 'Los problemas de la armonización de los sectores público y privado en el mercado unico', Situación 2, pp.92–111

Comín, F. (1988) 'Las administraciones públicas', in J. García Delgado, España: Tomo II, Economía, pp.431–69. Madrid: Espasa-Calpe SA

Donaghy, P. and M. Newton (1987) Spain: a guide to political and economic institutions. Cambridge: CUP

Edo Hernández, V. (1989) 'Las empresas públicas: concepto, delimitación y clasificación', Papeles de Economía Española 38, pp.68–77

El País (1990) Anuario El País, 1990. Madrid

Fariñas, J. et al. (1989) 'La empresa pública industrial española: 1981–1986', Papeles de Economía Española 38, pp.199–216

Fernández Rodriguez, Z. (1989) 'El alcance del proceso privatizador en España', Papeles de Economía Española 38, pp.243–6

García Fernández, J. (1989) 'La teoría de Stigler sobre la regulación como marco de la política empresarial pública 1973–1988', Papeles de Economía Española 38, pp.224–42

Intervención General de la Administración del Estado (1988) Cuentas de las empresas públicas para 1985. Madrid: Ministerio de Economía y Hacienda

Jonquiéres G. de. (1990) 'The break with French tradition', Financial Times 17 January,

p.24
Ministerio de Industria y Energía (MINE) (1989) *Informe Anual 1988*, Madrid
Mochón, F. *et al.* (1988) *Economía española 1964–1987 introducción al análisis economico.* Madrid: McGraw-Hill
Myro, R. (1988) 'Las empresas públicas', in J. García Delgado (ed.), *España: Tomo II, Economía.* pp.471–97. Madrid: Espasa-Calpe SA
Novales, A. *et al.* (1987) *La empresa pública industrial en España.* Madrid: Fundación de Estudios de Economía Aplicada
Ortiz Junquera, P. and A. Gómez Rodrigo (1989) 'La empresa pública en el contexto de la contabilidad económica', *Papeles de Economía Española* 38, pp.78–84
Papeles de Economía Española 38 (1989) *La empresa pública en España.* Madrid: Confederación Española de Cajas de Ahorros
Prowse, M. (1990) 'Putting a price on the quality of life', *Financial Times* 11 July, p.20
Ruiz Cañete, O. (1989) 'Empresa pública y transferencias estatales', *Papeles de Economía Española* 38, pp.85–100
Tamames, R. (1986) *The Spanish economy.* London: C. Hurst & Company
Tizón, A. (1989) 'La adaptación a la competencia del INI', *El País* 20 August, Sección Negocios p.2
Tsoukalis, L. (1981) *The European Community and its Mediterranean enlargement.* London: Croom Helm
Vickers, J. and V. Wright (1988) 'The politics of industrial privatisation in western Europe: an overview', *West European Politics* 11, October, No.4, pp.1–30

◆ Chapter 3 ◆

Agriculture, forestry and fishing

3.1 Agriculture, forestry and fishing in the economy

Agriculture, forestry and fishing continue to form important components of the economy, although their relative importance has declined as a result of the expansion of the economy and deep-seated problems. Their economic significance can be gauged by their contribution to the gross domestic product, to trade, to employment, to the processing industries that they sustain and to the market that they offer for manufactured products and services. Beyond this these primary activities permeate the life of the country, providing a reservoir of labour for economic expansion, a cushion of resources in times of recession, part-time employment, subsistence income and an invaluable recreation resource intimately connected with the physical environment.

The sector contributes a significant part of both national income and employment. Production represents between five and eight per cent of the gross domestic product, depending upon the climatic conditions experienced during the year. Within the total final value of production of agriculture and forestry (*producción agraria*), agricultural production (*producción agrícola*) contributes between fifty and sixty per cent, livestock production thirty to forty five per cent and forestry two to eight per cent (based on the years 1982 to 1988 inclusive; MAPA, 1989a). In terms of employment, the activities of agriculture, forestry and fishing involve between 1.5 and 2.0 million people (twelve to fourteen per cent of the labour force), of whom some 100,000 are directly engaged in fishing. To these statistics it is important to add the direct links that the sector has with the food processing industry, the largest manufacturing sector in Spain.

Agriculture, forestry and fishing products are also important components of trade, where they represent between ten and twenty per cent of both merchandise imports and exports (MAPA, 1988). The trade balance in agricultural and food products (*productos agroalimentarios*) is influenced by the size of annual harvests, nevertheless it has tended to deteriorate since membership of the European Community. Thus the rate of coverage of imports by exports declined from 101 in 1985 to ninety two in 1989. The source of the deficit is in food products (as opposed to primary agricultural products, which tend to record a surplus), where the rate of coverage deteriorated from 135 in 1985 to eighty in 1989. Major exports are fresh fruit and vegetables, cereals, wine and vegetable oils. Spain is a leading world exporter of table olives, olive oil, wine, almonds and cork. Major imports include feed grains (especially maize), fish, meat and dairy products.

An increasing proportion of agricultural product trade is with the European Community. Until recently this trade has been roughly in balance. However, food imports from EC countries have been growing faster than exports. Between 1985 and 1987 imports from EC countries rose from twenty two per cent of total food imports to forty two per cent, while exports to the EC increased over the same period from sixty five to sixty nine per cent (MAPA, 1989a).

While the sector remains of considerable importance to the economy, it has none the less experienced a substantial relative, and in some senses absolute, decline. The economically active population in agriculture, forestry and fishing plummeted from 4.9 million in 1960 (about forty per cent of the economically active population) to 2.4 million in 1980, then down further to 1.8 million (11.8 per cent) in the first quarter of 1990 (Table 3.1), the occupied population in 1990 being only 1.6 million. As a proportion of gross domestic product the sector has fallen by about ten percentage points since the early 1960s and by a larger amount in trade, reflecting the slower growth of the sector relative to others in the economy.

Table 3.1 The decline of employment in agriculture

Year	Economically active	Proportion of labour force	Year	Economically active	Proportion of labour force
1950	5,271,000	48.8	1980	2,362,700	17.8
1960	4,922,700	41.7	1985	2,242,500	16.5
1970	3,706,300	29.1	1990	1,766,400	11.8
1975	2,852,600	21.5			

Source: INE *Encuesta de la Población Activa* (various dates)

Decline in agriculture has been accompanied by a 'silent' restructuring process involving a radical transformation away from traditional agricultural practices towards more commercial production. Traditional agriculture was based on farming practices that were closely allied to the physical environment (for example using fallow to maintain fertility – as in the *año y vez* system – and dispersed plots to ensure product variety). Production methods were reliant upon abundant and cheap labour. Marketing was oriented either to local markets or subsistence requirements. This form of agriculture was protected by an extensive web of state intervention and product protection, which ensured the survival of small farms while providing an easy income on large farms. Rapid economic growth in the 1960s created a crisis in this system, as the labour force on which it relied melted away to leave behind a decaying rural economy suffering from labour shortages and rising labour costs (García Delgado, 1988). The adoption of capital to replace labour and draught animals (Table 3.2) and the increased reliance on off-farm inputs (mechanised equipment, new seeds, fuel, feed, fertilizers, pesticides and irrigation) increased other input costs. Simultaneously farm revenues were squeezed by inflation and weak product prices resulting from increased production, slow growth in demand and poor marketing. Problems were heightened in some sectors by changing patterns of demand. As incomes rose, those products with low or negative income elasticities of demand (such as cereals and field vegetables) faced declining or stagnant markets, while demand grew for those products with high income elasticities of demand (such as horticultural products, dairy products and meat). Agriculture was slow to adjust to these changing patterns of demand, as market controls impeded the translation of changing patterns of demand into appropriate pricing structures. Land-use competition also resulted in the abandonment of agricultural land, especially around the coast.

Table 3.2 Draught animals and mechanisation

Draught Animals (thousand head)	1960	1970	1980	1986	1987
Bulls and oxen	212	67	11	4	–
Cattle	1,063	1,035	306	162	–
Horses, mules and asses	1,469	914	394	241	–
Mechanised Equipment (thousand units)					
Tractors	–	260	524	658	679
Motorised cultivators	–	72	220	275	278
Combine harvesters (for cereals)	–	28	42	47	48

Sources: MAPA, 1988; Ortiz-Cañavate, 1989

New forms of agriculture are associated with more intensive production, specialisation and the increased reliance on capital and off-farm inputs. Farms are more dependent on markets for both inputs and outputs than they were under traditional farming systems. Production is more scientific and more commercially based, requiring careful cultivation techniques. Outputs are directed increasingly towards manufacturing and the tourism industry. Marketing has become more sophisticated, depending on specialised marketing channels. These changes in agriculture have been 'triggered by powerful market forces rather than by state policies' (García-Ramon, 1985).

The modern face of agriculture is illustrated by the commercial citrus fruit production in Valencia, mechanised cereal farms in Sevilla and horticultural production in southern Spain. Along the coast of Almería, Granada and Málaga, increased horticultural production has been achieved through the use of new techniques, particularly plastic to protect crops, either in the form of *invernaderos* (greenhouses), frequently coupled with '*enarenado*' (sand-bed) cultivation, or as black plastic sheeting over the soil. *Invernaderos* conserve moisture, provide proof against frost and ensure higher average temperatures, so bringing forward maturity and allowing many 'earlies' (which command higher prices than the main crop) to be produced. Covering the ground with black plastic has a similar effect and also inhibits the development of weeds. The *enarenado* system consists of: i) careful preparation of the ground, ii) application of a thick dressing of organic material and iii) covering the peat with some 100 mm of beach sand. The latter has two effects: it insulates the soil, thereby advancing the harvest, and it interrupts capillary movement of water through the soil, thereby reducing evaporation loss. The plants develop their roots in the top centimetres of soil below the layer of sand. In this area of soil they find the optimum conditions of aeration, nutrients and humidity for their development. This technique of farming has transformed semi-desert areas into areas of intensive horticulture and has spread widely around the Mediterranean coast. The Campo de Dalías in Almería is the most important centre along the south coast, with over 5,000 hectares under *invernaderos*. The coast of Huelva is a more recently established area, having developed a major export industry in strawberries in the 1980s.

New agricultural practices along the coast of southern Spain have been accompanied by new economic and ecological problems, which threaten continued success. Following a number of years of rapid expansion, markets have been saturated, not so much by the volume of production but more by the concentration of the harvest in May and June. Ecological problems are potentially more serious than economic ones. Rapid expansion of production has dramatically increased water demand, heightening problems of salinity (and possibly lowering the water table in the interior, leading to increased desertification). As a result, further expansion of the industry has had to be halted in many areas. Other problems have been associated with the intensive use of agri-chemicals: fertilizers, pesticides and fungicides. Less-often mentioned is the staggering visual blight on the landscape resulting from extensive stretches of coastline being enshrouded in plastic, a reflection (along with that of tourist development) of the priority given to economic growth and of private initiative uncontrolled by an effective planning system.

3.2 Changing patterns of agriculture

In capitalist economies, agricultural enterprises expand or contract according to their relative viability. Thus as input and product prices change, so too do agricultural patterns. In general irrigated areas, horticultural and livestock production have been expanding, while marginal dry farmed areas and their associated crops have been contracting. Of the total area of Spain (504,750 square kilometres), about ninety five per cent is not built on. Within this rural environment about forty eight per cent (203,900 square kilometres) is cultivated, sixteen per cent (66,800 square kilometres) is under pasture and thirty seven per cent (156,600 square kilometres; MAPA, 1989a) under some form of woodland. Of the cultivated area about seventy per cent is under herbaceous crops (cereal grains, legumes, roots, industrial crops, forage crops, vegetables) and thirty per cent under woody crops (citrus fruits, non-citrus fruits, vines and olives; Table 3.3).

Physical environmental conditions provide the framework within which different forms of agricultural enterprise are viable. For example, the pasture lands of the north coast of Spain (Asturias and Cantabria) contrast with the extensive cereal growing areas of the interior (Castilla and La Mancha), which again contrast with the sub-tropical products of the southern Mediterranean coast (Andalucía). Similarly, across much of the country (excluding the north coast and Galicia) the availability of water supplies determines the intensity of production. Where agriculture relies mainly on intermittent rain-fed water supplies, production tends to be extensive and centred around the traditional Mediterranean triad of cereals, olives and vines. Conversely, where regular water supplies are available, more intensive agriculture is possible (especially fruit and vegetables). On this physical environmental framework is superimposed the pattern of market areas, which are frequently associated with intensive agricultural production and production of perishable products.

Table 3.3 Land use in 1987

Land use	Dry Farmed (000ha)	Irrigated (000ha)	Total (000ha)
Cultivated area	17,284	3,106	20,390
Pasture	6,475	210	6,685
Forest	15,661	–	15,661
Other	7,734	–	7,734
Total	47,154	3,316	50,470
Cultivated area			
Cereal grains	6,869	1,012	7,881
Leguminous grains	375	56	431
Tubers for human consumption	151	148	299
Industrial crops	950	376	1,326
Forage crops	805	392	1,197
Horticulture	98	382	480
Sub total	9,249	2,368	11,617
Citrus crops	–	257	257
Non-citrus crops	649	251	900
Vines	1,460	54	1,514
Olives	1,979	114	2,093
Other woody crops	104	5	109
Sub total	4,192	681	4,873
Total cultivated area	13,441	3,049	16,490

Source: MAPA, 1989a

Herbaceous crops occupy more than seventy per cent of the cultivated area. Over two thirds of this area (eight million hectares) is sown to cereals, of which barley covers the largest area, followed by wheat. The total area under cereal production has remained relatively stable since 1971; however, the composition of crops grown has changed, with the area sown to wheat having decreased and that sown to barley having increased. Leguminous grains (including beans, chick-peas and lentils) have exhibited a long-term tendency to decline (the area under cultivation falling by forty six per cent between 1972 and 1986), reflecting the switch from natural means of maintaining fertility through fallow and crop rotations to the addition of artificial fertilizers. The area under rootcrop production has remained stable with about thirty per cent of production arising in Galicia, followed by León. Roots for human consumption are dominated by potatoes, very early varieties being produced in the Islas Canarias and along the coast of Andalucía.

Olives and vines are the other crops that dominate the landscape of central and southern Spain. The total area under olives has remained stable since 1935 at around two million hectares (of which over ninety per cent is under olives used for producing oil). The olive will grow on steep slopes and its long roots enable it to survive the summer droughts. Thus even where the trees are old and unproductive, they fulfil an important function in stabilising slopes. The plant bears fruit seven years after planting, reaching full production in fifteen years and thenceforth enjoying a long production life in which it requires relatively little attention. The olive formed an important component of many traditional agricultural systems, providing oil, wood for fuel, a construction material and olive waste for pig food. Modernisation has broken this system to leave olive growers more dependent on the olive itself. Olives frequently form a monoculture, covering extensive areas in Andalucía (the region embraces over fifty per cent of the total olive-growing area in Spain; Jaén alone covers over twenty per cent of the total area and Córdoba thirteen per cent), Extremadura (nine per cent of the total olive growing area of Spain) and in other parts of central Spain. The major area for table-olive production is around Sevilla (especially the Aljarafe area, where large table olives are generally grown on estates) and in Badajoz. Extensive areas have been replanted with new olive trees and some areas taken out of production. But large areas remain covered by unproductive trees, especially where there are few alternative crops or where neglecting the land has brought tax advantages.

Vines occupy over 1.5 million hectares, almost half of which are in Castilla–La Mancha. As with wheat and olives, vines are frequently grown as a monoculture (for example in Valdepeñas and Manzanares in Castilla–La Mancha and Penedés in Cataluña). The trend has been towards a decline in the area under cultivation, prompted by government policy. But, as with olives, many of the areas in which vines are grown are unsuitable for other crops. Poor soils and lack of attention have resulted in low yields. Where more careful cultivation is practised the vines yield table grapes (about five per cent of production) and high quality wines (many quality wines coming from areas covered by Denomination of Origin Regulation Boards los Consejos Reguladores de Denominaciones de Origen (CRDO).

Production of industrial crops has illustrated a strong long term increase in the area under production (from 738,000 hectares in 1972 to 1,319,000 hectares in 1988). In 1986 three quarters of this area was under sunflowers and fifteen per cent under sugar beet. Industrial-crop enterprises tend to be more capital intensive than other sectors and more closely tied to industrial production. Production of sunflowers has expanded dramatically since 1970 when guaranteed prices for oilseed products were introduced (from 165,900 hectares in 1970 to 920,700 ha in 1988). Sunflowers are grown throughout Spain under a wide range of environmental conditions (although eighty per cent of the area planted is in Andalucía and Castilla–La Mancha), nearly all being grown without irrigation. In Andalucía sunflowers have frequently replaced olives or are grown in rotation with cereals. The bulk of sugar production is obtained from sugar beet (some 190,400 hectares in 1988, especially in the Ebro Valley (Zaragoza), the Duero Basin (León and Burgos) and Andalucía (Granada, especially the Vega de Genil, Sevilla, the Guadalquivir Valley, Málaga, the Antequera Basin and Cádiz). The areas under sugar cane have declined steadily in the face of more profitable uses of the southern Mediterranean coastal land where it is grown (the crop occupying some 2,700 hectares in 1987 in Almería, Granada, Málaga and the Islas Canarias). Former sugar-cane fields are now more likely to support high-rise hotels or apartments.

Other industrial crops include cotton and tobacco, the former being the only textile fibre now of any importance in Spain. Cotton requires a frost-free environment, irrigation, and ample fertilizer and labour (prior to recent mechanisation). The area under production expanded in the 1980s from less than 50,000 hectares in 1979 to 134,800 hectares in 1988, expansion that has been related to the higher prices set under the Common Agricultural Policy and reduction in labour costs through mechanisation. Andalucía is the main region of production, with about forty per cent of the planted area in Sevilla, followed by Córdoba, Jaén and Cádiz. Tobacco is cultivated in non-irrigated areas of the north of Spain and in the irrigated lowland areas (*vegas*) of the interior in the south. During the 1980s there has been a steady expansion in the area under production from 18,400 hectares in 1979 to 28,500 hectares in 1988. About three quarters of the planted area is in Cáceres, followed by the Vega de Granada (especially the Rubio Valley).

Horticultural production is one of the most intensive agricultural enterprises. Although it occupies only a small percentage of the cultivated area, it contributes about fifty per cent of the value of crop production (*producción agrícola*). Production areas are closely related to transport arteries and urban areas, although improved transport has allowed production to develop away from markets, for example in the coastal areas of Almería and Huelva. A mild climate coupled with the availability of irrigation have been key environmental factors in the development of horticultural areas, resulting in production concentrated around the Mediterranean coast, in the Ebro Valley and in the Islas Canarias. Horticultural production has tended to expand steadily in the 1980s to around half a million hectares. Among the more important crops are artichokes, broad beans, cabbages, cauliflowers, cucumbers, asparaguses, lettuces, melons, onions, peas, peppers, runner beans, tomatoes, water melons, strawberries and flowers. One of the most widely planted crops is the tomato, with early varieties being grown in the Islas Canarias, Alicante, Almería, Málaga and Valencia. In the interior, horticultural products tend to be grown mostly for the domestic market, with the major exporting area being around the Mediterranean coast.

Citrus and non-citrus fruit are important export crops in addition to supplying the domestic market. They occupy some 250,000 hectares, over three quarters of which are under oranges (including mandarins), with most of the rest under lemons (grapefruit occupying a much smaller area). Production is concentrated around the Mediterranean coast and in the Ebro Valley, the major export region being Valencia. Orange varieties have changed in recent years towards sweeter ones, with more juice and fewer pips (for example the navel orange). In contrast to the limited range and concentrated pattern of citrus-fruit production, non-citrus fruits cover a diversity of products and are widely scattered, occupying almost 900,000 hectares, over fifty per cent of which is under extensive almond production. Non-citrus fruits offer a great diversity of products including apples, pears, apricots, cherries, plums and peaches from cooler climatic areas; figs, chirimoyos (custard apples), avocados, bananas and pomegranates from sub-tropical and semi-desert areas; and the dry fruits almonds, walnuts and hazelnuts. The almond-growing areas are distributed widely around the Mediterranean coast (especially in Alicante, the Islas Baleares, Granada and Murcia). In contrast, production of the chirimoyo is highly concentrated. Almost all of the 1,500 hectares under production are in Granada (municipality of Almuñécar). Similarly, production of bananas is almost totally confined to the Islas Canarias (with limited production from the Costa del Sol). Between 1981 and 1986 Spain was a net exporter of virtually all these crops.

Livestock production is another sector that has expanded (especially pigs), stimulated by increased consumer demand and access to imported feeds. Climatic conditions have always placed a restraint on production, especially of beef and dairy cattle, but this has been reinforced in the past by the protection (including import restrictions) afforded to potential animal feeds. The lifting of import restrictions has allowed greater imports of animal feed (imports that explain why there has been little increase in the area under forage crops such as alfalfa, vetch, clover and many cereals despite higher livestock numbers). Cattle production is concentrated principally along the north coast and in Galicia, where there is adequate rainfall to support pasture; elsewhere production must rely on cattle feed. In 1988 there were about 5 million head of cattle (a ten per cent increase on 1980), of which there were about 2.7 million cows (fifty per cent Frisians), 24 million head of sheep, 3.6 million head of goats and 16.6 million head of pigs (a forty-seven per cent increase on 1980). Dairy cattle are concentrated in the provinces of Barcelona, Madrid, Oviedo, Santander and Vizcaya (a high proportion of milk produced being processed into butter and cheese). Outside of the north, beef cattle are produced particularly in Andalucía (for example in the Guadalquivir Valley). Sheep are reared widely across Spain with Merino sheep being bred particularly for their wool in Extremadura. In La Mancha the milk from sheep is used to produce the famous Manchego cheese. Goats are the most widely kept animal (apart from the ubiquitous chicken) but are found especially in the central and south of Spain where they have been a characteristic element of the traditional farming scene, being bred for their skin, milk and meat.

3.3 Problems of agricultural production

Relatively low yields, low incomes and the continued drain of people away from agriculture are symptomatic of fundamental problems in agriculture. The cause of these problems lies partly in a difficult physical environment, but also in the way in which agriculture has evolved in response to a protectionist and interventionist political economy. Thus a distorted farm size structure, extensive monocultures, an elderly and low-skilled labour force, under-capitalisation, problems of finance, diffuse marketing arrangements and inadequate industrial development of agricultural products all characterised traditional agriculture. Tradition has been more deeply embedded in agriculture than elsewhere in the economy, slowing the rate of change.

3.3.1 The physical environment

The extent of agricultural activity in adverse environments can be gauged from the area of utilised agricultural land (*superficie agrícola utilizada* (SAU); this includes all the cultivated land, pasture, and land harvested during the period of the Census of Agriculture) recorded as being in less-favoured areas (*zonas desfavorecidas*: designated according to physical and economic criteria but notably mountainous and depopulated areas). According to a survey undertaken in 1987 by the Ministry of Agriculture (MAPA, 1989b), forty-six per cent of the total utilised agricultural land was in areas classified as unfavourable and twenty eight per cent in mountainous areas. Apart from spatial variations in soil conditions (including widespread soil erosion), the biggest single problem is the low and unreliable precipitation, roughly ninety per cent of the Spanish peninsular receiving on average less than 685 mm of precipitation per year. For example, a long period of drought over large areas of Spain in the early 1980s led to a series of poor harvests and consequent agricultural trade deficits, ended in 1984 by heavy spring rains and a record harvest. Those crops that rely on rain-fed water supplies are naturally most affected (especially cereals), but irrigated crops may be affected too, as irrigation water is reduced during prolonged periods of drought. Conversely, heavy rain hinders the development of olive flowers and dampness causes disease on olives, especially if it occurs in the autumn just before the harvest. Frost too is a common hazard, especially for citrus crops.

3.3.2 Farm size structure

One of the most intractable of problems in Spanish agriculture is a farm size structure distorted by a small number of very large farms and a multitude of very small ones. Farm size alone does not necessarily reflect efficiency, which depends on management, product mix, location, physical layout (degree of fragmentation), soil and so forth. Indeed the dichotomy between small and large farms partly reflects the contrasts between farming potential on irrigated and non-irrigated land. Nevertheless, large estates have frequently been associated with underutilisation of land and small farms are frequently unable to generate adequate incomes.

Using the standard definition of a farm to be a unit of operation and not of ownership, the 1982 Census of Agriculture recorded only 2.4 per cent of all holdings as 100 hectares or more, yet these large farms occupied 60.7 per cent of the total agricultural area. Conversely, 63.4 per cent of all the holdings were recorded as being less than five hectares in size, but they occupied only 5.4 per cent of the agricultural land (Table 3.4). In practice this degree of distortion may be misleading as the total agricultural area includes land not utilised for agriculture (for example woodland, scrub and mountainous land). If utilised agricultural land (SAU) only is considered, then according to the 1982 Census, holdings of 100 hectares or more occupy only 42.5 per cent of the farmland and holdings of less than five hectares occupy 8.0 per cent. A more recent survey specifically concerned with farm structure (MAPA, 1989b) found that farms of over 100 hectares occupied only 39.8 per cent of the utilised agricultural land, while those of less than five hectares occupied 8.4 per cent of the utilised agricultural land.

There are two explanations for the discrepancy between the figures for total agricultural land and utilised agricultural land. The first is that many large estates cover entirely unproductive land (for example in the province of Málaga many large estates are owned by municipalities and occupy high mountainous areas). The other explanation is that large tracts of land in large estates are underutilised. In both surveys, farms of 20 to 99.9 hectares occupy only about one third of the utilised agricultural land. These figures do not of course take into account ownership patterns which may be more distorted than those of farms, with individuals owning more than one holding, or the ownership of individual holdings being split between a number of people.

Table 3.4 Farm size structure

Farm Size (ha)	Percentage of holdings			Percentage of area			Percentage SAU	
	1962	1972	1982	1962	1972	1982	1982	1987
No land or less than 0.1	7.4	1.8	1.3	0.0	0.0	0.0	0.0	0.0
0.1–0.9	24.4	22.8	25.0	0.7	0.6	0.6	0.9	0.5
1.0–4.9	34.3	38.0	37.1	6.0	5.3	4.8	7.1	7.9
5.0–9.9	13.9	15.1	14.1	6.6	5.9	5.2	7.5	8.1
10.0–19.9	10.0	10.5	10.2	9.4	8.2	7.5	10.7	10.5
20.0–49.9	6.5	7.1	7.1	13.2	12.0	11.6	17.1	17.9
50.0–99.9	1.7	2.3	2.6	8.2	8.9	9.6	13.8	15.3
100.0–499.9	1.4	1.9	2.1	19.8	21.8	22.9	24.5	*
500 plus	0.4	0.5	0.5	33.7	37.3	37.8	18.3	39.8
Total	100.0	100.0	100.0	100.0	100.0	100.0	100.0	100.0

Note: Percentages are based on the total area of land included in the Census, except for the last two columns, which are percentages of the utilised agricultural land

* Farms in the 100.0 - 499.9 category are included in that for 500 plus

Source: MAPA, (Censo Agrario–various dates and 1986b)

The existence of large estates in the farm size structure has been of fundamental importance not just to the development of agriculture but to the evolution of the whole political economy. Traditionally (large estates) (*latifundia*) have been associated with extensive agriculture, insufficient capital investment and low levels of productivity, despite occupying some of the best lands (the land reform law of 1932 defined *latifundia* as estates of 200 hectares or more in dry farming or fifty hectares or more in irrigation, *dehesa* being mainly pastoral in the mountains and *cortijo* mainly arable in the lowlands; Martinez Alier, 1971). They are particularly characteristic of La Mancha (notably Ciudad Real), Extremadura (notably Cáceres) and western Andalucía (notably Cádiz, Córdoba and Sevilla). In the past, owners had little incentive to improve these lands: the lower the official classification of land, the lower the taxes (a situation that may change with the completion of the rural land catastral survey in the early 1990s and the tightening of taxation laws; Bruce, 1990). Frequently the land has been rented out for grazing and hunting, while absentee landowners lived in the cities. Apart from the economic consequences of *latifundia*, the social consequence was a landless peasantry denied any prospect of improvement (Giner and Sevilla, 1977). The *latifundio* was part of a feudal society, which withered only with the death of General Franco.

The presence of *latifundia* was an important political issue in the past, but in contemporary Spain the issue has been defused by the changing production environment: the Common Agricultural Policy, the decline of the agricultural population and the modernisation of agriculture. Emigration during the 1950s and 1960s released pressure on the land and diverted attention away from discontent over land ownership. By the time emigration was halted in the mid 1970s and a political regime installed that was more sympathetic with the problem, the problem itself had partly evaporated. The modern large estates are frequently intensively cultivated (especially where they are farmed by personally managing owners; Maas, 1983) and in many areas (for example in parts of Sevilla) they are being transformed into company farms practising the most modern agro-industrial techniques.

At the other end of the farm size spectrum is the small farm or *minifundio*, occupying only a few hectares (and frequently much less) and/or involving only a few head of livestock. Commonly these small farms are further fragmented into numerous dispersed plots (although fragmentation is also present on large farms), giving a variegated aspect to the landscape. In addition there may be multi-ownership of single plots and different usufruct rights in the same plot. Efficiency is precluded by limitations on economies of scale: the exclusion of machinery, the loss of land in field boundaries, the restrictions placed on raising loans to finance improvements, and the time taken to move from one plot to another. Atomisation of land holdings is common across Spain, but is particularly characteristic of the more mountainous areas of Andalucía and Galicia.

Restructuring of agricultural holdings has been substantial, even though small farms remain common. According to the Census of Agriculture, there has been a dramatic decline in the number of farm holdings since 1962 (although analysis of trends in farm structure must be treated with caution because of changes in definitions and coverage in the Census). Between 1962 and 1982 the number of farm holdings decreased by twenty one per cent (from 3,007,000 in 1962 to 2,559,000 in 1972 and thence down to 2,375,000 in 1982). Despite this decline, statistics on farm size provide little evidence that the small farm is disappearing from the landscape, although fragmentation does appear to be on the decline (García Delgado, 1988). But aggregate statistics mask important structural changes within different sectors of agriculture. Thus in cereal production (where economies of scale are critical) small farms has been declining. Overall the total number of land plots (*parcelas*) decreased by almost fifty per cent between 1962 and 1982 (from 39 million to 20 million), resulting in an increase of average plot size from 1.15 hectares to 2.16 hectares (Census of Agriculture). In 1962 the average number of plots per holding was 13.7 (Guedes, 1981), while in 1972 it was 10.0. These average figures conceal enormous spatial variations. Thus the average size of a plot (number of plots to total agricultural land) in 1982 varied from 0.26 hectares in Pontevedra to 18.4 hectares in Cádiz.

3.3.3 Enterprise combinations

In many parts of Spain agriculture has been heavily dependent on a single crop, with vast tracts of land given over to the monocultures of cereals, olives or vines, and fallow (non planted lands occupied twenty two per cent of the cultivated area in 1986). Irrigation is gradually breaking up this pattern. Monocultures include cereals in the Meseta (for example in the (region) (*comarca*) of Almazán they occupy eighty-seven per cent of the cultivated area), olives in Jaén (for example in the *comarca* of Campiña Sur olives occupy eighty per cent of the land area) and vines in Ciudad Real (for example in Valdepeñas). Such cropping patterns expose whole regions to the economic risks of a downturn in the fortunes of the crop produced, a risk that is reduced by enterprise diversification. At the other end of the spectrum many small farms have practised polycultures, providing a subsistence component to household income. Increased commercialisation is forcing greater specialisation.

3.3.4 The labour force

One of the most serious problems facing Spanish agriculture relates to the quality of the labour force. In general it is an elderly labour force with a low level of education and lack of agricultural training. A more youthful and better educated labour force is only slowly emerging, retarded by the continuing loss of young people from the land. Forty-six per cent of those working in farming are illiterate, and only 0.8 per cent have had higher education (*estudios superiores*). Only an estimated one in eighty-five people working in agriculture have had professional training (compared with one in eight in France and one in four in Holland; *El País*, 26 November 1989). The ageing of the agricultural labour force was reversed in the late 1970s and 1980s as young people found it difficult to find work away from rural areas. There have also been state (and European Community) incentives for young people to start agricultural businesses and thereby to retain people in agriculture (assistance has been available for young farmers to establish themselves, modernise farms, acquire land, obtain housing, etc.). Thus in 1983 13.5 per cent of the labour force were aged 20–29 and 13.5 per cent aged 30–39. By 1989 almost 20 per cent were aged 20–29 and 15 per cent 30–39. Against these figures thirty-five per cent are aged fifty or over. In other traditional industrial sectors, reconversion programmes have involved early-retirement programmes. In agriculture there was no such programme until after membership of the European Community.

Apart from the quality of the labour force, rising labour costs have been at the heart of the reorganisation of production and a critical factor in the crisis of traditional agriculture. Over the period 1964 to 1984 labour costs rose more rapidly than other farm costs, even during the period of rapidly rising energy prices in the 1970s (García Delgado, 1988). Not only has this resulted in the substitution of capital for labour (for example in cotton picking), but also in an increased reliance on temporary labour. Yet despite increased labour costs, negative wage differentials with other sectors still exists. Increased productivity in agriculture has generally not been accompanied by increased incomes, resulting in a continuing loss of labour.

3.3.5 Productivity

In relation to other European Community countries, productivity in agriculture remains low, partly because of relatively low levels of capital application. Low yields are particularly characteristic of cereals, but are also typical elsewhere, for example, in milk production, yields are only about sixty per cent of the European Community average. There has been a steady increase in mechanisation (associated with a decrease in labour and in the number of draught animals). The mechanisation rate (the horsepower of all motorised equipment per one hundred hectares) increased from 75.9 in 1970 to 176.6 in 1980 and thence to 224.0 in 1987 (MAPA, 1989a). In specific sectors there have been sharp increases in mechanisation. For example, in cotton the number of cotton harvesters increased from 299 in 1985 to 628 in 1986. But in comparison with other European Community countries, mechanisation remains low. Thus in 1986 there were three tractors per 100 hectares of utilised land (SAU) in Spain compared with five in France and twelve in West Germany (MAPA, 1989a). A similar picture exists in the application of agri-chemicals. Nitrogenous fertilizer consumption increased by 300 per cent between 1960 and 1985, yet in 1986 Spain used only forty-three kilograms per hectare (SAU), higher only than Portugal in the European Community (MAPA, 1989a).

3.3.6 Finance

More capitalistic farming methods have meant increased reliance on external finance and an increase in rural indebtedness (estimated to have increased from pta. 943 billion in 1984 to pta. 1,500 billion at the beginning of 1990; Maté, 1990a). The central problem for many enterprises has been that costs have risen faster than revenue. In addition, farming faces a particular financing problem because of the long time interval between investment and returns (and the cash-flow problem of income coming at one time of the year while expenditure is incurred throughout the year) and the indivisibility of many development projects. Simultaneously the financial returns on many agricultural investments would not normally allow farmers to borrow from the private sector. The Ministry of Agriculture provides grants directly (for example to subsidise the price of petrol and fertilizers, etc.) and in the past many farmers relied on government price supports and on the public sector for credit (notably the Agricultural Credit Bank (Banco de Crédito Agrícola, BCA) the Servicio Nacional de Productos Agrarios, SENPA, and the Instituto Nacional de Reforme y Desarrollo Agrario, IRYDA). Membership of the European Community has swept away this old system of support, while limiting many product prices to control surplus production. The net result has been a more competitive form of agriculture, increasingly financed through the private sector (controlling over eighty per cent of debt, about one third of which is through the rural savings banks).

3.3.7 Marketing

In the traditional production system, marketing is frequently chaotic, with output directed principally at the domestic market. Small family farms (generally with limited management ability and with limited power to negotiate prices) sell their products either directly in local markets or to merchants with small businesses. These merchants transport the products to their stores (which are generally small, badly prepared and without refrigeration facilities) and, after some brief selection and packing, they forward them to wholesale markets. Any surpluses are auctioned in small lots, without standardisation. The bulk of production tends to arrive in the market at the same time (for many products, in early summer), reducing product prices (in contrast, market prices tend to be high for the majority of products from December to April). In general there is a lack of information (transparency) about all aspects of the market.

The formation of marketing co-operatives has been one means by which farmers have endeavoured to improve their marketing position, but they have frequently not been very successful as a result of the inadequate discipline imposed by the co-operative. Producers may continue to decide independently the variety to be produced, the time of sowing, the cultivation methods to be used and the time of harvesting. When prices are high, all or part of the crop may be harvested and auctioned, resulting in market saturation and lower prices. Consequently, it may be impossible for a co-operative to offer consistent quality, quantity and price. For these reasons the big food-processing firms avoid these marketing networks by establishing their own farms or by having direct contracts with farmers.

3.4 Government intervention

The dominant theme in agricultural policy in the 1980s has been the adaption of the Spanish agricultural system to European Community requirements and the concomitant untangling of the extensive web of Spanish intervention measures developed during the Francoist regime. This has required the transfer to Brussels of part of the agricultural policy-making process and a rationalisation of assistance provided by the Ministry of Agriculture. Moreover, many of the functions previously carried out by the Ministry of Agriculture have been transferred to regional government organisations.

The major concern of national agricultural policy has been to modernise production structures and increase agricultural efficiency, thereby meeting internal demand for food and supporting an export industry able to meet foreign competition. Modernisation has included reform of production structures: irrigation, development of underground water supplies, farm modernisation, farm size structure improvements, training, and research and development. More broadly it has encompassed integrated rural development and the reconversion of some sectors of agricultural production (notably vines, olives, milk and cattle). Important programmes have included assistance to establish refrigeration equipment in milk producing areas, the provision of a modern network of municipal abattoirs (Plan General de Mataderos), the assistance provided in agricultural industrialisation zones (ZPLIA) and assistance to small agricultural enterprises (PYMES, *agroalimentarias*). Particular emphasis has been placed on promoting the formation of co-operatives for the purchase of inputs, the sharing of equipment and the marketing of produce. Many of these activities have been supported by the European Community.

3.4.1 Intervention in production and marketing

Prior to entry into the European Community, Spain operated an extensive intervention mechanism covering all stages of agricultural production and marketing. Areas planted were set, input and product prices were fixed and imports were controlled. Agricultural policy emphasised increased output, but this was restricted by the expansion of demand. Intervention inhibited the transmission of market signals to producers, leading to a mismatch between supply and demand.

Examples of intervention can be drawn from across the whole range of agricultural production. Intervention in wheat extends back to the nineteenth century, when production developed in the shelter of the rigidly protectionist laws prevailing between 1820 and 1869. Following strong competition from imports, further tariff protection was applied in 1891 and 1906, then in 1922 an absolute ban was imposed on foreign wheat imports. From 1937 wheat prices were supported by the National Wheat Service (Servicio Nacional del Trigo), which guaranteed to purchase all of the wheat crop at prices that would ensure the survival of small producers and simultaneously prove very rewarding to larger producers (*ad valorem* tariff barriers against wheat imports were also used to support prices). This agency was later broadened to the National Cereals Service (Servicio Nacional de Cereales), which in turn was enlarged in 1971 to the National Agricultural Produce Service (Servicio Nacional de Productos Agrarios, SENPA). SENPA guaranteed the purchase price for a range of crops (including soya seeds, sunflower seeds and rape seeds) and it subsidised seeds and fertilizer.

Agricultural product prices were supported from 1968 through the Fund for the Management of Agricultural Product Prices (Fondo de Ordenación y Regulación de los Precios y Productos Agrarios, FORPPA), an autonomous organisation of the Ministry of Agriculture. In the livestock industry there were guaranteed prices for all meats fixed at the abattoir and the Supply and Transport Commission (Comisaria General de Abastecimientos y Transportes) regulated prices in each product distribution channel (skins, frozen meat, etc.). In sugar production the Ministry of Agriculture determined the annual area of sugar planting for each region, fixed the price at which the sugar crop would be bought and the price at which sugar was sold to the public and to industry.

In tobacco the state intervened in cultivation and preparation through the National Tobacco Service (Servicio Nacional del Cultivo y Fermentación del Tabaco, SNCFT, established in 1944). Manufacturing and distribution were controlled by the Tobacco Monopoly (Monopolio de Tabaco) and through the Compañía Arrendataria de Tabacalera SA. Only the Islas Canarias lay outside the control of the tobacco monopoly.

Other elements of the control system included a network of wholesale markets in agricultural zones owned by the state and the local authorities (Empresa Nacional de Mercados en Origen de Productos Agrarios SA, Mercosa; for example, Mercogranada and Mercomediterraneo) and a network of retail markets (Mercasa).

Membership of the European Community has required that production and primary processing be liberalised. Frequently the national regulating organisations have taken on the responsibility of managing the pricing regime of the Common Agricultural Policy. In the case of a wide range of crops this is done by SENPA (with support for the pricing policy being channelled through FORPPA, which also manages intervention stocks) and in the case of tobacco by the SNCFT. In the case of Mercosa (now an agricultural-product distributor), the company has been privatised since 1990 and has embarked on a process of diversification and expansion into overseas markets (through a subsidiary, Mercodistribución). Similarly, Tabacalera has diversified into being a broad food-manufacturing company.

Co-operation between farmers is promoted as a means of increasing farm incomes through higher productivity and improved marketing. Apart from assistance available from the Ministry of Agriculture, assistance for this type of activity is also available from the European Community (through the European Agricultural and Guarantee Fund EAGGF, Guidance Section and European Social Fund). The phenomenon of association has been growing in recent years, but many of the associations that have been formed (including those for land improvement (Sociedades Agrarias de Transformación), producer associations (Agrupación de Productores Agrarios) and co-operatives) remain small in size and the extent of development is much less than in other European Community countries.

The Ministry of Agriculture also promotes the marketing of produce in a number of ways: for example, through setting up consumer panels to gain a better understanding of demand, through food-information campaigns and through the regulation and classification of horticultural and food products (the Fondo Nacional para la Normalización y Tipificación de Productos Hortofruticolas represents one specific action to achieve this end). The Ministry also attempts to promote quality assurance, for example through the national food classification institute (Instituto Nacional de Denominaciones de Origen). Classifications cover wine, cheese (e.g. Queso de Picón), sausages (e.g. Chorizo de Pamplona), asparagus (e.g. Espárrago de Navarra) and so forth. Finally, the Ministry undertakes certain inspection activities to ensure quality.

3.4.2 Restructuring and reconversion of agricultural production sectors

As part of the process of farm modernisation, the government has pursued a number of restructuring and reconversion programmes covering olives, vines, citrus fruit, milk, tobacco and livestock, designed to adjust production to demand. Producers must apply for assistance, which (in the case of crops) can be used to remove plants from unproductive areas and replant productive areas with improved stock.

In the case of olives at least twenty five per cent of the production area has been estimated to be on marginal land, difficult to convert to other uses. On these marginal lands, yields are low and mechanisation is difficult. The socio-economic implications of this crop have led government to intervene over a long period of time. Plans for reconversion and restructuring were begun in 1972 and further measures set in motion in 1982 (El Plan de Reestructuración del Olivar Mejorable y Reconversión de Comarcas Olivareras Deprimadas). Under this scheme 250,000 hectares of land then grown to olives were to be put down to other crops. Since 1986 help for improving the structure of the sector has been made through investment projects approved and partly financed by the European Community. In 1986 19,300 hectares were restructured (18,000 hectares in Andalucía) and 4,100 hectares reconverted (3,000 hectares in Andalucía).

Vines have been another sector that have suffered from overproduction and have thus been subject to restructuring and reconversion programmes designed to reduce excess production and improve the quality of wine. Other restructuring programmes have covered citrus fruit, milk and tobacco. In the case of citrus fruit, reconversion was necessary because of disease. The citrus virus 'tristeza' caused the death of more than 10 million trees in the early 1980s. Thus to combat the disease problem, and to maintain output in the sector, assistance was provided for the purchase of new, disease-resistant stock. Dairy farmers have also been able to apply to restructure production (which has been coupled with a plan to restructure the dairies). Intervention in tobacco cultivation was necessary to shift production to new varieties and to improve the production infrastructure (Plan de Reordinación de la Producción Tabaquera Nacional).

3.4.3 Agrarian reform

As mentioned earlier, farm size structure and organisation have been an important constraint on agricultural development. However, successive governments have avoided radical land reform and concentrated instead on irrigation, improving agricultural practices, land consolidation, colonisation and more general improvements in the rural environment. They have made little progress in breaking up large estates (Giner and Sevilla, 1977 and Naylon, 1973).

Following the death of Franco and the implementation of democratic government, renewed attempts were made to effect structural change. A law passed in 1979 permitted the expropriation of large estates where the land was found to be underutilised, but little progress was made, partly because the ideology of the Francoist regime still survived in the Ministry of Agriculture and partly because of the fear that radical reform might destabilise the emerging democracy. The Law of Agrarian Reform, (Ley de Reforma y Desarrollo Agrario) passed in 1983, provided new measures for the expropriation of land. The regional government of Andalucía was the first to implement the new legislation. In 1984 it designated land for reform in Antequera (province of Málaga). By the beginning of 1990 nine other areas (comarcas) had been designated for reform, but expropriation had made little progress (Maté, 1990b). The changing agricultural environment (especially European Community initiatives to take land out of cultivation and further falls in the agricultural labour force) has weakened the demand for such reforms (apart from amongst a declining group of militant agricultural workers). The designation of areas for agricultural reform is now seen more as a means of achieving farming improvements rather than one of achieving land redistribution. Thus designated areas are subject to land assessment and inventories, land improvement (irrigation and/or consolidation), reforestation, the formation of co-operatives, the commercialisation and industrialisation of products, and fiscal assistance.

Apart from the problem of *latifundia*, the central government has also attempted to tackle the problem of small and fragmented farms through land consolidation programmes. The first law on land consolidation was passed in 1952 (Guedes, 1981) and implemented by the Servicio Nacional de Concentración Parcelaria y Ordenación Rural (SNCPOR). Progress in this complex area of action was inevitably slow, although grants and loans were available at low interest rates for small farms to be increased in size and for all farmers to improve their properties. Vineyards, irrigated land, orchards and woodland are all difficult to consolidate, as are mountainous areas. Heterogeneity of land with different potential and trees of different ages and yields pose particular problems. Hence most headway has been made on uniform lands (for example the grain lands of León and Castilla, where settlement is nucleated). By 1977 4.7 million hectares had been concentrated, affecting 3,375 areas and 937,234 farmers; 13,688,688 plots of average size 0.35 hectares had been reduced to 1,790,971 plots of average size 2.64 hectares (Guedes, 1981). By 1982 consolidation had been extended to 5.2 million hectares (Tamames, 1983). Unfortunately, even after reform, farms tended to remain small in size (O'Flanagan, 1982). Significant increases in farm size will only occur as the number of farm owners decrease.

Responsibilities for agrarian reform have now largely been transferred from the central government (IRYDA, which was formed in 1971, subsuming the roles of both the colonisation institute, the INC, and the land consolidation organisation SNCPOR) to the regional governments (for example, in Andalucía the Instituto Andaluz de la Reforma Agraria (IARA)). These regional agencies continue the work of agrarian reform: crop development, farm modernisation, the introduction of new farm systems, irrigation and settlement. However, in a democratic society (where under the Constitution private property is protected) structural change is inevitably slow, with limited opportunities to break up large estates or consolidate small farms.

Apart from the general programmes of agrarian reform, specific areas now qualify for assistance under both state and European Community schemes. Specific support is available for agriculture in mountainous areas (*indemnizaciones compensatorias de montaña*, ICM) which embrace 3,000 municipalities and an area of 20 million hectares (the Spanish administration gave pta. 7,500 million to farmers in these areas in 1988, pta. 6,008 million paid by central government, pta. 1,300 million by regional government plus pta. 200 million in País Vasco). The scheme complements that for areas unfavourable for farming.

3.4.4 Irrigation

In the past, irrigation schemes have been used by the state as the main means of promoting rural development. Irrigation has been installed across the whole of Spain, especially in the main river basins: the Ebro, Guadiana, Guadalquivir and Tajo. Between 1960 and 1987 the irrigated area (covering both public and private irrigation schemes) increased by seventy per cent from 1.83 million hectares to 3.1 million hectares. Irrigation enables more intensive production (higher yields per crop, multiple cropping, year-round production), a greater diversity of crops and more-consistent output. The principal problems of irrigation are concerned with its cost in relation to the benefits derived from increased agricultural output and employment, the relationship between those who pay for irrigation works and those who benefit from them, the ecological impact of irrigation on surrounding areas (for example the over-use of underground aquifers), and the management and technical problems associated with the implementation and running of irrigation schemes.

Major public works associated with irrigation schemes (dams, reservoirs and irrigation canals) are carried out under the direction of the Ministry of Public Works (Ministerio de Obras Públicas, Dirección General de Obras Hidráulicas) through the water authorities (*confederaciones hidrográficas*). Schemes are set in motion by the Ministry of Agriculture, through IRYDA, in conjunction with the regions (where they are of national concern) and/or by the regions themselves. The regional agencies in conjunction with IRYDA then implement the irrigation schemes and are responsible for agrarian development (including any colonisation). Assistance from central and regional government agencies is also available for the improvement and development of private irrigation.

3.4.5 Conservation of nature

The national rural environmental agency is the Instituto Nacional para la Conservación de la Naturaleza (ICONA), which on its formation in 1971 subsumed the roles of the Patrimonio Forestal del Estado, the Servicio de Pesca Continental, Caza y Parques Nacionales and the Servicio Nacional de Conservación de Suelos. Thus it has broad responsibilities for the environment: for the protection of flora and fauna, the protection of river basins and water, for forestry and the conservation of soils. Like IRYDA it is an autonomous organisation of the Ministry of Agriculture and, as with IRYDA, its role has been reduced by the formation of regional government agencies such as the IARA and the Agencia de Medio Ambiente in Andalucía. Generally ICONA provides a link between the regional agencies and the central government, channelling national programmes down to the regions. Amongst the gravest ecological problems are those of desertification, soil erosion and pollution. Thus ICONA continues work on a project to reduce desertification (*Lucha contra la desertificación del mediterráneo*), preparing maps of the erosion situation in each of the river basins, and on programmes to combat forest fires.

3.5 Application of the Common Agricultural Policy

The incorporation of Spain into the European Community added about thirty per cent to the cultivated area of the existing ten member states, thirty per cent to the employment in agriculture and thirty per cent to the number of farm holdings. Agricultural production in Spain now represents about twelve per cent that of the EC. The Islas Canarias, Ceuta and Melilla chose to remain outside the customs union of the Community and thus to remain outside the Common Agricultural Policy (CAP). The CAP covers ninety five per cent of Spanish agricultural production in its price-support section (in 1989 Spain received European Currency Units (ECU) 1,823 million compared with 6,210 million for France) in addition to providing assistance for modernisation under its Guidance Section (in 1989 Spain received ECU 204 million, the third-largest sum after Italy and Greece) and broader rural development under the European Structural Structural Funds. In a sense therefore, Spanish agriculture is now more heavily protected than in the past.

The addition of Spain brought conflicts with other Mediterranean producers and added substantially to the problems of agricultural restructuring and maintaining price support within the Community. It also brought problems for third countries trading with Spain; for example, the United States feared the loss of a substantial maize market, and other third country Mediterranean producers (for example Israel and north African countries) feared greater competition for their products in European Community markets.

The objectives of agricultural policy in the European Community are to: i) increase the productivity of agriculture, ii) seek an equitable standard of living for the agricultural population, iii) achieve stability of markets, iv) guarantee security of food supplies and v) achieve reasonable prices to consumers (Treaty of Rome, Article 39). This policy has been implemented through the Common Agricultural Policy drawing on the EAGGF. The price support element of the EAGGF (Guarantee Section) has absorbed the majority of all funding; funds going especially into cereals and milk products. The Guidance Section has complemented national funding for agricultural improvements including funding for hill farmers, training, modernisation and early retirement. The growth of spending under the CAP and its effect of stimulating excess supply (increased output at a time when population growth has been almost static) have resulted in pressures for reform. Reform has included more realistic product pricing, quantity restrictions and land set-aside schemes. Simultaneously the Guidance Section of the CAP has been incorporated into the European Community Structural Funds, where agricultural improvements are now viewed in the broader context of rural development.

The reformation of Spanish agricultural policy necessary to make it compatible with the Common Agricultural Policy began before 1986. There were four main differences between the Spanish intervention system and that in the CAP. In Spain there was a more rigid system of intervention. Thus sales of a number of products (wheat, tobacco, sugar beet and hops) had to be directed through a public agency. Secondly, in Spain the state controlled trade in cereals, vegetable oils, milk products, cotton, tobacco and meat, which together represented a substantial proportion of total agricultural trade. Thirdly, the breadth of state intervention was less in Spain. Finally, there were a smaller range of structural measures in Spain than under the CAP.

To accommodate Spanish agriculture, a two pronged transitional arrangement was agreed: one extending over seven years and one extending over ten years. The classical model is one of seven years (with completion by 1 January 1993) applying to all products, except for fresh fruit and vegetables, and vegetable oils, which allows only very limited imports during the first four years. Institutional price regimes will gradually be brought into line (although if the initial difference was less than three per cent the price adjustment was instantaneous). Preferential state assistance incompatible with that in the European Community will be eliminated and the free circulation of products between Spain and the European Community will be established. Tariffs will gradually be reduced (by 12.5 per cent per year) and other trade restrictions, including the state control of agricultural trade, will be ended. Finally, there will be a gradual adjustment to the Common External Tariff, with the exact conditions varying according to products. A special safeguard clause will exist for ten years (until 1996) during which protectionist measures may be taken with the agreement of the European Community to prevent serious market problems. For fresh fruit and vegetables the transition comprises two stages extending over ten years. In the first four years domestic market protection was maintained while Spain adjusted its internal market mechanisms to those of the European Community. From 1 January 1990 the second stage of six years began during which trade restrictions with the European Community will gradually be removed. For vegetable oils there is a special regime also covering ten years, based on maintaining the status quo for five years (until 1 January 1991), thence following the classical model.

The impact of membership of the European Community continues to reverberate through the Spanish agricultural system (Banco Bilbao Vizcaya, 1990). In general, membership has been beneficial to producers of fruit and vegetables, cotton, rice, sunflowers, olive oil and wine. However, for the latter two products production restrictions may create problems and the liberalisation of the vegetable-oil market in 1993 is likely to see a fall in the demand for olive oil as other oils (notably sunflower and soya oil) become more competitive. Membership of the CAP has caused the greatest problems for milk producers and for cereal growers (although as soft wheat was considered a sensitive product, protection for it was extended over a further four years). Tight regulations on product quality have also had an impact. Thus the export of pork was prohibited up until 1989 because of the disease porcina africana. Overall, entry into the European Community has increased competition and resulted in substantially higher trade with Community countries, especially greater exports of horticultural products and greater imports of dairy products, meat and fish.

3.6 Forestry

For a country the size of Spain, the area of productive woodland is relatively small and timber yields are low, reflecting a long history of forest clearance (for example for agriculture and the sheep pastures of the Mesta), timber extraction (for shipbuilding and construction) and inadequate forest management. Of the total area of Spain 15.7 million hectares are classified as forested land (*terreno forestal*). Within this forested area, woodland (*superficie arbolada*) occupies 11.8 million hectares: 5.4 million under conifers, 3.7 million under broad-leaved trees on high mountains, and 2.2 million under broad-leaved trees on low mountains. Of the woodlands only 6.8 million hectares contain useful timber (Fernández Tomás, 1985), and even these tend to have a low-density tree cover. In fact only 2.5 million hectares of woodland show good or average density stands of timber. Potentially the most productive areas for forestry are the low lands (below 600 m) in Galicia and Cantabria

The forest-products industry offers employment in rural areas and a source of exports, in addition to meeting growing domestic demand. Total wood production was almost 16 million cubic metres in 1986, output having increased by over a third since the mid 1970s. The greater proportion of output is derived from eucalyptus and conifers. Despite increased production, consumption tends to exceed production and hence there is normally a deficit on the balance of trade, with imported products tending to be of a higher value than exports.

Production of timber and timber products has been increasing (Table 3.5), mainly a result of the planting of fast-growing tree species, especially eucalyptus. Rapid-growing species can produce an average of more than eight cubic metres of wood per hectare per year. The eucalyptus can produce ten to twenty-five cubic metres per hectare per year in a ten to twenty year growth cycle, compared with pine (pinus pinaster, maritime pine) which can only produce five to twelve cubic metres per hectare per year after taking eighteen to twenty-four years to reach maturity. Spain and Portugal are the only two producers of eucalyptus pulp in Europe. Apart from rapid growth, the tree has grown in popularity with paper producers because its fibres are short and easy to dry. By 1970 the state had planted 137,941 hectares and private growers 50,172 hectares. Since 1975 private investment has led the way, with private speculators having planted 203,082 hectares by 1985, while the state programme had increased to 232,691 hectares (current figures, especially for private growers, are much higher). Production has been further stimulated by European Community subsidies and the reduction of tariff barriers. As a result, Spain became a major exporter of eucalyptus fibre in the 1980s. The mixed public/private company Ence (Empresa Nacional de Celulosas) is now the world's largest producer of eucalyptus pulp with a substantial proportion of sales going to exports (more than sixty per cent of sales in the first six months of 1989; Financial Times 26 July 1989). It has 120,000 hectares under eucalyptus making it the second-largest grower after the government (Financial Times, 25 August 1989).

Table 3.5 Forest products

Year	Wood (000 m³)	Sawn wood (ooo m³)	Wood pulp (000 tonnes)	Paper and board (000 tonnes)	Cork (000 tonnes)	Resin (000 tonnes)
1960	4,513	—	—	—	86.3	47.2
1965	5,705	1,779	301	658	126.2	46.7
1970	8,627	2,098	599	1,280	109.5	43.1
1975	11,340	2,313	919	1,853	82.5	38.2
1980	11,892	2,094	1,219	2,566	87.8*	26.4
1985	13,899	2,264	1,394	2,913	73.5	24.0
1986	15,635	2,235	1,466	3,153	81.9	12.1
1987	14,259	—	1,568	3,252	67.9	15.3

* 1979 figure

Sources: MAPA (Ministerio de Agricultura–various dates)

The extraction of timber is closely related to the primary timber-processing industries of sawmilling and wood pulp. In turn these are linked to the manufacturing of paper and board, and furniture. Sawmills are widely distributed across the forested area (in 1983 there were 3,149 sawmills with a capacity of 6.73 million cubic metres, employing 23,000), with particular concentrations in Galicia (thirty-two per cent of sawmills and thirty-three per cent of capacity), Castilla–León (twenty per cent of sawmills and seventeen per cent of capacity) and Valencia (nine per cent of sawmills and eight per cent of capacity). Valencia is also the most important region for board, plywood and veneer mills. These industries are characterised by numerous very small plants. Fibre board and particle board mills are larger and more modern, including some of the most modern plant in Europe. Furniture is a major industry in Spain with important exports and an estimated employment of over 150,000 people in more than 20,000 plants, Cataluña and Valencia being the most important regions.

The paper industry has been expanding in the 1980s on the basis of growing domestic demand, which increased from 2.77 million tonnes in 1983 to 3.53 million tonnes in 1987. Part of this increased demand has been met by imports, which increased over the same period from 411,000 tonnes to 743,000 tonnes (Financial Times 24 February 1989). Despite this growth, consumption remains below the European Community average (in 1984 paper consumption in Spain was 77 kg per head, about half the EC average; in the USA it was 268 kg per head). This has been a major factor attracting foreign multinational companies into the Spanish paper industry. Wiggins Teape bought the paper producer Celulosas de Asturias in 1986. Scott Paper of the USA expanded its Spanish operations in 1987 by buying a pulp mill from the state-owned Ence, and the Kuwait Investment Office has control of the Catalan paper group Torras Hostench. Jefferson Smurfitt of Ireland and Feldmuehle of Germany were other paper companies investing in Spain in the late 1980s.

The paper industry has been characterised by small plants and fragmented ownership, but, as in other sectors, increased competition has brought restructuring and the increased participation of foreign multinational companies. In the early 1980s forty-four per cent of plants had production capacities of less than 5,000 tonnes per year and less than one per cent had capacities of more than 50,000 tonnes (Financial Times 24 February 1989). The industry, was not offered a government-sponsored restructuring plan, thus restructuring with the closure of many of the smaller plants has resulted from market forces. Nevertheless small size remains a characteristic of the industry, with no Spanish paper company in the world's top 100 in 1989. Cataluña, País Vasco and Valencia are particularly important centres of production.

Other traditional forest products, especially cork and resin, have tended to decline in importance. Cork is obtained from the cork oak (*alcornoque* – Quercus suber) which is estimated to cover 421,000 hectares, mainly in western Andalucía (especially Cádiz with 79,750 ha, Huelva and Sevilla), Extremadura (Badajoz and Cáceres), and Gerona (Abreu Pidal, 1985). The cork oak once formed the core of an agricultural system (Parsons, 1962a and 1962b) but its importance has declined as labour costs have increased and cork substitutes (notably plastic)) have appeared. Resin is produced from the maritime pine and as a by-product of the cellulose industry. Like the cork industry, the resin industry has also declined, with the number of factories falling from thirty-eight in 1974 to seventeen in 1983, while production capacity decreased from 60,000 tonnes to 40,000 tonnes (Abreu Pidal, 1985).

Apart from their commercial use, the forests are an integral part of the natural ecosystem and provide an invaluable leisure facility; as such they require careful management. Exploitation of the forests threatens not only the forests themselves but the whole forest ecosystem. The pattern of woodland ownership provides only limited opportunities for the state to become directly involved in woodland management. Sixty-six percent of the woodland area (*superficie arbolada*) is privately owned, leaving about 3.97 million hectares owned by public agencies, of which only 0.47 million hectares (four per cent) are owned by the state (much less than in other EC countries). Where the state is involved, it operates through ICONA. Past failures to provide adequate management may be partly attributable to the lack of support given to this agency by the central government.

Reforestation and the prevention of forest fires are an important part of forest management. Between 1975 and 1985 an average of 83,000 hectares (0.7 per cent of the woodland area) were replanted each year. Much of this replanting is associated with fast-growing pines and eucalyptus, which provide quick economic returns. However, this policy has impoverished the forest and it is claimed that the eucalyptus dries up the soil (increasing the risk of forest fire) and saps the soil of nutrients. Grade 1 and 2 forests can no longer be cut down for eucalyptus and regional governments are now supposed to be much stricter about planting applications. But many private landowners continue to plant without permission. By comparison with reforestation, between 1976 and 1985 there were on average 6,500 fires per year, affecting 125,000 hectares per year, causing losses of 440,000 cubic metres of wood (0.1 percent of total woodland) per year. Most worrying has been the trend towards an increased number of fires (Rico, 1985).

3.7 Fishing

The Spanish fishing industry is the largest in Europe outside of Norway, supporting an important fish processing industry and sustaining part of the shipbuilding industry. In 1989 there were 1,572 fishing vessels of 100 gross registered tonnes (GRT) or over, the total fish catch in 1988 was 1.02 million tonnes (including about ten per cent from fish farms); the whole fishing fleet in 1987 was recorded at about 663,000 gross registered tonnes; and there were about 100,000 fishermen (Larrea Ereño, 1989). Nevertheless, the fishing industry is a modest part of the total agriculture, forestry and fishing sector, contributing less than ten per cent of the value of final production (production valued at pta. 224 billion in 1987) and of employment in the sector. As in agriculture, fishing has become increasingly commercial but there remains a semi-subsistence element supplementing the incomes of many families.

The growth of the industry was based on the considerable length of Spanish coastline: 5,968 kilometres, of which 3,359 kilometres border the Atlantic and 2,580 kilometres the Mediterranean (3,904 kilometres are around the peninsular and the rest around the islands). The most important waters are those of the Atlantic coastline (Islas Canarias and Cantabria), which are much richer than those of the Mediterranean. However, because of the narrow coastal platform around the coast (depths of less than 400 metres extending only thirty to fifty kilometres from the coast, except in the Gulf of Cádiz and Valencia, where the coastal shelf extends eighty to one hundred kilometres) and the depletion of fish stocks, the fish catch must be enhanced by fish caught in more distant waters (about two thirds of the total catch).

The north west (Galicia) is the leading fishing region, accounting for about fifty to sixty per cent of the total fish unloaded in Spanish ports by weight (Table 3.6), about one third of the fishing vessels (measured by GRT) and one third of employment. It is also the major centre of shipbuilding for the fishing industry and of the fish-processing industry. The fishing industry focuses on Vigo and La Coruña, the two largest fishing ports in Spain. Outside of the north-west, fishing is also important along the rest of the northern Spanish coastline, in Cantabria (for example in Bermeo, Pasajes, San Sebastían and Gijón) and Vizcaya. Other Atlantic coastal areas in southern Spain and around the Islas Canarias also support an important fishing industry (Las Palmas de Gran Canaria is the third-largest fishing port in Spain). The provinces of Cádiz (major ports in Algeciras and Cádiz) and Huelva (major port is Huelva) are the base for the fishing fleet in north-African waters, as well as providing local fishing banks. In the Mediterranean, the Tramontana region (Cape Palos to Cape Creus) is the most significant (fishing ports including Castellón de la Plana, Tarragona, Barcelona, Villanueva y Geltria and Valencia). Elsewhere in the Mediterranean, fishing is either based on small catches for very localised markets or larger vessels must travel to waters off the coast of Africa or to the Atlantic (fishing ports include Alicante, Cartagena, Málaga and Palma de Mallorca).

Table 3.6 Distribution of fish catch unloaded in 1989

Area	Total fish catch		Frozen fish	
	Volume (tonnes)	Value (pta. billion)	Volume (tonnes)	Value (pta. billion)
Cantábria	92,283	29.4	—	—
North-west	573,803	98.2	254,259	37.3
Sub-Atlantic	94,162	40.5	22,051	15.8
Southern Mediterranean	8,667	—	—	—
Levante	25,447	9.3	192	0.1
Tramontana	77,342	23.5	—	—
Baleares	2,545	—	—	—
Canarias	72,745	18.1	33,534	14.4
Total	960,831	230.1	310,039	67.6

Note: The figures do not include fish transshipped on the high seas (*transbordos en alta mar*) or those landed in non-Spanish ports

* Includes fresh and frozen fish and those from fish farms: In 1989 a total of 97,454 tonnes of fish from fish farms, of which 96,901 tonnes from the north-west

Source: *El País*, 1990

Overfishing and fishing restrictions have resulted in stagnation in the industry and decline in some sectors (Table 3.7), although figures for fish unloaded in Spanish ports do not include those unloaded onto other ships at sea, those unloaded at foreign ports or those unloaded by Spanish vessels flying other flags. For example, the cod catch dropped from 170,000 tonnes in the 1960s to about 11,000 tonnes in 1983. As a consequence the industry has been unable to meet the domestic demand for fish and fish products (fish form an important element in the Spanish diet, amounting to thirty kg of fish per capita per year or 1.1 million tonnes), leading to a substantial and growing annual trade deficit in fish. This deficit amounted to pta. 119 billion in 1988 compared with pta. 50 billion in 1986 (Larrea Ereño,1989), with imports covered only forty per cent by exports compared with eighty per cent coverage in the mid 1980s. For example, imports of frozen hake (*merluza*) increased from 22,500 tonnes in 1986 to 65,000 tonnes in 1988, and frozen squid from 9,800 tonnes to 44,000 tonnes (Maté, 1990c).

The response has been a gradual process of restructuring, involving the modernisation of the fishing fleet, a shift towards higher-value added fish products, and the promotion of fish farming. However, the industry continues to suffer from an atomistic ownership structure coupled with small average size of vessels (especially in Andalucía, where in the early 1980s sixty one per cent of boats were less than twenty gross registered tonness; Osuna Llaneza, 1985) and old ships (in 1983 forty seven per cent of the fishing fleet was more than twenty years old).

Table 3.7 Volume of fish unloaded in Spanish ports, 1961–89

Period	Volume (tonnes)	Period	Volume (tonnes)
1961–65	786.0	1986	1,056.2
1966–70	1,171.0	1987	1,071.2
1971–75	1,273.8	1988	1,047.6
1976–80	1,218.9	1989	974.8
1981–85	1,167.6		

Source: *El País*, 1990

The fishing industry is now regulated by the European Community (through the European Community fishing policy and the system of quotas – total authorised captures) and administered in Spain through the Fund for Regulating the Market in Fish and Marine Products (Fondo de Regulación y Organización del Mercado de Productos de la Pesca y Productos Maritimos, or FROM), established in 1980, which operates in a similar way to FORPPA. Outside of western Europe the extension of territorial waters – from twelve miles to 200 miles – and the imposition of fishing quotas and licenses have severely restricted fishing (especially around north and west Africa – Morocco, Senegal, Angola, Namibia, – the United States and Canada).

Apart from the imposition of fishing restrictions, other aspects of European Community regulations have affected the fishing industry. For example, the fish-canning industry has suffered from competition from third countries where costs are lower (Maté, 1990d). In 1984 exports of canned fish were 35,000 tonnes and imports 8,800 tonnes; in 1988 exports were 25,000 tonnes and imports 27,800 tonnes. There is a long tradition of fish canning in Spain (especially in Galicia). In 1980 there were 375 factories with a production capacity of 351,000 tonnes; by 1988 there were only 180 factories with capacity of 360,000 tonnes (although production in 1988 was only about 200,000 tonnes), employing about 40,000 people. Sixty per cent of production in 1988 was of tuna and sardines. The slow process of reducing tariffs (over ten years from 1986; on tuna the tariff was twenty five per cent in 1986 and eleven per cent in 1990) is designed to protect other Community countries from a flood of Spanish imports. Simultaneously, non-Community producers (for example Morroco) have lower costs; both lower labour and material costs (being free to buy vegetable oil and cans on the world market).

Fish farming (both seawater – especially mussels – and freshwater – dominantly trout) offers one possibility of reducing the substantial import of fish. Recent developments supported by government funding build on a long history of fish farming in many parts of the country, especially in Galicia where production of mussels represents ninety six per cent of the Spanish total and fifty per cent of the world total. About three quarters of fish farms are in the north of the country (for example along the river Arosa). There also exists considerable potential for development in the Ebro delta and in Huelva. But the growth of the industry is threatened by competing water uses and pollution.

3.8 Restructuring of agriculture, forestry and fishing

Restructuring in agriculture, forestry and fishing has been less publicised than that in other sectors of the economy. Nevertheless, restructuring has been substantial in a sector where archaic production structures have persisted for longer than in most other parts of the economy, protected by the state and by the inertia of activities that have been as much a way of life as a means of livelihood. The clearest indication of change has been the continuing decline in employment as labour-intensive production methods have given way to mechanisation. Beyond this, qualitative changes have brought the eclipse of subsistence production, replaced by new production techniques, new products and more-efficient marketing methods. Whole landscapes have changed as farmers have responded to movements in crop prices, as dry-farmed areas have been transformed by irrigation, as the land has been buried beneath plastic sheeting, as eucalyptus woodland spreads, and as fishing ports have been converted into marinas. Agriculture, forestry and fishing are now part of the international economy, regulated by the European Community, relying on imported inputs and selling their products on international markets and to multinational companies. Nevertheless, fundamental weaknesses remain in the production structure, weaknesses that will be exposed by competition, forcing further restructuring.

References and Bibliography

Abad, C. (1985) 'La industría alimentaria española: caracterización de la concentración y la internacionalización de las mayores empresas', *Estudios sobre Consumo* No. 6 December, pp. 63–120

Abreu Pidal, J. (1985) 'Resina, corcho y frutos forestales', *El Campo*, No.98, pp.66–73

Aceves, J. and W. Douglass, (1976) *The changing faces of rural Spain*. Cambridge, Mass.: Halsted Press, John Wiley

Banco Bilbao Vizcaya (1990) 'La agroindustria y el Mercado Unico de 1993', *El Campo* No.115

Barceló, L. and J. Alvarez-Coque (1987) *El futuro de la política agrícola común y la economía española*. Madrid: Ediciones Mundi-Prensa

Barceló Vila, V. (1987) 'La modernización de la agricultura española y el bienestar', *Información Comercial Española* ICE No.652, pp.13–27

Bosque Maurel, J. (1973) 'Latifundio y minifundio en Andalucia Oriental', *Estudios Geográficos*, No. 132–133, pp.457–500

Bruce, P. (1990) 'The party ends for Spain's rural taxpayers', *Financial Times* 5 April 1990, p.3

Bull, W. (1936) 'The olive industry of Spain', *Economic Geography* 12, pp.136–54

Cabo, A. (1982) 'Agricultura y ganaderia', in M. Teran *et al* (eds), *Geografía General de España*. Chapter XVII Barcelona: Editorial Ariel SA, pp.323–81

Camilleri, A. (1984) *La agricultura española ante la CEE*. Madrid: Instituto de Estudios Econímicos Madrid

El País (1990) *Annuario El País, 1990*

Enggass, P. (1968) 'Land reclamation and resettlement in the Guadalquivir Delta – Las Marismas', *Economic Geography* 144, pp.125–43

Fernández Tomás, J. (1985) 'Aspectos económicos de nuestros bosques', *El Campo*, No.98, pp.21–4

García Delgado, J. (1985) 'La agricultura en la España contemporánea: temas dominantes', *Pensamiento Iberoamericano: Revista de Economía Política*, No.8, pp. 488–91

García Delgado, J. (1988) 'La agricultura: Cambios estructurales en los últimos decenios', in J. García Delgado (ed.), *España, Tomo II, Economía*. Chapter 2, pp. 119–152, Madrid: Espasa-Calpe SA

García-Ramon, D. (1985) 'Old and new in Spanish farming', *Geographical Magazine*, March, pp.128–33

Giner, S. and E. Sevilla, (1977) 'The latifundio as a local mode of class domination: The Spanish case', *Iberian Studies* 1, No.2, pp.47–57

Guedes, M. (1981) 'Recent agricultural land policy in Spain', *Oxford Agrarian Studies* 10, pp.26–43

Instituto Nacional de Estadísticas (INE) (1989) *Encuesta sobre la estructura de las explotaciones agrícolas, 1987*. Madrid

Instituto Nacional de Estadísticas (INE) (1985) *Censo agrario de España, 1982. Tomo 1, resultados nacionales*. Madrid

Larrea Ereño, S. (1989) 'La producción pesquera española desde la implantación del limite de las 200 millas nauticas', *Situación* No.3, pp.5–38

Laxe, F. (1988) *La economía del sector pesquero*. Madrid: Espasa-Calpe SA

Maas, J. (1983) 'The behaviour of landowners as an explanation of regional differences in agriculture: Latifundists in Seville and Cordoba (Spain)', *TESG (Tijdschrift voor economische en sociale geografie)* 74, No. 2, pp.87–95

Majoral, R. (1987) 'La utilización del suelo agrícola en España: aspectos evolutivos y locacionales', in *El Campo* 104 pp.13–26

Manuel Naredo, J. et al. (3rd ed. 1985) *La agricultura en el desarrollo capitalista español, 1940–1970*. Madrid: Siglo veintiuno editores

Manuel Naredo, J. (1986) *Historia agraria de la España contemporánea*. Madrid: Editorial Crítica

Martinez Alier, J. (1971) *Labourers and landowners of southern Spain*. London: George Allen and Unwin

Mata, R. (1981) 'Notas sobre la situación actual de la gran propriedad', *Estudios Geográficos* 42, No. 163, pp.139–65

Maté, V. (1990a) 'Las deudas del campo', *El País* (Sección Negocios) 3 June, p.34

Maté, V. (1990b) 'Reforma agraria, del rojo al verde', *El País* (Seccíon Negocios) 25 March, p.12

Maté, V. (1990c) 'Volver a casa: la flota congeladora', *El País* (Seccíon Negocios) 1 April, p.22

Maté, V. (1990d) 'El entierro de la sardina', *El País* (Seccíon Negocios) 25 March, p.27

Ministerio de Agricultura (MAPA) (1987) *Adhesión de España a la CEE*

Ministerio de Agricultura (MAPA) (1988) *La agriculture, la pesca y la alimentación, 1987*

Ministerio de Agricultura (MAPA) (1989a) *Manual de estadística agraria, 1989*

Ministerio de Agricultura (MAPA) (1989b) *Encuesta sobre la estructura de las explotaciones agrícolas, 1987*

Naylon, J. (1959) 'Land consolidation in Spain', *Annals Association American Geographers* 49, pp.361–73

Naylon, J. (1973) 'An appraisement of Spanish irrigation and land-settlement policy since 1939', *Iberian Studies* II, No. 1, pp.12–18

O'Flanagan, T. (1980) 'Agrarian structures in north western Iberia: responses and their implications for development', *Geoforum* Vol. 11, pp.157–69

O'Flanagan, T. (1982) 'Land reform and rural modernization', *Erdkunde* 36, pp.48–53

Ortiz-Cañavate, J. (1989) 'Situación actual de la mecanización agraria en España', *El Campo* 111, pp.3–9

Osuna Llaneza, J. (1985) 'La pesca Andaluza', *El Campo*, 99, pp.87–95

Parsons, J. (1962a) 'The cork oak forests and cork industry', *Economic Geography*, Vol. 38, No. 3, pp.195–214

Parsons, J. (1962b) 'The acorn-hog economy of S.W.Spain', *Geographical Review*, Vol. 52, No. 2, pp.211–235

Pérez Touriño, E. (1983) *Agricultura y capitalismo. Analisis de la pequeña producción campesina*. Madrid: Ministerio de Agricultura, Servicio de Publicaciones Agrarias

Reig, E. (1988) 'La adhesión española al Mercado Común Agrícola', in J. García Delgado (ed.), *España: Tomo II, Economía*, Chapter 3, pp.153–176 Madrid: Espasa-Calpe SA

Rico, F. (1985) 'Incendios', *El Campo*, 98, pp.149–53

Ruiz-Maya, L. (1986) 'Evolución de las estructuras agrarias a través de los Censos de 1962 y 1982', *Revista de Estudios Agro-sociales* No.138, pp.45–74

Ruiz-Maya, L. (1987) 'Evolución de la concentración de la tierra (1962–1982)', *Agricultura y Sociedad* No.44, pp.93–135

San Juan, C. (1987) *Eficiencia y rentabilidad en la agricultura española*. Madrid: Ministerio de Agricultura, Serie Estudios

Tamames, R. (15th ed. 1983) *Estructura económica de España. Vol.1, Primera Parte: El sector agrario*. Madrid: Alianza Editorial SA

♦ Chapter 4 ♦

Minerals and Mining

4.1 The mining industry

Despite a rich variety of resources and important mineral deposits, the mining industry accounts for only about 0.5 per cent of the occupied population (76,200 at the end of 1988), about one per cent of GDP and two per cent of industrial output (value of sales was pta. 400 billion in 1988; MINE, 1989b). In relative terms it is similar in size to the fishing industry. However, as with other primary activities, the importance of the industry extends beyond the measurement of extraction alone. Products from the mining industry provide the basis for the construction industry and important segments of manufacturing industry: for example metal manufacturing, oil refining, cement, ceramics and fertilizers. Many minerals (notably the energy minerals) are of strategic importance, in that their loss could undermine the whole economy. Finally, minerals (especially hydrocarbons) are important in the trade balance, which is characterised by a deficit in trade in energy and metallic minerals and a surplus on non-metallic minerals and quarry products. Mineral exports tend to be of relatively low-value products (quarry products), frequently those that have been restricted in their extraction in developed countries through environmental considerations.

Energy products represent the largest component of the mining industry. Even with the low energy prices prevailing in the late 1980s, energy products contributed about two thirds of the value of production and two thirds of the employment in mining (Table 4.1). Within the energy sector, coal and lignite generate about eighty per cent of the value of energy mining output (1987) and most of the employment. In metallic-mineral mining, zinc and precious metals are most important in terms of value of output, contributing over half the value of metallic-mineral production in 1987, followed by iron, pyrites, lead and copper, and then, of far lesser importance, tin and mercury (Table 4.2). Of non-metallic minerals, sulphur, potash and salt are major products (potash contributing about one quarter of the total value of non-metallic-mineral output; Table 4.3). Limestone is the most important quarry product, both in terms of value of output and the number of people employed in its extraction, followed by slate, granite and marble.

Development of the mining industry has been restricted by a combination of physical-resource limitations (limited or poor-quality raw materials), more-attractive investment opportunities outside mining in the 1960s, and the severe

Table 4.1 Characteristics of the mining industry, 1987

Sector	Mines	Employment (at end 1988)	Production (pta. billion)
Energy products	243	48,879	226.5
Metallic minerals	45	6,310	47.9
Non-metallic minerals	245	5,985	42.0
Quarry products	2,963	15,075	65.3
Total	3,496	76,249	381.8

Sources: MINE, 1989a employment data MINE, 1989b

Table 4.2 Characteristics of metallic mineral mining, 1987

Product	Production (000 tonnes)	Metal content (000 tonnes)		Value (pta. billion)	Mines	Employment (at end 1988)
Iron	4,500 (4,159)	2,109		6.6	8	929
Zinc	500 —	273	(275)	13.7	*	*
Lead	132 —	82	(73)	4.8	10	2,270
Copper	66 —	16	(10)	3.2	6	1,050
Tin	11,500 —	77†	(59)	0.1	7	116
Pyrites	2,177 (2,290)	1,011	—	5.5	6	1,035
Mercury	— —	—	—	1.5	2	135
Precious metals	— —	—	—	12.3	3	775
Other	— —	—	—	0.2	3	‡
Total	— —	—	—	47.9	45	6,310

Note: Production figures in brackets are for 1988

* Figures included with those for lead, † Metal content in thousand kg

‡ Figures included in those for precious metals

Sources: MINE, 1989a; employment and production data for 1988 from MINE, 1989b

crisis in the industry during the late 1970s and early 1980s. During the period of economic growth in the 1960s the mineral sector was neglected because of the easy availability of minerals on the international market, the higher returns in manufacturing industry, services and property development, and industrial-policy measures that were not appropriate to the mining sector. Following the first oil shock, renewed attempts were made to stimulate mining; for example, the Law of Mines (Ley de Minas, 1973) made geological reserves public property, exploitable by concessions for thirty years. There followed intensive exploration by Spanish and foreign companies but with little result except in the Iberian pyrites zone, where exploration and development had been underway since the late 1960s. In this zone three new mines were developed after 1970: Cerro Colorado, Aznalcóllar and Sotiel. In each case the discoveries were made in

Table 4.3 Characteristics of non-metallic-mineral mining and quarrying, 1987

Product	Production (million tonnes)	Value (pta. billion)	Mines	Employment (at end 1988)
Non-metallic minerals				
Potash salts	—	10.7	4	2,350
Other	—	31.3	241	3,635
Sub total	—	42.0	245	5,985
Quarry products				
Limestone	85.2	26.0	737	4,387
Other	—	39.3	2,226	10,688
Sub total	—	65.3	2,963	15,075
Total	—	107.3	3,200	21,060

Sources: MINE, 1989a; employment data MINE, 1989b

association with existing workings, or previous mines. (Across the border in Portugal there have also been some recent major discoveries; for example the polymetallic sulphide deposits at Neves Corvo were discovered in the late 1970s and the mine opened in 1988 with a planned output of 135,000 tonnes of copper in concentrates and 5,000 tonnes of tin by 1991, production that will be worth far more than the output from all Portugal's other mines; anon., 1989.) Further attempts to encourage mineral development were made at the end of the 1970s through the introduction of the National Mineral Supply Plan (Plan Nacional de Abastecimiento de Materias Primas Minerales, 1979–87), but it was difficult to promote investment in a climate of retrenchment in mineral production. Since the mid 1980s there has been a strong recuperation in non-metallic minerals and quarry products but continuing problems in coal and metals, where weak prices and rising costs of production have brought large segments of the industry near to closure, necessitating major restructuring, closures, amalgamations and improvements in productivity. As a result, a pattern of large mines has emerged (Table 4.4).

The scale of adjustment necessary has threatened whole communities, prompting stiff union opposition and government intervention at both state and regional level. The problems have been most serious in the coal mining areas of Asturias and in the metal mines of Huelva. In Huelva, Rio Tinto Minera (RTM, a subsidiary of Explosivos Rio Tinto (ERT) and part of the Ercros group) has been saved from complete closure only by government intervention.

Despite restructuring, many of the contemporary characteristics of mining echo those identified in the nineteenth century: i) a multitude of small-scale workings ii) lack of profitability and hence a lack of investment, and iii) the presence of foreign ownership (Mallada, 1890). The industrial structure retains the presence of a large number of small firms and mines, frequently displaying high production costs and operating with a low level of technology, sometimes the result of a long process of decapitalisation. In 1987 there were 3,496 mines, of which about four fifths corresponded to quarry products. There is also a lack of

Table 4.4 Mines producing more than 150,000 tonnes of ore per year, 1990

Mine	Province	Mining method*	Size†	Product
Santiago	La Coruña	P	2	Copper
Cerro Colorado/ Alfredo	Huelva	P	1	Copper, silver, gold
Sotiel	Huelva	Uª	3	Copper, lead, zinc
La Zarza	Huelva	Uª	4	Copper, pyrite
Tharsis	Huelva	P	3	Copper, pyrite
Filon Sur	Huelva	P	5	Gold
Rodalquilar	Almería	P	5	Gold
Transacción	Huelva	P	5	Gold
Agruminsa	Vizcaya	P	1	Iron
Franco Belga	Vizcaya	P	3	Iron
Marquesado	Granada	P	1	Iron
La Cruz	Jaén	U	5	Lead, silver
Almadén	Ciudad Real	P	3	Mercury
Cardona	Barcelona	U	2	Potash
Llobregat	Barcelona	U	3	Potash
Suria	Barcelona	U	3	Potash
Barruecopardo	Salamanca	Pª	2	Wolfram
Aznalcóllar	Sevilla	P	1	Zinc, copper, lead
Reocin	Cantabria	P	2	Zinc, lead
Troya	Guipúzcoa	U	3	Zinc, lead
Mantos de Silicatos	Murcia	P	2	Zinc, lead, silver
Rubiales	Lugo	U	3	Zinc, lead, silver

*U: Underground; P: Open pit; ª: Operation suspended

†1: Over 3 million tonnes; 2: 1 to 3 million tonnes; 3: 0.5 to 1 million tonnes;

4: 0.3 to 0.5 million tonnes; 5: 0.15 to 0.3 million tonnes

Source: Anon (1990) *Mining Magazine*, January

vertical integration, with notable weaknesses in links to mining equipment manufacturers.

Foreign penetration of the mining industry has a long ancestry, covering ownership of production resources, supply of mining equipment and control over foreign marketing. For example, the British companies Rio Tinto Zinc and Tharsis played an important role in developing the mining industry in Huelva (Rio Tinto Zinc was formed in 1873 after buying the Rio Tinto mines from the Spanish government), the Belgium company Solvay opened up the salt deposits in Cantabria and the potash deposits in Cataluña, and Rothschild played a key role in marketing mercury production. As a result, the production of raw materials in the past may have contributed less to Spanish development and more to the benefit of foreign manufacturing industry (Tamames, 1983). Currently foreign ownership of mineral resources is most clearly illustrated in the case of the mining industry of Huelva, dominated by the Ercros group, whose principal shareholder is the Kuwait Investment Office. Foreign ownership of production resources also partly explains the foreign domination of the mining-equipment industry, a feature also explained by the small size of the Spanish market, which has restricted the development of competitive domestic manufacturers. The severe crisis that affected the mining industry in the 1970s and early 1980s frightened off much foreign investment, leaving the state to absorb failing mining companies. But in the late 1980s foreign investment returned, especially in construction materials. For example, the Swedish Boliden group took over the company Andaluza de Piritas, SA in 1988, the British company Steetley have bought into construction material companies, and Richard Costain has set up a mineral and extractive industrial development company.

The mining industry can be subdivided into metallic minerals, non-metallic minerals and quarry products. While this is not a perfect classification, it does have the advantage of grouping most minerals according to the industrial sectors that they supply. Thus metallic minerals feed the metals industries, non-metallic minerals the chemical and fertilizer industries, and quarry products the construction industry. The fortunes of each mining sub sector are thus closely bound up with these industries.

4.2 Metallic-mineral-mining

The metallic-mineral-mining industry was the most severely affected by the economic crisis. Rising costs of production and falling market prices sent many companies into bankruptcy. Problems have frequently been compounded by the loss of markets to substitute products (for example in mercury) and by more competitive imports (for example in iron ore).

4.2.1 Iron

Iron mining has been in long term decline since the 1960s, a decline that accelerated in the early 1980s to leave only a handful of mines. In the 1960s there were about 200 mines employing more than 9,500 people. By 1970 the number of mines had fallen to seventy-two and by 1976 to twenty-nine with 2,676 people employed. Contraction in the number of mines and employment was especially severe in the early 1980s as rising production costs (labour, fuel and transport) coincided with weak prices, resulting especially from cut-backs in the iron and steel industry. Rationalisation of the iron and steel industry squeezed domestic demand and brought specific problems to particular areas. For example the Compañía Minera de Sierra Menera, SA (CMSM), which mined the deposit of Ojós Negros/Setiles (Teruel/Guadalajara), was closely linked to iron making at Sagunto until the closure of the Sagunto plant. In 1988 iron mining employed little over 900 people in eight mines, the largest of which is in Granada (Table 4.5). Total production has fallen to 4.2 million tonnes of iron ore, yielding less than two million tonnes of metal (MINE, 1989b).

Imported ores are generally more competitive (partly a result of the strength of the peseta) than domestic ones, leading to a deficit on the balance of trade, which accounts for a significant element of the total balance of mineral trade deficit. In addition to low export volumes, the value of exported iron ore has also tended to be low (mainly fines), while imports have tended to be of higher-value material

Table 4.5 Iron-ore production in 1985 and 1987

Province	Number of mines		Employment		Iron-ore output
	1985	1987	1985	1987	(1985) (millions of tonnes)
Granada	1	1	409	345	3.7
Guadalajara	1	0	52	0	0.4
Huelva*	1	1	149	205	0.0
Murcia	1	1	6	5	0.2
Cantabria	2	0	118	0	0.2
Soria	1	2	30	20	0.2
Teruel	1	0	133	0	0.5
Vizcaya	3	3	108	331	0.9
Total	11	8	1,005	986	6.1†

Note: In 1987 total output was 4.5 million tonnes

* The mine in Huelva was being developed in 1985

† Total iron metal content of ore estimated at 2.8 million tonnes in 1985

Sources: Koerting Wiese, 1986; MINE, 1987; MINE, 1989a

(mineral and pellets). Successive proposals for pelletisation plants in Spain have been rejected, although Ensidesa has invested in pelletisation plant abroad (the pelletisation plant of Hispano-Bras, Brazil, which became operational in 1979 with a three million tonne capacity, includes a 49.7 per cent holding by Ensidesa). Hence Spanish iron mineral output can only be used in iron-sintering plants. In 1988 1.7 million tonnes of iron ore were exported (almost all from the mine in Granada and mostly to the EC). Imports amounted to 5.6 million tonnes (over fifty per cent of national requirements), especially from Brazil (where Ensidesa has mining interests), Venezuela (Ensidesa and Alto Hornos de Vizcaya, AHV), Liberia (Ensidesa) and Australia (Ensidesa).

Iron-ore deposits are generally of relatively low iron content and contain many impurities. Total reserves are estimated at 369 million tonnes. Possible resources may amount to a further 1,700 million tonnes. The largest reserves (82 million tonnes) are found in the south-east, centred on the Alquife and Marquesado haematite deposits in Granada. The deposits, worked by open-caste methods, are situated on the northern slope of the Sierra Nevada on the flood plain of the Marquesado. Ores average fifty-four per cent iron content, with no phosphorous or sulphur impurities. The Alquife mines were opened with British capital, but eventually passed to the Compañía Andaluza de Minas SA (CAM). Production increased from two million tonnes of iron ore in 1971 to three million tonnes in 1975 and reached 3.7 million tonnes in 1987.

In the north-west there are reserves of 21 million tonnes in Galicia, León and Asturias (Koerting Wiese, 1986). These reserves of magnetites and haematites (averaging forty-eight per cent iron, generally of high phosphoric content and containing silica and alumina) are found in Silurian and Devonian sediments in a series of parallel arcs extending from Astorga (León) to Ribadeo (Lugo). The largest deposits are thought to be near Ponferrada (León) and are worked by Minero Siderúrgico de Ponferrada (part of the Banco Central group). In the north there are reserves of 60 million tonnes (thirty-five to forty per cent iron content) in limestones in Vizcaya and Santander. Haematite ores extending from Durango to Santander are now mostly worked out. In the Centro-Levante region there are reserves of 60 million tonnes. The most important deposits (forty-four per cent iron content with silica and alumina) are found in Silurian limestones in the Sierra Menera (Teruel and Guadalajara). Included in this area are the mines of Albarracín and Moncayo. In the south-west there are reserves of 40 million tonnes (mainly magnetites of iron content thirty-eight to sixty per cent) in Badajoz, Huelva and Sevilla. Reserves of iron pyrites in this zone are put at 100 million tonnes.

Iron is also produced from iron pyrites (from Huelva), mainly by plants in Vizcaya but also through the state-controlled company Presur in Huelva. Metalquímica del Nervión, SA have a factory in Axpe-Erandio that extracts iron chemically from iron pyrites brought from Huelva. Production (capacity amounting to almost half a million tonnes annually in the mid 1980s) is sold to Ensidesa and AHV. INI, through its company Presur, is trying to re-open the deposit of Cala (Huelva) following the cessation of the activities of Minera de Andivalo. Apart from producing iron concentrate, an experimental beneficiation plant in Fregenal de la Sierra has been established. At the beginning of 1986 600,000 tonnes of concentrate (sixty per cent iron) per year were being produced at Cala.

Current problems facing the iron-mining industry are limited domestic demand, the poor quality of domestic ores, high production costs, high transport costs and competition from imports. The two integrated iron and steelworks of Ensidesa and AHV have an installed capacity for sintering 6.8 million tonnes of iron fines. This forms the ceiling of domestic demand, although actual demand is below this because of the poor quality of domestic supplies, which continues to impede their use (despite work by Ensidesa to develop new production technology).

Delivered costs are swollen by high transport costs, which form a significant proportion (possibly fifty-five per cent) of the cif (cost, insurance, freight) price of iron-ore. High transport costs often mean that imported iron mineral is cheaper. Generally iron mineral is transported by the state railway RENFE: for example from Marquesado to Almería 94 km, Montiel to Sagunto 204 km– where CMSM have deep water port facilities– Olvega to Sestao 315 km, and Fregenal to Huelva 93 km). In each case iron-ore transport represents a high proportion of all the traffic on the line (eighty per cent in the case of CAM).

4.2.2 Copper

The copper-mining industry entered a serious crisis in the late 1970s and 1980s as production costs increased and copper prices fell in response to lower demand, occasioned both by weak demand generally and product substitution (for example optical fibre in telecommunications). By 1987 the copper price in dollars had fallen below that in 1950. Multinational companies responded by cutting their labour force, closing mines, introducing more energy-efficient technology and taking advantage of large-scale production. In Spain the two major copper-mining companies, ERT and Tharsis, experienced serious financial problems and the industry has only been protected from complete collapse by government intervention and investment in new facilities by state-owned mining companies.

The copper industry comprises copper produced from scrap and copper produced from copper ores. Smelting, or the chemical treatment of ores, is the first stage of the production process. For example Metalquímica de Nervión (Bilbao) uses a chemical process to treat pyrites residuals to produce copper (3,600 tonnes in 1984). Blister copper is produced from copper pyrites that are smelted in a blast furnace with coke to produce black copper, which is then further refined to blister copper (ninety-eight per cent copper). In Huelva there is an oxygen furnace (built in 1970) that enables the use of ores with high levels of sulphur impurities. To achieve economies of scale the plant also draws on imports. Electrolytic refining is the final stage in the production process. Refineries are located in Huelva (Rio Tinto Minera: capacity 105,000 tonnes) and in the north of Spain (Electrolisis de Cobre in Palencia: capacity 32,000 tonnes, and Ercosa in Bilbao: capacity 26,000 tonnes; all figures refer to the mid 1980s).

Copper is found either dispersed in the form of copper pyrites (chalcopyrite) or massively in the form of chalcocite, which is exploited mostly for sulphur. Precious metals are not generally found in association with Spanish ores. Almost all the blister copper in Spain is produced from the copper pyrites deposits in Huelva. These deposits form part of the Iberian Pyrites Zone, which extends for some 250 km from the Guadalquivir in Spain to the valley of the river Sado and the Atlantic coast of Portugal. The Spanish deposits are exploited by UERT (Unión Explosivos Rio Tinto) and Tharsis. All of the pyrites zone is designated as a National Reserve and divided into exploration blocks. In 1985 61,000 tonnes of copper mineral were produced in Spain (66,000 tonnes in 1987), mostly by UERT (55,000 tonnes from copper ore and the rest from blister copper and the chemical treatment of pyrites), providing direct employment for over two thousand people. There are mines producing copper ore in the provinces of Sevilla, in Huelva and in La Coruña (Santiago mine). In addition, blister copper is produced in mines in Huelva and in one mine in Vizcaya, providing employment for a little over 200 people. The most important copper mine is the open-caste Cerro Colorado (Huelva: opened in 1971 and owned by ERT). Production from the mine was about 28,000 tonnes of copper mineral in the mid 1980s and recoverable reserves were estimated at 670,000 tonnes. Another three mines in the Iberian Pyrites Zone are at Aznalcóllar (Sevilla; formally owned by Andaluza de Piritas but now owned by the Swedish Boliden group; it is an open-caste mine with total production in the mid 1980s around 9,000 tonnes), Sotiel (Huelva; owned by the INI subsidiary Minas de Almagrera, an underground mine that has been developed since 1984 and had production in the mid 1980s of 500 tonnes but had production suspended in 1990) and Cala (Huelva; being developed by the INI subsidiary Presur to an output in the mid 1980s of over 2,000 tonnes). Outside of the south-west there are mines owned by ERT in La Coruña (open-caste mines of Arinteiro and Bama at Santiago de Compostela, output 8,500 tonnes and estimated reserves of 81,000 tonnes); and the Alfredo deposits, producing 10,660 tonnes and reserves estimated at 84,000 tonnes.

4.2.3 Lead

The crisis affecting the mining industry in the 1980s has resulted in concentration within the lead industry to leave only ten mines in 1987, producing about 80,000 tonnes of lead metal (about three quarters of EC production but only two per cent of world production). Frequently lead is now only produced as a by-product of zinc or in association with precious metals. Lead consumption increased from 77,000 tonnes of refined lead in 1970 to 110,000 tonnes in 1980 and 117,000 tonnes in 1985. But consumption is now relatively static as substitutes emerge. Similarly, in the world market consumption has been relatively static since the late 1970s, leaving weak prices. In real terms the price of refined lead in January 1986 was only forty-one per cent of its price in 1976.

Lead metal is produced from the smelting of lead ores (essentially galena– lead sulphide). There are two principal companies involved in smelting. They are Sociedad Minera y Metalúrgica de Peñarroya-España (owned by French capital), who are the owners of the Santa Lucia smelter in Cartagena (Murcia), and Compañía La Cruz (Banco Central group), which has a new smelter in Linares (Jaén). Lead-metal production in 1985 was 164,000 tonnes (fourteen per cent of the volume produced in the other EC countries, and about two per cent of world production).

National production of lead concentrate is insufficient to meet the demands of the lead-smelting industry in Spain, hence lead concentrate must be imported (for example from Morocco). At the same time consumption of lead in Spain is below the output of lead smelters, hence part of the lead produced is exported (50,000 tons in 1985).

4.2.4 Zinc

Zinc mining is closely related to that of lead and thus it too has been part of the metal-mining crisis despite increased consumption. Zinc-metal production increased from 86,100 tonnes in 1960 to 98,100 tonnes in 1970, 179,300 tonnes in 1980 and 275,000 tonnes in 1988 (thirty-five per cent of EC production but only three per cent of world production). At the beginning of 1986 the zinc price in real terms was only fifty per cent that of 1976. Part of zinc production is exported, leaving zinc smelters in Spain having to import zinc mineral (zinc and copper are the two major metal exports, valued at about pta. 31 billion each in 1988).

Zinc metal is obtained mainly from zinc blend (ZnS; ninety per cent of world production) and is normally accompanied by lead. In 1985 zinc metal was mined by five mining companies. Asturiana de Zinc SA has various mines, but by far the biggest is Reocin in Cantabria, the most important zinc mine in Spain (in 1981 the company had taken over from the Belgium company Real Compañía Asturiana de Minas, which had monopolised the industry up until the 1960s). Exploración Minera Internacional España SA (Exminesa), with Canadian and South African capital, owns the Rubiales mine in Piedrafita del Cebrero in Lugo, which produces lead and silver as well, and the Troya mine in Guipúzcoa opened in 1986 (this company is probably now the largest zinc producer in Spain). The Swedish Boliden group took over the Aznalcóllar mine in Sevilla in 1988, which also produces important quantities of lead, copper and silver (Fox, 1990). Sociedad Minera y Metalúrgica de Peñarroya-España SA owns two mines, the more important of which is Mina de Silicatos in Cartagena. Empresa Nacional Minas de Almagrera, SA owns the Sotiel mine in Huelva, which produces copper and silver as well. A further two per cent of production comes from the Metalquímica del Nervión plant. Some 3,000 people were employed in the mid 1980s by the five mining companies mentioned above.

The two principal producers of zinc metal in Spain are Asturiana de Zinc (production in 1984 160,000 tonnes) and Española del Zinc (production in 1984 35,000 tonnes) with production capacity of 200,000 and 60,000 tonnes a year respectively. Their zinc-smelting factories are in San Juan de Nieva-Avilés (Asturias) and Cartagena (Murcia). The Metalquímica factory in Bilbao has a capacity of 8,000 tonnes. In 1988 a total of 275,000 tonnes of zinc metal was produced, a substantial increase on the 206,000 tonnes in 1984.

4.2.5 Mercury

Spain is one of the world's leading producers and exporters of mercury, increasing its market share in the early 1980s by maintaining production in the face of falling prices. Thus production of mercury metal remained static at about 40,000 to 50,000 flasks (about one fifth of world production; one flask is about 34.5 kg of mercury), although by the turn of the decade production had fallen to about 25,000 flasks. Normally ninety per cent of mercury production is exported. Reserves will allow production at existing levels at least into the early twenty-first century.

In the 1970s there was widespread publicity concerning the health hazards of mercury, leading to its substitution by other less-toxic products. This exacerbated the pattern of falling demand. Three private mercury producers in Asturias/León ceased production (although from 1980 mercury has been produced from zinc concentrate by Empresa Asturiana de Zinc SA). In the mid 1980s prices remained weak (less than $150 a flask in 1985). In the mines the health hazard was recognised by the adoption of special employment conditions. The normal regime has been to work six hours per day for only eight days per month. Retirement has been at fifty and workers have been exempt from taxes and national service. They have also received a small plot of land.

The mercury deposits at Almadén (Ciudad Real) are amongst the largest in the world. They have been known since the fourth century BC and are known to have been in production since 1499. In the early twentieth century, marketing was handled by Rothschild, which also controlled mines in Istria (Italy) and California. In 1981 administration of the mines and the marketing of the mercury was placed in the hands of the Empresa Nacional de las Minas de Almadén y Arrayanes (under the DGPE), which was also given responsibility for other mercury deposits in Spain (in Asturias, Granada, Castellón and Badajoz).

Three deposits are being worked by Minas de Almadén: Almadén (estimated reserves of 65,000 flasks, currently supplying about twenty-five per cent of the company's production), El Entredicho (seventeen km from Almadén, open-caste, seventy-five per cent of company production and reserves estimated at 500,000 flasks) and Las Cuevas (in development, 8 km from Almadén, production from underground deposits with reserves estimated at 200,000 flasks). All the raw material is processed in plants at the mines, which have also processed residual mercury since 1985.

From being an important source of state revenue, the mines have become a liability with chronic deficits. Falling demand has been accompanied by cuts in employment, with employment in the mining company falling to around 700 in 1990 (a figure that is likely to fall much further and only a small proportion of whom are directly employed in the mines; Rivera, 1990). Dependence of the local region (covering some 30,000 people) on the activities of the mines has prompted government investment to ameliorate the situation. Investment has included an exploration programme that led to the discovery of two new mercury deposits and one of lead and zinc at Navalmedio, a mercury-waste treatment plant, and an economic development programme for the region of Almadén involving state investment in new activities and further investment in mercury mining. Further plant for treating and storing toxic industrial waste have been proposed (as one of three sites suggested under the National Dangerous and Toxic Waste Plan (Plan Nacional de Residuos Tóxicos y Peligrosos)), met by environmental opposition but matched by support from those who wish to see employment expand. The status of the mining company has also been changed to make it more commercially oriented: from an autonomous organisation of the state to a state limited company.

4.2.6 Tin and precious metals

Tin deposits are found mainly along the border with Portugal, but few mines have been worked since 1959, when tin prices fell following the easing of import restrictions. Most tin and cassiterite (tin ore) is imported. The three major companies in tin smelting are Metalúrgica del Estano (with smelters in Villaverde in Madrid and Villagarcía de Arosa in Pontevedra), Ferroaleaciones Españolas (with smelters at Medina del Campo) and Metalúrgica del Agueda (at Villaralbo in Zamora).

Production of precious metals is small, with production normally associated with other minerals. The gold mines at Rodalquilar (near Cabo de Gata, Almería) are exploitated whenever the gold price justifies production and gold is also produced in Huelva. Silver is produced in Huelva, Jaén, Murcia and Lugo.

4.3 Non-metallic-mineral mining

Non-metallic-mineral mining provides inputs to the fertilizer and chemical industries. Both these industries were subject to severe pressure during the economic crisis and have undergone restructuring. In the late 1980s demand for chemicals and fertilizers recovered, but in a more open economy domestic sources of supply face greater competition from imports. A scarcity of commercial phosphate deposits in Spain already requires fertilizer manufacturers (producing superphosphates) to rely on imports (mostly from Morocco).

4.3.1 Potash

Large reserves of potash in Spain support an industry that produced 0.75 million tonnes of potash in 1988, constituting both an important raw material for the domestic fertilizer industry and a significant export. Spain is the seventh-largest world producer of potash, after the two giants (the USSR and Canada, which has reserves of 45,000 million tonnes), West Germany, France and the USA. Total world production in 1982 was 27.4 million tonnes. The Ercros group, INI and the regional government of Navarra control Spanish production.

Reserves of potash are estimated at about 107 million tonnes, concentrated in the Ebro Valley between Cataluña and Navarra. In Cataluña production is centred around the Cardona and Llobregat valleys (reserves about 75 million tonnes) and the mineral is exploited by Minas de Potasas de Suria (owned by INI) and Potasas de Llobregat (part of the Ercros group mining the Sallent and Balsareny deposits; in 1990 Ercros was seeking to sell these operations to INI). Deposits are located relatively close to the coast, allowing easy export by mineral lines to the port of Barcelona. In Navarra, Potasas de Subiza SA (jointly owned by the regional government of Navarra and INI) exploit deposits near Pamplona. Organisational concentration is reflected in the producers' association Potasas Españolas.

The Cadener and Suria deposits in Cataluña were the first to be worked in Spain in 1912. The developers of the mine formed the company Minas de Potasas de Suria in 1920 with capital from the Belgium company Solvay, which quickly became the outright owner. In 1929 another company was formed in Cadener, which later became part of Unión Española de Explosivos (UEE), now part of the Ercros group. Operations in the Llobregat Valley began soon after that, falling under the control of French and German companies. After the Second World War the state holding company INI took control of the German holdings, forming the company Fodina in 1952. Fodina then acquired interests in other potash companies. From 1969 the Llobregat deposits were being worked by Explosivos Riotinto and the INI company Fodina. In 1972 Fodina ceded the working of its deposits to Potasas de Suria. Recession forced the integration of the two companies in 1982 (and the withdrawal of Belgium capital), leaving INI as the major partner in Potasas de Suria. If the sale of the activities of Ercros in potash mining are completed, virtually all potash production will be concentrated in the hands of INI.

In Navarra, Potasas de Navarra was established in 1960 by the state holding company INI to work the potash deposits in the Sierra del Perdon, large-scale production beginning in 1964. High extraction costs, limited reserves, labour disputes and weak market prices brought deteriorating economic circumstances, which forced INI to close the company in 1986. To save the industry, a new company (Potasas de Subiza) was formed by the regional government of Navarra (Foral de Navarra) and INI to work the Navarra deposits.

Membership of the European Community has forced the break-up of a highly regulated market (which resulted in fertilizer prices being generally above world market prices) and, coupled with the pressures of recession, has prompted mergers in the Spanish fertilizer industry to leave one major company, Ercros. Until 1970 domestic demand was relatively small (reflecting the backwardness of Spanish agriculture), forcing a reliance on exports. The structure of the domestic fertilizer market was oligopolistic, with the fertilizer manufacturers ERT and Cros accounting for about three quarters of demand. As ERT obtained its supplies from within the company, the major consumer was Cros (others included Energía e Industrias Aragonesas, Inabonos, the state company Enfersa, SA. Mirat and Induca).

From 1971 marketing of potash was in the hands of the monopoly Coposa (Comercial de Potasas, SA), which was formed by the producing companies. Coposa divided the domestic market between producers and controlled all exports except those to China (which were exported by Marfusa through the port of Tarragona). Coposa gave Spanish producers more power in international bargaining and provided a channel for presenting the producers' case to the government on import protection and domestic prices (which were set by the government and tended to reflect the profitability of INI's potash operations).

4.3.2 Sulphur

In 1988 2.3 million tonnes of iron pyrites (sulphur ore), which forms the basic material for the production of sulphuric acid, were produced. There are large reserves of iron pyrites in Spain, of which it has been estimated that sixty per cent were under the control of the British company Tharsis (established in 1866) and twenty-four per cent under the control of UERT. The most important reserves are found in Huelva (deposits contain 46–51 per cent sulphur). There are also major reserves in Cartagena. Other major centres of sulphur production are at Libros and Riodeva (south of Teruel), Hellin (Albacete), Benahadux (Almería), Lorca and Maratella (Murcia).

4.3.3 Common salt

Production of common salt in 1988 amounted to 3.1 million tonnes, the largest proportion coming from rock salt, for which Cantabria is the most important single location (Polanco de la Sal, Cabezón de la Sal and Monte Corona; linked to the Solvay company). The remainder (usually between 300,000 and 500,000 tonnes) comes from sea salt produced at various locations around the Mediterranean (especially Torrevieja in Alicante, San Roque and San Fernando in Cádiz and Cabo de Gata in Almería). Production of sea salt is concentrated in the hands of a few companies (dominated by La Nueva Compañía Arrandateria de las Salinas de Torrevieja y La Mata). Apart from the supply of table salt, the mineral is a basic one in the chemical industry.

4.4 Quarry products

After energy, quarry products constitute the most important sector of mining by both value of sales and employment. Products include limestone, marble, slate, granite, clay and aggregates of various types. Quarrying occurs throughout Spain, although high transport costs mean that there is particular pressure to extract materials near to market areas. Activity is bound up with that of the construction industry and has thus been more buoyant than the other sectors of mining. Indeed, the frantic pace of construction in many areas (especially in the 1960s, early 1970s and late 1980s) has put particular pressure on sites for mineral extraction, frequently leading to environmental degradation.

4.5 Restructuring of the mining industry

The recession in the mining industry (outside that of quarry products) has been accentuated by the decline in many traditional industrial markets, by product substitution and by the lifting of import restrictions. As a result, small mines are being closed to leave a pattern of larger, more highly automated mines. Increasingly the more-profitable mines contain an element of foreign capital, which after deserting the industry in the 1970s has been returning to incorporate Spanish mining activities into international production systems.

References and Bibliography

Anon. (1989) 'Neves Corvo', *Mining Magazine*, September, p.184–90

Anon. (1990) *Mining Magazine*, January

Castejon Montijano, R. (1986) 'El síglo crucial de la minería española (1850–1950)', *Papeles de Economía Española* 29, pp.30–48

Costa Campi, M. (1986) 'Minería potásica', *Papeles de Economía Española* 29, pp.240–70

El País (1990) *Anuario El País, 1990*, Madrid

Fox, K. (1990) 'Aznalcóllar', *Mining Magazine*, January, pp.20–5.

Gea Javaloy, R. (1986) 'El sector del plomo en España', *Papeles de Economía Española* 29, pp.271–81

Gea Javaloy, R. (1986) 'El sector del zinc', *Papeles de Economía Española* 29, pp.321–31

Harvey, C. (1981) *The Rio Tinto Company*. London: Alison Hodge

Koerting Wiese, G. (1986) 'La minería del hierro', *Papeles de Economía Española* 29, pp.332–47

Mallada, L. (1890) *Los males de la patria y futura revolución española*. Madrid: Manuel Tello

Ministerio de Industria y Energia (MINE) (1987) *Estadística minera de España, 1986*

Ministerio de Industria y Energía (MINE) (1989a) *Estadística minera de España, 1987*. Madrid

Ministerio de Industria y Energía (MINE) (1989b) *Informe anual sobre la industria española, 1988*. Madrid

Morera Altisent, J. (1986) 'La minería del cobre', *Papeles de Economía Española* 29, pp.303–20

Muñoz, J. *et al.* (1976) 'Minería y capital extranjero', *Información Comercial Española* No.514, pp.59–89

Rivera, A. (1990) 'Almadén se plantea el tratamiento de residuos como medio de subsistencia', *El País*, 8 July

Romero Alvarez, J. and Oliveros Rives, J. (1986) 'El mercurio', *Papeles de Economía Española* 29, pp.282–302

Tamames, R. (1983) *Estructura económica de España, Vol.1*. Madrid: Alianza Editorial

Terán, M. (1978) 'La minería y las industrias extractivas', in M. Terán, *et al.* (eds), *Geografía general de España*, pp.404–28 Barcelona: Editorial Ariel SA

Velarde Fuertes, J. (1986) 'Ante la nueva minería española', *Papeles de Economía Española* 29, pp.2–29

◆ Chapter 5 ◆

Energy

5.1 Energy in Spain

A crucial characteristic of the Spanish economy centres on the limited capacity to meet energy requirements from domestic sources and a consequent reliance on imports, especially of oil. In 1988 the degree of self-sufficiency in primary energy was only thirty-nine per cent and fifty-four per cent of primary energy requirements were derived from oil (Table 5.1). Dependence on imported oil was one of the major causes of the severe economic crisis in the early 1980s and remains a latent threat to the economy.

Table 5.1 Structure of primary energy consumption, 1950–88

Energy Source	1950	1960	1970	1975	1980	1985	1988	
Oil	8.9	27.9	62.2	70.9	68.6	53.2	54.2	(44.7)
Coal	73.6	47.0	22.3	15.5	18.3	25.6	18.8	(15.5)
Nuclear	0.0	0.0	0.5	2.5	1.5	8.4	13.4	(11.1)
HEP and other	17.5	25.1	14.7	9.7	9.4	9.9	9.5	(7.8)
Natural gas	0.0	0.0	0.3	1.4	2.2	3.0	4.2	(3.5)
Total	100.0	100.0	100.0	100.0	100.0	100.0	100.0	(82.6)

Note: Figures in brackets refer to primary-energy consumption in millions of tonnes oil equivalent

Sources: MINE, 1989b Papeles de Economía 29, 1986

Primary-energy production is shared by coal, nuclear power and hydroelectricity (Table 5.2). Domestic oil supplies are very small (less than three per cent of requirements), as are those of natural gas. Coal supplies are reasonable but of poor quality. Hydroelectricity continues to grow but its contribution to overall production is subject to variations in precipitation. Nuclear power has expanded rapidly but further development has been halted by growing political opposition and shifts in energy production costs. As a reflection of these characteristics, energy policy continues to seek a reduction in energy imports, diversification of energy sources and energy conservation. In terms of the organisation of the industry, energy-market liberalisation is reducing the extent of state control and

Table 5.2 Structure of primary energy production, 1975–88

Energy Source	1975		1980		1985		1988	
Coal	41.3	—	39.4	—	45.7	(13.6)	33.7	(10.8)
Nuclear	10.3	—	6.8	—	21.1	(6.3)	34.6	(11.1)
HEP	36.1	—	48.3	—	24.9	(7.4)	24.5	(7.8)
Oil	12.4	—	5.3	—	7.4	(2.2)	4.6	(1.5)
Natural Gas	0.0	—	0.2	—	1.0	(0.3)	2.6	(0.8)
Total	100.0	(16.4)	100.0	(22.0)	100.0	(29.7)	100.0	(32.0)

Note: Figures in brackets refer to production in millions of tonnes oil equivalent

Sources: MINE, 1989b; *Papeles de Economía* 29, 1986

opening up the industry to foreign penetration.

The final-energy market in Spain is characterised by relatively low levels of consumption per unit of GDP (in relation to other European Community countries), a high degree of penetration by electricity (Table 5.3), and spatial concentration. In 1985 energy consumption per capita was 1.29 toe (tonnes oil equivalent) and final-electricity consumption 0.23 toe. In the European Community the figures were 2.35 toe and 0.35 toe. Electricity consumption per head in 1988 was 3,326 KWh in Spain, higher only than Greece and Portugal (5,218 KWh per head in the UK; *El País*, 1990). The energy market is concentrated in four major areas: Barcelona, Madrid, País Vasco and Comunidad Valenciana, which together account for about forty per cent of demand (Martos Martínez, 1987).

Table 5.3 Structure of final-energy consumption, 1975–88

Energy Source	1975		1980		1985		1988	
Oil	74.8	(31.4)	75.4	(38.1)	68.3	(34.3)	69.0	(38.8)
Electricity	13.8	(5.8)	15.3	(7.7)	17.8	(8.9)	17.6	(9.9)
Coal	9.4	(4.0)	7.0	(3.5)	10.4	(5.2)	8.2	(4.6)
Gas	2.0	(0.8)	2.3	(1.1)	3.5	(1.8)	5.2	(3.0)
Total	100.0	(42.0)	100.0	(50.5)	100.0	(50.2)	100.0	(56.2)

Note: Figures in brackets refer to final-energy consumption in millions of tonnes oil equivalent

Sources: MINE, 1989b; *Papeles de Economía* 29, 1986

5.1.1 National Energy Plans

The first round of world oil-price rises at the end of 1973 highlighted the excessive dependence of Spain on imported oil and the poverty of existing use of domestic energy resources. The ensuing energy crisis spawned a series of national energy plans (Plan Energético Nacional, PEN), all of which have aimed at energy conservation, reducing dependence on energy imports and expanding the role of domestic resources. However, the strategies adopted have shifted in the light of changing political and economic realities. Thus the First National Energy Plan (approved in January 1975 for the period 1975 to 1985) assumed continued strong growth in energy consumption to be met largely through a massive nuclear-energy programme. The Second National Energy Plan (approved in 1979 for the period 1978 to 1987) revised energy demand downwards, attached less urgency to reducing oil consumption and scaled down nuclear-energy plans. The switch to increased coal usage in electricity-generating stations was to continue and further diversification of the energy base was to be achieved through the increased use of natural gas. The substantial oil-price rise in 1979 necessitated an early revision of the Plan, to focus on reducing oil consumption to forty-five per cent of primary energy requirements by 1990 (Revision of the Second National Energy Plan, 1981–90).

The Third National Energy Plan (1984–92) provided a thorough review of energy policy following the 1982 general elections. It sought four kinds of medium term action: i) absorption of current surplus capacity by a) scaling down energy investment and b) raising prices to cover costs of production; ii) financial improvement of energy utilities and reform of the institutional mechanisms for transferring earnings among the various utilities; iii) improvement in the efficiency of energy use and iv) reduction of the vulnerability of Spanish energy supply by increasing the use of coal and hydroelectricity and reducing the import dependency associated with the use of oil. National economic growth and the growth of energy consumption were further revised down from the previous plans to an average of 3.5 per cent per annum (GDP growth) 1986–92, with an elasticity of energy demand of $0.73 \times$ GDP (compared with the actual elasticity of 0.95 in the period 1971–81).

A fourth plan was initially due in 1986 but uncertainty in the energy market on both the supply and demand side have resulted in its delay (publication due in late 1990 was further delayed by the Gulf crisis). An economy expanding more rapidly than expected, continuing weak oil prices (until the Gulf Crisis in 1990) and problems in the nuclear industry have been amongst the factors that have had to be taken into account.

5.2 Coal

In 1988 the coal-and-lignite-mining industry employed about 48,600 people (MINE, 1989b), with production of coal and lignite accounting for about twenty per cent of primary-energy requirements and about thirty-three per cent of domestic primary-energy production. After a period of expansion in the late 1970s and early 1980s, production has stabilised (at around 15 million tonnes of hard coal and anthracite, and 20 million tonnes of lignite; Table 5.4) and coal has come under renewed pressure from other energy sources (including oil as oil prices have fallen), particularly away from the coalfields. Domestic coal production has also suffered from increased import penetration, with imports rising from three million tonnes in 1975 to over eight million tonnes in the late 1980s (Table 5.5), due largely to increased demand from power stations and steelworks. Environmental problems have also become a more important issue in the coal industry, both in terms of extraction (especially open-caste workings) and use (emissions from power stations and cement works leading to air pollution and acid rain). Spanish coal remains costly to produce as a result of numerous interlocking factors. The coal itself tends to be of low quality, is frequently dirty (containing many impurities, especially a high proportion of sulphur), friable and of low calorific content. Production costs in underground mines are high due to difficult geological conditions involving thin and faulted seams, making the use of modern mechanised equipment difficult. Small-scale production and low productivity continue to characterise the industry, while labour difficulties, often associated with poor working conditions, are endemic. Transport too is frequently a problem, adding to the delivered cost of the coal.

Table 5.4 Characteristics of energy extraction, 1987

Energy product	Production (million tonnes)	Value (pta. billion)	Mines	Employment
Coal	8.7	80.7	84	31,839
Anthracite	5.4	45.4	118	11,523
Sub-bituminous coal and brown lignite	20.5	59.5	34	7,096
Crude oil	1.6	28.0		
Natural gas	750.0*	8.8	5	356
Uranium concentrate	—	2.9	2	280
Other	—	1.2	—	—
Total	—	226.5	243	51,094

* Millions of cubic metres

Source: MINE, 1989a

Table 5.5 Coal production and imports (mtce), 1950–88

Year	Hard coal	Anthracite	Lignite*	Coal imports
1950	9.5	1.5	1.3	—
1960	11.3	2.5	1.8	—
1970	7.9	2.8	2.8	3.5
1975	7.5	3.2	3.4	4.0
1980	9.1	4.1	15.4	5.7
1985	10.5	5.9	23.6	8.4
1986	9.5	5.3	22.2	—
1988	9.0	5.2	17.6	8.7

* Includes sub-bituminous coal

Sources: García Alonso, 1986 and 1987; MINE, 1989b

5.2.1 Coal resources

Given present levels of output and on the assumption of no new deposits, hard-coal and anthracite supplies should be available for forty to fifty years, brown lignite for thirty years and black lignite for eighty to ninety years (from the mid 1980s). Ninety per cent of 'probable' hard-coal and anthracite reserves are located in Asturias and León (360 million tonnes and 355 million tonnes respectively of national 'probable' reserves, estimated at around 790 million tonnes; García Alonso, 1987), especially in the central basin of Asturias – El Bierzo-Villablino, – where seventy per cent of Spanish coal is produced. The central Asturias Basin alone produces fifty per cent of all Spanish coal. Major producing districts are found in the Nalón Valley (districts of Langreo, San Martín del Rey Aurelio and Leviana) and Caudal Valley (Mieres and Figaredo), and in the Camocha depression south of Gijón. In the provinces of León and Palencia mainly anthracite is produced, León producing seventy per cent of the total mainly from the valleys of Bierzo, Fabero-Bembibre, Villablino and Caboalles, which are linked by rail to Ponferrada. For other hard-coal production, Villablino (province of León) is the major centre, followed by a zone bordering the railway from La Robla (twenty-five km north of León) to Bilbao. Outside this northern area the most important coal deposits are at Puertollano (Ciudad Real), which supply local power stations and industry, as well as providing the nearest supply for Madrid, and in the province of Córdoba at Belmez, Peñarroya and Espiel.

The major deposits of lignite are located in the province of La Coruña, which contain an estimated eighty-four per cent of all 'probable' brown-lignite reserves (national 'probable' reserves 537 million tonnes) and Teruel with seventy-two per cent of all 'probable' black lignite reserves (national 'probable' reserves 525 million tonnes). Other important deposits are in the province of Barcelona ('probable' reserves of black lignite 40 million tonnes) and Granada ('probable' reserves of brown lignite 88 million tonnes; García Alonso, 1987). Teruel is the leading producer of lignite with the most important centres being at Utrillas (linked to Zaragoza by rail), Aliaga and the group of Ariño-Alloza-Andorra that provide supplies to the Escatron power station. In Cataluña the basins of Berga, Figola and Pobla de Lillet in the upper Llobregat Valley produce a high-calorific lignite. In La Coruña, Portocraibo supplies the power station of Puentes de García Rodríguez. Large new deposits were found in Orense in 1982.

5.2.2 Development of the coal industry

Following the Civil War, hard coal and anthracite production expanded from 6.7 million tonnes in 1939 to 11.5 million tonnes in 1960. Apart from hydroelectricity, it was virtually the only domestic energy source available to sustain autarchic industrialisation.

The change in economic policy after 1959 opened the way for oil imports and a fundamental restructuring of energy use away from coal. Oil was relatively cheap, more convenient and cleaner to use, and the basis of the new petrochemical industry. Coal was left with only power stations and iron- and steel works as customers. Even in these two industries it faced competition from other sources of energy and imported coal. During this period of crisis in the industry, production was sustained only by the rapid expansion of electricity generation and iron and steel production. Coal and anthracite output fell from 13.8 million tonnes in 1960 to below 10 million tonnes in 1973 (essentially hard-coal production fell while anthracite production remained stable). Employment in coal and lignite mining fell from over 100,000 people in 1959 to 58,000 in 1971. Atomisation of production impeded planned rationalisation. Nevertheless economic circumstances forced closures and amalgamations, reducing the number of coal and anthracite mining companies from 391 in 1959 (eighty-four per cent of which were producing less than 25,000 tons per year) to 121 in 1970 (of which sixty per cent were producing less than 25,000 tons per year). Similarly, in lignite mining the number of companies fell from 135 in 1959 to forty-one in 1970 (García Alonso, 1987).

The government took a number of steps to accommodate the impact of economic change on the coal industry. One of these steps was to reach an agreement with the industry over production targets in exchange for a package of government assistance including official credit and import-tariff protection (this form of joint action – *acción concertada* – was introduced from 1965). This action met with little success. A second step was to partially nationalise the industry by initiating the fusion of seventeen loss-making Asturian coal-mining companies into the state-owned company Hunosa (Empresa Nacional Hullera del Norte, SA, established in 1967). The process of fusion was difficult and protracted, continuing into the 1970s. In 1970 Hunosa employed 25,000 people at thirty-one mines, producing four million tonnes of mostly coking coal (Terán, 1978).

The sharp increase in oil prices beginning in 1973 and continuing in the early 1980s led to renewed interest in coal by producers (as coal prices rose), consumers (as coal prices fell below those of oil; coal prices to power stations and coke ovens were fixed by the government but other coal prices were free) and the government (for both strategic and balance-of-payments reasons). The government introduced a number of policies to stimulate the use of coal, including the conversion to coal of existing large, industrial, energy consumers (especially cement works, ceramic factories and power stations). Many power stations were converted to coal (for example Los Barrios, Algeciras) with the help of official credit to cover up to seventy per cent of the investment necessary for conversion. Under the Second National Energy Plan there was an acceleration in the construction of coal-fired power stations, leading for example to the construction of Puentes de García Rodríguez (1,400 MW) and Teruel (1,050 MW) power stations. Installed capacity in coal-fired power stations increased from 3,060 MW in 1976 to 9,640 MW in 1985 (Garcí Alonso, 1987).

These policies resulted in a substantial growth in coal production between 1975 and 1985 (coal and anthracite production rose from 10.7 to 16.4 million tonnes and lignite production from 3.4 to 23.6 million tonnes, Table 5.5). Increased demand for coal (demand doubled from 14 million tonnes coal equivalent (mtce) in 1976 to 27.5 mtce in 1985; García Alonso, 1987) was accompanied by increased coal imports (up from 4.0 million tonnes in 1975 to 8.4 million tonnes in 1985 (handled through three major ports: Algeciras (Cádiz), Carboneras (Almería), and Gijón (Oviedo), a switch in the composition of coal demand, a change in the structure of electricity generation and a reduction in fuel-oil consumption. Power stations substantially increased their absolute levels of demand, accounting for over eighty per cent of coal production in 1985 (including virtually all lignite). Industrial demand also increased in absolute terms (notably in the cement industry and in ceramics), although this was tempered by contraction in some traditional heavy industrial markets (notably in the iron and steel industry) associated with industrial contraction and energy conservation.

5.2.2 Coal-industry structure and restructuring

The industrial structure of coal mining remains littered with small firms. During the 1960s there was a substantial decline in the number of firms in the industry as primary-energy demand switched to oil, but the wave of industrial expansion in the 1970s increased the number of firms by fifty per cent between 1974 and 1982. Small size is most common in hard coal and anthracite mining. In 1985 there were 168 hard coal and anthracite firms, of which sixty per cent produced less than 25,000 tons per year (García Alonso, 1987).

In hard-coal production there are a few large firms, mostly public ones, and a multitude of largely family-run small firms. The major public company Hunosa employs about seventy per cent of all employees in this sub sector (employed 19,671 in 1987) and produces about forty-five per cent of the total output. In anthracite production all the companies are private, with production concentrated in the companies that exploit the large anthracite deposits of Bierzo and surroundings. However, the average size of firm in the sector and average output remain relatively small. In 1990 there were an estimated 250 firms in the coal industry producing eight per cent of European Community coal output but employing thirteen per cent of the European Community coal labour force. Further exposure to competition in the industry will bring continued rationalisation, especially amongst the small firms in both hard coal and anthracite production.

In the lignite sector the average size of company is relatively large and virtually all production is open-caste. In 1985 there were twenty-eight companies of which thirteen produced ninety-eight per cent of total lignite output. These thirteen companies had an average labour force of more than 500 people and production of over 1.6 million tonnes a year. As in hard coal and anthracite, public sector companies are very important, especially Endesa which works the lignite deposits of Teruel and Puentes de García Rodríguez to supply its power stations.

Rationalisation in the coal industry has been very slow in comparison with other countries in the European Community, especially in relation to the contraction of the labour force. Between 1959 and 1974 the labour force declined from 100,000 to 50,000. By 1990 it had declined little further to about 43,000, shedding only some 1,300 jobs after 1985. Despite some mechanisation and the opening of new mines, productivity continues to be below that in other north-west-European countries. In 1985 productivity was only 205 kg per man hour in underground hard-coal mines and 369 kg per man hour in underground anthracite mines. The greatest contributions to productivity have come from open-caste developments such as the lignite workings at Puentes de García Rodríguez, Meirama and Ariño, the hard-coal workings at Prado de la Guzpeña, Coto Cortés, Valdesmario and Puertollano, together with smaller, less-important ones in anthracite. The slow pace at which rationalisation has proceeded stems essentially from the extent of public-sector involvement in the industry, linked to the political problems of pit closures in areas dependent on coal mining.

Further substantial rationalisation is certain in the early 1990s, a process that may have become politically easier with the transfer of responsibilities to the

European Coal and Steel Community, which has partly subsidised continuing heavy losses. Thus a major restructuring plan was requested in 1990 by the EC if futher European assistance was to be forthcoming (a similar condition to that which has been applied to the shipbuilding industry, where cuts of up to thirty per cent in the labour force have been requested). Labour-force cuts are likely to involve about 9,000 workers (twenty-one per cent of the labour force) in addition to further mine closures.

5.3 Oil

Expansion in oil refining and oil consumption in the 1960s and early 1970s came to a halt during the 1970s as crude-oil prices increased and energy consumption switched to non-oil sources. This caused a crisis in the refining sector and a rapid deterioration in the energy trade deficit, while prompting oil exploration and production within Spain. Lower oil prices in the late 1980s (attributable both to low dollar prices and a strong peseta exchange rate) have diluted the urgency for domestic exploration, while rekindling demand in refined-oil products. The most significant events in the oil industry are currently those affecting its organisation, as the oil market is progressively liberalised.

5.3.1 Oil production and resources

Despite substantial exploration, domestic oil production remains minimal (less than three per cent of supplies in 1989), with the bulk of crude-oil supplies (55.4 million tonnes in 1989) being met by imports (49.4 million tonnes in 1988). In 1985 Hispanoil (now Repsol Exploración) produced 4.7 million tonnes overseas, bringing total Spanish production to seven million tonnes. Within Spain exploration first succeeded in oil production as early as 1900 at Huidobro (Burgos). But large-scale exploration did not really begin until legislation was passed in 1958 (Hydrocarbon Law), which reserved 3.5 million hectares of land for exploration and provided incentives for foreign companies. Even then exploration was not very intensive, resulting in only a small quantity of oil being produced in 1964 from the La Lora region (Burgos), which was used by local industry. The 1958 legislation was fundamentally changed in 1974 and with higher oil prices there was much greater investment in oil exploration, involving both foreign and national oil companies. However, few commercial reserves have been discovered, resulting in oil production rising from 0.2 million tonnes in 1972 to two million tonnes in 1974, thence to a peak of only 2.98 million tonnes in 1983. Since then oil production has fallen back to 1.0 million tonnes (1989). Oil is produced offshore on the continental shelf of Tarragona (Casablanca field 0.9 million tonnes), and both onshore and offshore in País Vasco (Ayoluengo field 0.05 million tonnes and Gaviota field 0.13 million tonnes respectively). Production offshore of the Ebro delta has now ceased. The most promising on-shore geological areas are the Guadalquivir Valley and the Sub-Pyrenees basins.

5.3.2 Oil refining

Oil refining is divided between one large public-sector company, Repsol Petróleo (including Petronor), which accounts for about sixty per cent of capacity, and three relatively small private companies. There are nine crude-oil refineries (excluding a small specialist refinery owned by Asfaltos Españoles, Aesa) with an effective capacity of about 62 million tonnes (Table 5.6). The first oil refinery was installed by Cepsa in 1930 in Tenerife outside the control of the state oil monopoly, Campsa. In 1944 Campsa authorised a refinery at Escombreras (Cartagena) that began operating in 1949. No further refineries were added until the 1960s, when refineries were built at Puertollano, Huelva, La Coruña, Bilbao, Algeciras and Castellón. By 1975 the industry had grown to roughly its present size.

Table 5.6 Distribution of oil-refining capacity, 1987

Company	Refinery	Authorised capacity (millions of tonnes)	Effective capacity (millions of tonnes)	Output in 1985 (millions of tonnes)
Repsol Petróleo	Puertollano	7.0	6.0	4.8
	Tarragona	11.0	8.0	5.7
	Cartagena	10.0	5.0	3.5
	La Coruña	7.0	6.0	4.2
	Sub total	35.0	25.0	18.2
Cepsa	Algeciras	8.0	—	6.2
	Tenerife	8.0	—	4.0
	Sub total	16.0	14.5	10.2
Petronor	Somorrostro, Bilbao	12.0	11.0	8.9
Petromed	Castellón	6.0	6.0	3.7*
ERT	Huelva	4.0	4.0	2.6
Asesa	Tarragona†	1.4	1.5	1.0
Total		74.4	62.0	44.6

† Treatment of crude oil for manufacturing asphalt

* In 1989 Petromed refined 3.4 million tonnes at its refinery in Castellón

Source: Diverse sources

Adjustment to the refining crisis of the early 1980s was slow, although there were organisational changes as multinational companies withdrew. For example, Gulf Oil sold its interest in the Huelva refinery to UERT and Exxon sold its interests in Petromed. Refiners reacted to reduced domestic demand by increasing exports, which rose from 2.4 million tonnes in 1980 to 4.9 million tonnes in 1985. Between 1980 and 1986 refining capacity in Spain was reduced by only seven per cent (MINE,1987) compared with thirty-one per cent in the European Community. Furthermore there were no refinery closures, unlike in other parts of western Europe where the industry was controlled by multinationals.

Decline in demand has been fundamentally a decline in heavy oil products (fuel oil for power stations etc.), where substitutes and energy savings have been possible. In contrast there has been an expansion in demand at the light end of the market (for aviation and motor fuel). Thus refiners in other countries switched to lighter products by investing large sums of money in upgrading refineries with catalytic cracking facilities able to take advantage of a greater variety of crude oils (increased flexibility in supply) and able to produce a greater proportion of light-oil products. In Spain this provision of catalytic cracking facilities was slow, despite government measures introduced in 1980 to encourage this restructuring of output (the Refinery Conversion Plan) (Plan de Conversíon de Refinería).

5.3.3 Oil industry structure and restructuring

The oil industry is split between the public and private sectors. The public sector is represented by the Repsol group, formed in 1987 from the various public companies involved in the hydrocarbon sector owned by INH (Instituto Nacional de Hidrocarburos).

The INH was formed in 1981 under the Ministry of Industry and Energy to co-ordinate the dispersed interests of the state in the hydrocarbon industry. Prior to its formation, state control was exercised in a variety of companies through both the Ministry of Economy and Finance (especially through Campsa) and the Ministry of Industry and Energy (especially through INI). INH acquired the state interests and rights in the following (Figure 5.1): i) two mixed (public/private) refining companies, Petroliber (with a fifty-four per cent INH holding) and Hispanoil (with a 100 per cent INH holding); ii) the oil distribution company Campsa (initially INH had a fifty-four per cent holding, increased to 60.5 per cent by 1985) and iii) the former INI companies EMP (Empresa Nacional de Petróleo SA; initially a ninety-two per cent holding), Eniepsa (100 per cent holding), Enagas (100 per cent holding) and Butano SA (initially a fifty per cent holding with the other fifty per cent belonging to the Campsa affiliate Corporación Española de Hidrocarburos (CEH); the INH holding was increased to 100 per cent by 1985). These companies participated in a further twenty-seven companies. Thus through Campsa and its affiliate CEH, INH had interests in the companies Asesa, Proas and Petronor; and through EMP in the petrochemical companies Paular, Alcudia, Calatrava and Montoro.

Co-ordination of public-sector interests in hydrocarbons facilitated a policy of restructuring, reducing costs, investing in distribution networks (e.g. modernising service stations) and improving the image of public-sector companies through advertising campaigns. The process of restructuring began in 1983 and was completed with the formation of Repsol in 1987 (Figure 5.1).

In exploration and crude-oil production there were initially two public-sector companies: Hispanoil (formed in 1965, initially with seventy per cent INI capital, becoming wholly owned by INI in 1975), concerned with overseas exploration and production, and Eniepsa (owned by INI), concerned with exploration and production within Spain. In 1985 Hispanoil acquired Eniepsa and the mineral-exploration rights of Campsa. In 1986 Hispanoil was operating in fifteen countries and producing oil in six (with major deposits in Dubai). The company also produced gas from the Gaviota and Serrablo fields.

Figure 5.1 Evolution of INH, 1981–90

```
Eniepsa (1985)          ┐
Hispanoil (1985)        ├── Hispanoil (1987) ──────────── Repsol Exploración
Campsa (minerals) (1985)┘

Petroliber (1985) ──┐        Petronor (1989) ──┐
EMP ────────────────┴── EMP (1987) ────────────┴── Repsol Petróleo

Calatrava (1983) ┐
Alcudia (1983)   ├── Alcudia (1987) ──────────── Repsol Química
Paular (1983)    ┤
Montoro (1986)   ┘       Bioquímica Española (1987) ┘

Campsa (1984) ──────────── Holdings of EMP and
                           Petroliber (1987) ──────────── Repsol Distribución
                           and Petronor (1989)            (owns 70% Campsa)
                           Gas Butano (1987) ──────────── Repsol Butano
                           Enagas ─────────────────────── Enagas
```

Campsa (Compañía Arrendataria del Monopolio de Petróleos SA)
EMP (Empresa Nacional de Petróleo SA)
INH formed in 1981; Repsol Group formed in 1987
(1985) : Date of incorporation into the group shown in the column to the right

In refining INH bought the holding of Phillips in the petrochemical company Calatrava in 1984, thereby increasing its participation in EMP to ninety-nine per cent. EMP was formed in 1973 from the three companies with INI participation: Repesa (Refinería de Petróleos de Escombreras), with a refinery at Escombreras, Cartagena (established in 1949); Empresa Nacional Calvo Sotelo, with its refinery at Puertollano (established in 1965); and Enptasa (Refinería de Tarragona) with its refinery at Tarragona (established in 1974). In 1985 EMP acquired the company Petroliber (Compañía Iberica Refinados de Petróleos, SA, which was owned fifty-four per cent by INH, twenty-eight per cent by Deutsche Marathon Petroleum and eighteen per cent by other private interests). This acquisition brought a fourth refinery located in La Coruña (established in 1966). Together the four refineries have a crude oil refining capacity of 25 million tonnes.

In petrochemicals the company Alcudia absorbed Calatrava and Paular in 1983. In 1986 Alcudia acquired the participation of Arco in Montoro and merged all four petrochemical companies in 1986 under Alcudia, with plants in Santander, Puertollano and Tarragona producing a wide range of products (especially plastics, rubber, carbon black, styrene and butadiene). Alcudia thus became the only subsidiary of EMP and a medium-size petrochemical company by European standards, exporting a large proportion of its production.

Oil distribution in Spain has been a state monopoly since the 1920s. Campsa (Compañía Arrendataria del Monopolio de Petróleos SA) was founded in 1927 by José Calvo Sotelo to administer a monopoly in oil (Monopolio Español de Petróleos), which was supervised by the Ministry of Economy and Finance. This monopoly covered the whole of Spain, except the Islas Canarias, Ceuta and Melilla, where multinational companies have been able to market oil products.

All oil sold in Spain (except in the excluded areas) was thenceforth sold through Campsa. The objective was to increase state tax revenues and to protect the oil industry from foreign domination. Campsa remained primarily concerned with oil refining and distribution, with little interest in downstream integration into petrochemicals.

Entry into the European Community required that Campsa be reformed to break up its monopoly. Reorganisation of the company was also necessary to enable it to compete more effectively against the multinationals. In 1984 ownership of the monopoly was transferred to Campsa and ownership of Campsa was divided among all the major oil companies in Spain, according to their refinery capacity. This left INH with a controlling share. In 1989 Repsol held 70 per cent, Cepsa 14.6 per cent, Petromed 7.5 per cent and ERT 5.7 per cent (Bruce, 1989). Under the reorganisation, the private refiners have made over to Campsa the service stations that they used to manage under concessions. Campsa will maintain its exclusivity over the distribution and sale of nationally produced petrol and fuel and imports from non-European Community countries. In 1989 Campsa agreed in principle to allow some multinationals to use its pipeline and tanker fleet, but they will only be able to use it for imported products.

Campsa is one of Spain's largest companies by value of sales, distributing and marketing oil in Spain (outside the Islas Canarias, Ceuta and Melilla). The company owns an extensive supply network, a large transport fleet (including road, rail and sea transport) and all of the country's oil pipelines. Faced with the prospect of competition, Campsa is actively trying to improve its image and modernise and extend its distribution network. Campsa owns about one third of the 3,650 service stations (in 1989) and brands most of the others, which are run by small private concessionaires. The pipeline network is being extended to the northern and Mediterranean coastal regions currently supplied by sea, adding to the company's competitive advantage in distribution. The existing network links La Rota to Zaragoza (817 km double pipeline). The new network will link Algeciras to La Rota, Miranda to Pamplona and Zaragoza, Tarragona to Barcelona and Gerona, Sevilla to Coria del Rio and Puertollano to Almodovar. After 1992 all domestic refinery output will still have to be sold to Campsa.

The formation of Repsol in 1987 marked the most recent stage in the rationalisation of the oil industry. This new company is the seventh-largest oil company in Europe (although in 1987 its sales were worth only sixteen per cent of those of BP) and the largest industrial organisation (by sales) in Spain. The company has six divisions (Figure 5.1): Repsol Exploración (formally Hispanoil; in 1989 Repsol owned thirty per cent of its own crude supply and is seeking forty per cent), with reserves in Colombia, Indonesia, Dubai, Gabon and Egypt, and small stakes in the North Sea; Repsol Petróleo (formally EMP); Repsol Química (formally Alcudia); Repsol Butano (formally Gas Butano); Repsol Distribución (formally EMP Distribución), which owns seventy per cent of Campsa); and Repsol Derivados (formally Bioquímica Española).

Petronor (Refinería de Petróleos del Norte SA) has been controlled since 1989 by Repsol (it includes an interest by Petromex, providing a foothold for Mexico in the EC). The company owns one refinery at Somorrostro, eighteen km from Bilbao. In 1984 Petronor refined 7.7 million tonnes of crude oil, partly for export; new investment has included a plant for producing lead-free petrol.

In the private sector the largest company is Cepsa (Compañía Española de Petróleos, SA), controlled by Banco Central (with a significant holding by the petroleum company of the United Arab Emirates). Cepsa is a vertically integrated company involved in production (for example in Venezuela), transportation, refining, petrochemicals and distribution, as well as non-oil-related activities. In refining it has an effective crude-oil-refining capacity of 14 million tonnes split between two refineries, one in Santa Cruz de Tenerife and one in the Campo de Gibraltar. The latter has a catalytic cracking plant built in the 1980s and is the centre of Cepsa's petrochemical complex (including asphalt and carbon black production). Faced with the prospect of increased competition, the company first diversified into non-oil-related activities (acquiring the operations of the food and drinks companies Aguas de Lanjarón and Condepols in 1984), and then sought alliances with foreign companies in relation to its core business of oil refining, lubricants and petrochemicals. In essence Cepsa is a regional oil company in the European Community with interests in Portugal, France and Spain.

The other private oil refiners are Petromed (Petróleos del Mediterraneo, SA; part of the Banco Banesto Group), which owns a refinery at Castellón; and Ertoil (almost entirely controlled by the banking group Hispano–Urquijo until the Kuwait Investment Office gained control in 1988, it is now part of the Ercros group), which owns a refinery in Huelva and through the rest of the Ercros group has access to diverse other oil and mineral interests, including the petrochemical complex in Huelva.

Internationalisation is the principal challenge facing Spanish oil companies in the coming years, necessitating further restructuring in the wake of increased competition. Strategies adopted have included product diversification, alliances with foreign companies and expansion into foreign markets. The three private companies have not been able to merge to form a single, strong, Spanish refining group (an initial merger between Cepsa and Petromed was effectively halted by the failure of Banco Central and Banco Banesto to reach an agreement themselves to merge). It has also been suggested that Cepsa should buy the whole Rabida petrochemical complex at Huelva from Ercros. In contrast the companies have sought to become more international. For example, in 1989 Cepsa formed a joint venture with BP to produce and market maleic anhydride (used to produce plastic resins, lubricants and agricultural chemicals). The company has also merged its business in resins with the European activities of Dai Nippon. Petromed reached an agreement in 1987 with BP to create a mixed distribution and marketing company in Spain (BPMED), giving BP the potential to gain access to the Campsa pipeline and a network of service-stations. This agreement was criticised as breaking the objective of the new Campsa to retain the dominance of Spanish companies in marketing oil in Spain, once again illustrating the rivalries between Spanish companies.

Foreign multinational companies have found it difficult to gain entry to the Spanish market. Spanish companies have been refurbishing and expanding their service station networks, while sites for foreign companies have been hard to obtain. But indirectly foreign companies have been buying holdings in Spanish oil companies, for example through the part privatisation of Repsol. These holdings will provide access to the pipeline network.

5.3.4 State intervention in the oil industry

The oil industry has been very tightly controlled by a plethora of state intervention, exemplified by the state monopoly over the purchase of most important oil products and the sale of oil products in mainland Spain and the Islas Baleareas (through the Monopolio de Petróleo and Campsa respectively). Other forms of intervention have covered: i) ownership and participation in oil companies; ii) determination of oil input prices to refineries; iii) the requirement that all of the oil from Hispanoil was purchased by refineries; iv) sources of supply regulated through a commercial quota system (this percentage of oil products that the refineries are obliged to buy through the state – the *'Cuota de Comercio'* – was reduced from sixty to forty-five per cent of total purchases in 1983 and down to twenty-eight per cent in 1986); v) the requirement that crude oil was transported in Spanish registered vessels; vi) control over the market price for many oil products (determined in part by the level of taxes applied to the ex-works price: the twelve per cent VAT, the special oil tax (*Impuesto Especial de Hidrocarburos and Renta de Petróleos*); and vii) a broad influence through energy policy.

Thus state intervention moulded the development of the industry. In exploration, companies benefited by having a tied market. Production was a very profitable activity from the early 1970s to the early 1980s. However, the lack of vertical integration in the 1980s meant that profits from refining could not be used to support production. In refining, state intervention prevented vertical and horizontal integration of the industry, as oil companies concerned themselves mainly with refining. Vertical integration allowed multinational companies to take advantage of different levels of profitability at different stages of production. The horizontal integration in multinational companies also allowed economies of scale and in recession enabled rationalisation to proceed with selective closure and investment programmes. This was not possible in Spain.

State intervention has also been criticised as: i) protecting relatively small companies, operating refineries well below an economically competitive size; ii) impeding responsiveness to market conditions (Spanish refineries have generally produced heavy-oil products that are high in sulphur and generally of relatively low value); iii) protecting inefficiency, especially high-cost structures, as the pricing policy adopted by the administration was based on a formula that covered production costs; and v) leaving experience of distribution and marketing exclusively to Campsa, which itself has little experience of marketing in a competitive environment.

5.3.5 The oil industry and the European Community

Membership of the European Community has required the harmonisation of Spanish energy policy with that of the EC, including the policy to reduce dependence on oil and imported energy, environmental legislation, compliance with EC industrial policy in restructuring oil refining and EC competition policy in reorganising Campsa and breaking up the oil monopoly. In restructuring oil refining the EC (EC of twelve) cut its refining capacity by thirty-six per cent (from 934 million tonnes to 598 million tonnes in the mid 1980s) and completely closed forty-four refineries between 1977/79 and the beginning of 1987. During the same period in Spain there were no complete refinery closures and capacity was cut by only fourteen per cent (Fernández, 1987). The Spanish refiners' association Aserpetrol argued that the dispersed pattern of refineries in Spain would lead to significant increases in product distribution costs if any one refinery were closed. Capacity reductions were made largely by the public sector, it being difficult for private firms to reduce capacity below a certain level without plant closures and the withdrawal of firms from the sector. More contentious than capacity reductions have been the negotiations over the liberalisation of the oil market required by the EC. The prospect of a more liberal market has acted as a catalyst for many of the changes that have occurred in the industry (although even when the transition is complete, foreign companies will still not be able to sell oil in Spain that has been refined in Spain; this will remain the preserve of Campsa). Repsol Exploración will be able to sell its oil to any customer. Oil-product prices began to be freed from 1988 with most becoming free by 1990, subject to the administration being able to fix a minimum and a maximum price.

In distribution, foreign companies are beginning to establish service stations. Under the new Road Law (Ley de Carreteras) the minimum distance between service stations has been reduced (by about a half) and anyone may apply to the Ministry of Industry and Energy to operate one. In 1989 there were relatively few stations in Spain (3,643, compared with over 30,000 in France and 20,000 in the UK). Campsa owned about 1,200 stations in 1989 and was expanding provision (to around 2,000 by the end of the century). Total (which was the first to break the monopoly of Campsa) is seeking to install thirty-five service stations by 1992 and to have about 200 (five per cent of the market) by the year 2000. BP opened its first service station in Valencia in November 1989 through the company BPMED; by the end of the century it hopes to have about 400 stations in Spain, controlling ten per cent of the market. Agip and Texaco opened their first service stations in Madrid in 1990, and Mobil has formed a joint company with the drinks firm Larios to establish a network of service stations in Andalucía. Repsol is hoping to have 400 service stations by 1992. Cepsa hopes to have fifteen per cent of the market by the year 2000. Competition has brought a diversification of the range of services offered along with improvements in the appearance of service stations. In addition, both Repsol and Cepsa have begun to look outside Spain for service stations. Cepsa has owned service stations in Portugal since the 1960s and is currently expanding into France. Repsol has service stations in Portugal (six by the end of 1989), has bought service stations in Britain and is seeking to expand into France (*El País* 17 September 1989).

5.4 Gas

The gas market is divided into town gas, liquefied gas (GLP) and natural gas, the latter two being monopolies of state enterprises. Further growth in gas supplies will come from natural gas. Natural gas was favoured in the Third National Energy Plan as a means of diversifying energy supplies and because there are domestic reserves. A national gas grid has been established and gas tariffs set that are competitive with other fuels.

5.4.1 Town gas

Town (manufactured) gas is on the decline as supplies are replaced by natural gas. Town gas is produced from coal (which was the source of the first town gas produced in Spain, in Barcelona in 1842), oil and natural gas, and distributed over relatively small areas to essentially domestic and small commercial users. In 1955 about 0.4 million tonnes of coal were used to produce town gas but from the mid 1950s many gas manufacturers began to switch to oil. The spread of liquefied gas in the late 1950s limited the further growth of town gas. A number of small companies (some sixteen private companies in the mid 1980s) manufactured gas, serving most of the large towns in Spain. In 1985 town-gas suppliers provided 2.4 billion therms. Gas Madrid is the largest supplier. The town-gas companies are currently converting their installations to the use of natural gas and there is a process of rationalisation between the town-gas suppliers and Enagas (for example in 1988 Gas Madrid sold its interests around Valladolid to Enagas, in return for the gas activities of Enagas in Madrid).

5.4.2 Liquefied gas

Liquefied gas (*gas licuados del petróleo* – GLP) is butane/propane gas that liquefies under moderate pressure. Liquefied gas was first imported by Campsa in bottles from France in 1934. In 1953 GLP began to be produced at the Cepsa refinery in Tenerife and in 1955 at the Repesa refinery at Cartagena. Consumption of GLP increased from only 900 tonnes in 1957 to 2.2 million tonnes in 1985, serving 13.3 million consumers. In 1985 fifty per cent of input requirements came from domestic refineries, nine per cent from Enagas and forty-one per cent from imports.

The former distributor Gas Butano SA was established in 1957 (originally with fifty per cent participation from Campsa, and the other fifty per cent by INI, Cepsa, Texaco and Standard Oil of California; later it became wholly owned by INH). Repsol Butano (formed in 1987 from Gas Butano SA) is the state-owned monopoly importer and distributor of liquefied gas (except in the Islas Canarias and Ceuta and Melilla). It is the largest liquefied-gas distributor in Europe. Under the Gas Protocol (Protocol de Intenciónes para el Desarrollo de Gas en España, 1985) and the Gas Plans (Planes de Gasificación), Repsol Butano now also participates in the distribution of natural gas (acquiring interests in local distributors such as Gas Madrid SA). At the end of 1986 it had thirty-seven factories with an overall capacity for producing 635,000 bottles of GLP per day. With the promotion of natural gas and the increasing penetration of electricity, the growth in sales of GLP has slowed.

5.4.3 Natural gas

Natural-gas consumption has been expanding rapidly as the gas grid has been extended and energy pricing policy has been set so as to ensure competitiveness (the price of natural gas to consumers is set by the government in the form of a uniform system of tariffs). Expansion of natural gas has been viewed as part of the strategy of diversifying energy supplies and reducing reliance on imports. However, although at the beginning of the 1990s some thirty per cent of consumption is supplied from domestic resources, unless new supplies of natural gas are discovered and exploited the industry will be wholly dependent on imports by the turn of the century.

Expansion of the natural gas market has been much more rapid than forecast in the Third National Energy Plan. The Gas Supply Plan (Plan de Gasificación, 1986) envisaged the supply of natural gas increasing to 53.8 billion therms in 1992, of which 15.5 billion therms (twenty-nine per cent) were to come from domestic supplies. The Gas Plan (Plan del Gas) approved in 1988 predicted growth to 6.3 per cent (56 billion therms) of energy requirements by 1992 and seven per cent by 2000, largely displacing fuel oil in the industrial energy market. The industry estimate consumption growing even faster reaching 71 billion therms by 1996, ninety per cent greater than in 1988, giving natural gas seven per cent of the national primary-energy market. In 1989 consumption had already reached 55.5 billion therms. The bulk of natural gas is consumed by industry (especially the power stations, integrated steelworks and fertilizer plants) and commercial customers (eighty-six per cent in 1989), this is where further growth is likely to come from, with domestic use of natural gas remaining relatively small.

Natural-gas supplies are dominated by the state company Enagas (Empresa Nacional de Gas), set up in 1972 as a wholly owned subsidiary of INI (later transferred to INH). It was formed to acquire and import natural gas, to construct a gas pipeline network and to distribute natural gas in Spain (a monopoly in which there were clearly areas of conflict with the existing monopoly conferred on Gas Butano for GLP supplies). Thus it acquired Gas Natural, which had been set up in 1965 by Compañía Catalana de Gas y Electricidad (together with a number of Spanish banks and the multinational Exxon). Gas Natural first imported gas in 1969 from Exxon in Algeria. A regasification plant was built in Barcelona (which began supplying natural gas in 1971, imported from Algeria and Libya) and the Barcelona town-gas network was converted to natural gas. Other companies (existing town-gas companies, for example Catalana de Gas, Gas de Euskadi and Gas Madrid) are also involved in the distribution of natural gas within particular localities, mainly to domestic and commercial consumers.

The framework for the development of natural gas supplies in Spain was established in 1985 by the Gas Protocol. Under this protocol Enagas assumed responsibility to: i) construct the trunk gas pipelines and regasification plants in Huelva, Cartagena and Mallorca; ii) provide the supply of natural gas; and iii) supply large industrial consumers (those using over 10 million therms per year) directly, except in Cataluña and País Vasco, where Catalana de Gas and Gas de Euskadi assumed this responsibility and that of developing the respective regional gas-supply networks. Small industrial users and the domestic market would be supplied by the various gas distribution companies, and gas-supply tariffs would be the same throughout Spain. Thus there has been some rationalisation of the industry through the transfer of resources between companies. For example the rights that Enagas had in various gas distributors (such as a thirty-three per cent stake in Gas Navarra) were transferred to Gas Butano.

5.4.4 Natural-gas resources and supplies

Existing domestic gas supplies are only likely to last until the end of the century. The first natural gas supply in Spain came from the Castillo field in the province of Alava in 1963. Production from the Serrablo field in the Pyrenees (province of Huesca; reserves estimated at 2.5 billion cubic metres) started in 1982 and supplies were connected to the national gas grid in 1984. In 1989 the field supplied 12.7 million cubic metres of gas. In 1986 the Gaviota field (offshore from Bermeo, Vizcaya; estimated reserves 12 billion cubic metres) was connected to the gas grid and now constitutes the source of almost all domestic natural gas (supplying 1.49 billion cubic metres, ninety-nine per cent of domestic production, in 1989). This field may eventually supply some 14 billion therms per year. A small amount of gas is also supplied from the Ayoluengo field. In southern Spain the Guadalquivir field has estimated reserves of 0.46 billion cubic metres and was due to be connected to the Huelva–Sevilla gas pipeline in 1987 to supply up to 1.8 billion therms per year (not in production in 1989). In the Gulf of Cádiz there are reserves estimated at three billion cubic metres but there are no current plans for the development of this field.

Algeria and Libya have been the source of foreign gas supplies in the past (in 1989 all imports were from Algeria). In an attempt to diversify these supplies an agreement has been made to develop the Troll gas deposit in Norway, which will supply gas from the mid 1990s; an outline agreement has been reached with the USSR to supply 1,000 to 1,500 million cubic metres of gas for twenty-five years annually from 1992; and a connection with the French network linking the Lacq deposits to Serrablo has been proposed.

Within Spain, natural gas is distributed through the gas grid, which was first expanded in the 1970s following the increasing price of oil. Difficulties over supply contracts and institutional factors (relating to established gas producers) slowed growth. The initial network comprised 1,135 km of trunk pipeline (72 kg/cm^2) and 500 km of primary pipeline (16 and 4 kg/cm^2). The network joined: i) Barcelona–Ebro–Tivisa–Zaragoza (with a branch to Serrablo) ii) Tudela–Logrono– Haro (with branches to Burgos and Vitoria, and the Gaviota field) and iii) Barcelona–Reus–Tarragona–Tivisa–Castellón–Valencia. A further 118 km were brought into service in 1986 linking Bermeo and Lemona, and Haro to Burgos. In 1987 Madrid was linked to the pipeline from Burgos. Further connections have provided more than two thirds of the economy and Spanish industry with the option of using natural gas. More distant possible strategic investments include: i) a link to the French gas grid (Lacq to Serrablo in Plan del Gas, 1988), thereby tapping the European grid and sources of supply in the Soviet Union ii) a pipeline under the Straits of Gibraltar to link directly with supplies in north Africa (SEGAMO pipeline), iii) linking the whole network together through a pipeline between Madrid and Sevilla (Plan del Gas, 1988) and iv) the construction of underground storage facilities.

The gas network also draws on imported liquefied natural gas, which is processed in one of three regasification plants. A plant in Barcelona supplied the whole gas network until the late 1980s, when two further regasification plants were brought on stream: one in Cartagena (completed in 1988) to supply the local market (including a fertilizer plant), and one in Huelva (completed in 1988) to supply the gas link to Sevilla (and a fertilizer plant in Huelva).

5.5 Electricity

Following rapid expansion in the 1960s and 1970s (Table 5.7), the electricity-generating industry has undergone a significant process of restructuring in recent years, involving diversification of energy sources (especially a switch to coal and nuclear energy with the almost complete elimination of fuel oil), measures to increase efficiency and improve financial structures, and organisational change.

Table 5.7 Growth of electricity generation in Spain, 1950–89

Year	Production (GWh)	Installed Capacity (MW)
1950	6,853	2,553
1960	18,614	6,567
1970	56,490	17,924
1975	82,482	25,467
1980	110,483	31,144
1985	126,680	41,436
1986	128,349	42,052
1987	132,707	42,052
1988	138,904	44,000
1989	147,500	—

Sources: Adapted from *El País*, 1990; MINE, 1988; *Papeles de Economía* 29, 1986

Serious financial problems were encountered in the early 1980s, which had their roots in optimistic forecasts of growth in demand made at the beginning of the 1970s. Thus the National Electricity Plan (Plan Eléctrico Nacional 1972–1981, presented to the Ministry of Industry and Energy by Unesa) (Unidad Eléctrica SA) sought major new facilities. Demand was forecast to be 117,800 KWh in 1978 (actual 77,850 in 1977), rising to 154,600 KWh in 1981 (actual 101,460 KWh). This Plan led to major investment (especially in nuclear power), which left overcapacity in the industry in the late 1970s and early 1980s. Much of this investment was financed from outside the industry, increasing exposure to high interest rates and exchange-rate fluctuations. Thus increased debt coincided with slower-than-expected growth in demand.

The completion of the development cycle begun in the early 1970s, increased electricity demand and financial restructuring have returned most of the industry to an operating profit (although it continues to carry a heavy capital debt, estimated in mid 1990 to be $5 billion). However, increasing electricity demand requires a new cycle of investment to begin in the early 1990s (with demand for an additional 3,000 MW by 1995 and between 7,000 and 10,000 MW by the year 2,000; Luisa Huidobro, 1988 and Trincado, 1988). Plans made in the mid 1980s tended to underestimate the growth in demand. The Third National Energy Plan envisaged electricity consumption growing at 3.3 per cent annually in the period

1984 to 1992 (whereas actual growth in the three years 1983 to 1985 averaged 4.2 per cent).

In the late 1970s and early 1980s electricity generation and generating capacity were switched to non-oil energy sources. Thus in 1988 139,010 GWh of electricity were generated (Table 5.8): 52,550 from coal, oil and gas (thirty-eight per cent, almost all from coal with very little from oil and gas compared with the 37.4 per cent from oil and gas in 1980; Huidobro, 1988); 50,410 GWh from nuclear stations (thirty-six per cent compared with five per cent in 1980); and 36,080 GWh from hydroelectricity (twenty-six per cent, compared with twenty-one per cent in 1987 and 1986). Fuel oil had virtually been eliminated from electricity power generation. In terms of installed capacity (42,052 MW in 1987), fifty per cent is in conventional power stations (coal twenty-five per cent), thirty-six per cent in hydroelectric stations and fourteen per cent in nuclear stations (Table 5.8). By 1992 Spain could bring on stream an additional 2,000 MW through the completion of the two frozen nuclear power stations. Beyond that, additional capacity will be necessary in the mid 1990s, for which investment must begin before 1990. According to the Third National Energy Plan, the most favourable situation would be 3,665 KWh per capita by 1992 (compared with the 6,279 KWh in West Germany in 1987).

Table 5.8 Structure of installed electricity generating capacity and electricity generation

Year	Coal	%	Oil and other	%	HEP[a]	%	Nuclear	%	Total	%
Electricity generation capacity (000 MW)										
1988	10.5	25.5	7.9	19.2	14.9	36.3	7.8	19.1	41.1	100.0
1992*	10.2	23.6	5.5	12.7	19.9	46.0	7.7	17.8	43.3	100.0
Electricity Generation (000 GWh)										
1986	56.3	43.8	8.0	6.2	27.4	21.4	36.7	28.6	128.3†	100.0
1989	71.8	48.7	‡	‡	19.6	13.3	56.1	38.0	147.5†	100.0

[a] Hydroelectric power

* Projected under PEN 3

† Gross output

‡ Figures included in coal

Sources: *El País*, 1990; Huidobro, 1988; MINE, 1988; Nadal, 1989

Liberalisation of the energy market is gradually opening the door to increased foreign investment. For example, in 1989 Unión Eléctrica-Fenosa, Spain's fourth-largest electrical utility (with a fifteen per cent share of the market) was negotiating to sell a minority of its equity (five per cent) to West Germany's Rheinisch-Westfalisches Elektrizitätswerk. This would be the first entry of foreign capital into Spain's electricity sector. Other Spanish electricity utilities are looking either to merge or to seek foreign private partners. But foreign investment has been retarded by the uncertainty that hangs over the future of the industry. The government favours concentration around two or three Spanish-owned companies.

5.5.1 The structure of electricity supply

Electricity is supplied through a large number of regionally based private utilities (involving substantial holdings by the banks) and one major state group, Endesa (Empresa Nacional de Electricidad), which has acquired holdings in many of the private companies: Endesa includes Empresa Nacional Hidroeléctrica del Ribagorzana, Gas y Electricidad SA, Unión Eléctrica de Canarias SA, Eléctricas Reunidas de Zaragoza SA and Empresa Nacional Carbonífera del Sur SA (Table 5.9). The ten largest utilities account for about eighty per cent of production. There is also a high degree of interrelationship between the utilities, many of them being financed from the same sources, particularly major banks. Co-ordination of the industry is achieved through state control over the high-tension grid, state control over electricity tariffs, and a system of compensation for variations in electricity-generating costs.

Table 5.9 Electricity utilities, 1988

Utilities	Sales (pta. million)	Employment
Endesa	457,502	15,678
Hidrola *	257,080	6,662
Iberduero	252,751	6,962
Unión Fenosa	202,732	6,205
Cia. Sevillana	171,491	6,433
Fecsa†	165,798	4,185
Enher	86,704	2,313
Hidroeléctrica del Cantábrico	65,315	1,120
Eléctricas Reunidas de Zaragoza	40,406	1,139
Hidruña‡	39,788	1,062
Eléctrica de Viesgo	33,114	1,003
Unión Eléctrica de Canarias	31,918	1,945
Gas y Electricidad	31,266	1,982

* Hidroeléctrica Española

† Fuerzas Eléctricas de Cataluña

‡ Hidroeléctrica de Cataluña

Source: El País, 1990

Serious financial problems in the industry led to rationalisation. For example, in 1984 the three largest companies (Iberduero, Endesa and Hidroeléctrica Española SA) agreed to take over smaller loss-making companies in exchange for government assistance. Asset swaps have also been undertaken (for example, interests in power stations) to allow a more rational pattern of production. In addition, many companies were forced to dispose of assets. For example, Fecsa (Fuerzas Eléctricas de Cataluña), one of the most seriously affected companies, was forced to sell its interests in property and minerals as well as in electricity.

Co-ordination of the industry is achieved partly through through Redesa, which since 1986 has co-ordinated the generation and supply of electricity in

Spain (assuming the functions previously exercised by Aseléctrica, an association of electricity industry utilities). Through Redesa the state controls the high-tension grid. Individual utilities can transfer electricity to, or acquire electricity from, the national grid on a swap pool basis, with a flat sale price for the acquiring companies. Nationalisation of the high-tension grid necessitated compensation to the electricity industry utilities amounting to pta. 61 billion. This represented part of the investment needed to cope with an asset swap programme designed to concentrate electricity production in the hands of companies that had a large market share but insufficient production. For example, Cia Sevillana acquired thirty-three per cent of the coal burning Litoral (Almería) plant from Endesa, and 50 MW of the Almaraz nuclear plant from Unión Eléctrica-Fenosa SA (bringing the Sevillana share in this plant up to 670 MW). Secondly, co-ordination is achieved through the association of private electricity industry utilities in Unesa (Unidad Eléctrica SA). Thirdly, there is a unified system of tariffs fixed by the government (Sistemas de Tarifas Tope Unificadas, established in 1953). Fourthly, the electricity utilities have a contract with Endesa to purchase all of this public company's output (thus they are not free to purchase the cheapest electricity available). The power purchased is split amongst the utilities in proportion to their respective share of the end-user market. Finally, co-ordination is achieved through a fund that is used to compensate for the varying costs of electricity generation between utilities.

5.5.2 Nuclear energy

In 1963 a law on nuclear energy was passed that opened the door to the development of nuclear power in Spain. In the same year authorisation was given for the development of the first nuclear-power station (José Cabrera Zorita), which began operating in August 1969. In 1971 Santa María de Geroña and in 1972 Vandellós 1 started operating; these three power stations represented the first generation of nuclear power in Spain (combined generating capacity of 1,200 MW).

The main push towards the development of nuclear energy came at the beginning of the 1970s with the authorisation in 1973 for a further seven nuclear-power stations, which on completion would add 6,500 MW. The energy crisis led to increased support for nuclear power in the First National Energy Plan, which envisaged a major expansion of nuclear power to twenty-three per cent of all primary-energy requirements and fifty-six per cent of electricity generation by 1985. However, in the revised Second National Energy Plan the role of nuclear energy was reduced to supplying fifteen per cent of primary-energy requirements and thirty-seven per cent of electricity by 1987. Nevertheless, support was given for continuing work on the second generation of reactors and for a third generation of plants.

Enthusiasm for nuclear energy waned in the 1980s, initially in the light of slackening demand and high construction costs, but increasingly amidst worries over safety (inflamed in the mid 1980s by accidents at Three-Mile Island and Chernobyl and then by a fire at Vandellós 1 in 1989), technical problems (such as corrosion in Asco 1 and Almaraz and problems over the disposal of nuclear waste), and lower conventional-energy prices. Thus the Third National Energy

Table 5.10 Nuclear-power stations

Power station	Location	Type	Installed Capacity (MW)	Authorised	In service	Ownership (1989)
First generation (installed capacity in operation 1,120MW)						
José Cabrera	Guadalajara	PWR	160	1963	1969	U.Fenosa
Sta. M. Garoña	Burgos	BWR	460	1963	1971	Iberduero (50%) E.Viesgo (50%)
Vandellós I†	Tarragona	GCR	500	1967	1972	E.de France (25%) Fecsa (23%) Enher/Endesa (23%) H.Cataluña (23%) F.E.Segre (6%)
Second generation (planned installed capacity 6,555 MW in operation 4,695 MW)						
Almaraz I	Cáceres	PWR	930	1971	1981	Hidrola (36%) C.Sevillana (36%) U.Fenosa (11.3%) Iberduero (16.7%)
Almaraz II	Cáceres	PWR	930	1972	1983	As above
Lemóniz I	Vizcaya	PWR	930	1972	Frozen	Iberduero (100%)
Lemóniz II	Vizcaya	PWR	930	1972	Frozen	Iberduero (100%)
Ascó I	Tarragona	PWR	930	1972	1983	Fecsa (60%) Enher/Endesa (40%)
Ascó II	Tarragona	PWR	930	1972	1985	Fecsa (40%) Enher/Endesa (40%) H.Cataluña (15%) F.E.Segre (5%)
Cofrentes	Valencia	BWR	975	1972	1984	Hidrola (100%)
Third Generation (planned installed capacity 7,914 MW, in operation 2,022 MW)						
Valdecaballeros I	Badajoz	BWR	975	1975	Frozen	Hidrola (50%) C.Sevillana (50%)
Valdecaballeros II	Badajoz	BWR	975	1975	Frozen	As above
Trillo I	Guadalajara	PWR	1,040	1975	1988	U.Fenosa (46.5%) Iberduero ((46.5%) H.Cantábrico (7%)
Trillo II	Guadalajara	PWR	1,032	1976	Frozen	Enher/Endesa (60%) U.Fenosa (40%)
Vandellós II	Tarragona	PWR	982	1976	1990	Enher/Endesa (72%) Hidrola (28%)
Vandellós III	Tarragona	PWR	950	1976	Abandoned	Fecsa (100%)
Sayago	Zamora	PWR	1,030	1976	Abandoned	Iberduero (100%)
Regodola	Jove (Lugo)	LWR	930	1976	Abandoned	U.Fenosa (60%) E.Viesgo (20%) H.Cantábrico (20%)

Note: Total installed capacity in 1988 7,837MW

* BWR: Boiling Water Reactor; GCR: Gas-Cooled Reactor; LWR: Light Water Reactor; PWR: Pressurised Water Reactor

† Vandellós I withdrawn from service in 1989 following an accident on 19 October 1989

Sources: *El País* 3 December 1989; *El País*, 1990; Iranzo Martin, 1987

Plan envisaged only four more power stations in addition to those operating in 1984, and a number of construction programmes were suspended. In 1989 there were nine nuclear stations in operation with an installed capacity of 7,837 MW, accounting for over thirty per cent of electricity generation (Table 5.10).

Nuclear power has stimulated development of the uranium industry in Spain. The National Uranium Company (Empresa Nacional del Uranio SA) was created in 1971 to develop uranium mining, participating in a project in the Republic of Niger. In 1974 the National Plan for Exploration and Investigation of Uranium (Plan Nacional de Exploración e Investigación de Uranio) was aimed at increasing exploration for uranium in Spain and overseas. Spain participated in overseas exploration, especially in Canada, South Africa, west Africa and Colombia. In recent years uranium concentrate has been extracted in Salamanca (termino de Saelices el Chico, Ciudad Rodrigo) and in Badajoz (Don Benito), with a combined capacity of 300 tonnes of uranium oxide per year (although only some 269 tonnes were produced in 1985). Under the Third National Energy Plan, production was planned to increase to 1,000 tonnes by 1990 (eighty per cent from Salamanca), including a project to recover uranium from phosphoric acid in Huelva (project Fuesa, based in the factory of Fosfórico Español SA in the former development pole of Huelva). Nationally controlled uranium-concentrate facilities meet over three quarters of domestic demand, but there are no enrichment facilities in Spain and no plant for treating residuals. Nuclear waste is stored at power-station sites, although some low-level waste is stored in the El Cabril mine in Córdoba.

5.5.3 Hydroelectricity

Hydroelectricity is an important source of electricity production because of its low cost and renewable and indigenous nature. Hence capacity continues to be increased, reaching about 18,000 MW at the beginning of the 1990s (20,000 MW planned by 1992 under the Third National Energy Plan). However, electricity generation from this source varies considerably from year to year, with variations in the pattern of precipitation and river flow regimes. Thus in the ten-year period 1976 to 1985 (inclusive), the lowest output was 23,178 GWh (twenty-one per cent of total electricity generation in 1981), the highest 47,473 GWh (forty-five per cent of total electricity generation in 1979), the ten-year average being 33,000 GWh (thirty per cent of electricity generation). Loss of power from hydroelectricity requires utilities to switch to higher-cost sources (coal and oil), thereby reducing profits.

As electricity supply has been in the hands of private utilities, the rate of development of hydroelectricity has depended on its relative profitability in relation to other sources of electrical energy. Thus development has been most rapid when assisted by state aid. During the 1970s the utilities tended to invest in nuclear- and coal-fired stations, and in the early 1980s the strained financial position of many utilities combined with low growth in electricity consumption to restrict investment.

There are both physical and human-resource constraints on hydroelectric developments. Relief, precipitation and drainage are obvious physical constraints, leaving the drainage areas of the north, Ebro and Duero with the greatest potential. But restrictions on hydroelectric potential also arise from competing uses of water in river basins, such as domestic and industrial consumption, fishing (and fish farming), irrigation and flood control.

Development of water resources depends on the legal arrangements governing water use. In this respect an important change was made in 1985. The Water Law (Ley de Aguas) is designed to stop the irrational use and contamination of water resources. Under the old Water Law passed in 1879, subterranean water had been regarded as part of land ownership, while surface water belonged to the state. This enabled Spain to produce a national water policy and become a pioneer in the management of its rivers and to develop hydroelectric installations. But soaring demand, new pumping techniques and modern knowledge about the water cycle connecting underground and surface water made the old law obsolete. Thus the new law makes underground water too part of the public domain (although it leaves existing wells in private ownership, protects the rights of well owners and offers them 75-year concessions). The new law should improve the co-ordination of water use within river basins.

5.6 Renewable energy sources and energy conservation

The need to reduce reliance on imported energy has been the principal stimulus for programmes designed to promote renewable energy and energy conservation. At the beginning of the 1990s, such energy sources constitute about two per cent of primary energy production (mostly from biomass). Renewable energy sources cover:

i) Biomass energy: Estimated reserves are in the form of forest and agricultural residuals and urban waste. Currently there are two plants in Barcelona (25,000 tonnes of oil equivalent, toe) and one in the Islas Baleares (1,400 toe).

ii) Mini-hydroelectric stations: Seventy per cent of potential resources lie in northern Spain.

iii) Geothermal energy: Possible sites have been identified in Madrid, Burgos, Barcelona, Orense and Murcia as well as in the Islas Canarias.

iv) Solar energy: More than seventy per cent of Spain has over 2,500 hours of sunshine per year, yet relatively little energy is expected to be generated from this source. Experimental solar plants have been built in Almería (where there are two 0.5 MW generators, ceded to Ciemat (Centro de Investigaciones Energéticas Medioambientales y Technológicas) from the International Energy Agency in 1986), Manzanares (Ciudad Real; 0.1 MW) and Valdepeñas, where the GAST (Generador Solar Torre, Solar Power Generator) wind-and-solar plant is located (20 MW). Although generating potential may be small, there are numerous domestic and commercial applications, including solar batteries and solar panels for hot-water systems, in addition to the established use in conjunction with plastic and glass shelters in agriculture.

v) Tidal energy: As yet there are no schemes in Spain.

vi) Wind energy: In 1990 there was an installed wind based generating capacity of about 5.3 MW, including generators at Tarifa (belonging to Endesa), Granadilla (Tenerife), and at Cabo Villano, La Coruña. It has been suggested that existing capacity could be expanded to 70MW by 1993.

A renewable energy plan emerged in 1986 (Plan de Energías Renovables, PER) from the Third National Energy Plan. The PER envisaged an increase in renewable resources from 0.9 per cent of primary energy supply in 1988 to 2.7 per cent in 1992. A second PER was finalised in 1988 (PER 1989) for the period up to 1995, incorporating the resources available from the European Community for developing renewable energy (particularly under the Valoren programme). This second PER envisages the increase of renewable energy to provide about four per cent of primary energy consumption (800,000 toe) by 1995. Biomass and urban waste are considered to offer the greatest potential (forecast 190,000 toe and 330,000 toe respectively by 1995) along with mini-hydroelectric stations (forecast 200,000 toe).

5.7 Restructuring the energy base

Since the beginning of the 1970s there has been a substantial restructuring of the energy base, with growth in the use of nuclear power, coal, hydroelectricity and natural gas. But despite this progress in energy diversification, supply remains heavily dependent on imports. Without an expansion of the nuclear-power programme, and with little prospect of a significant increase in renewable energy, the only policy to contain imports would appear to be energy conservation.

In the coal industry substantial further restructuring will be necessary to achieve efficiency and staunch the financial haemorrhage that characterised the industry in the 1980s. The prospects for deep-mined coal are especially bleak. Oil supplies will continue to be almost wholly imported, while the oil industry witnesses the spread of multinational companies and Campsa is adapted to meet European Community competition rules. Natural gas will increase its penetration of the market, but will also continue to be supplied largely through imports, the sources of which must be diversified. The future role of nuclear power remains undecided, with work on a number of stations still shelved and no new stations planned. In electricity generation, significant further rationalisation is likely, leaving only a few major companies.

References and Bibliography

Anon. (1988) 'Un Plan del Gas con horizonte en el año 2000', *Economía Industrial* 259, pp.7–12

Badosa Pagés, J. (1986) 'El gas natural en España', *Papeles de Economía Española* 29, pp.88–109

Banco de Bilbao (1979) 'Energía', *Situación* 7, No.8

Banco de Bilbao (1984) 'National energy programme', *Situacion* July, pp.28–32

Banco de Bilbao (1987) *Informe Económico, 1986* Bilbao

Bruce, P. (1989) 'Selling Spain's oil company to the world', *Financial Times*, 31 March, p.20

Castillo Bonet, M. (1983) 'El carbón en perspectiva', *Papeles de Economía Española* 14, pp.171–194

Coll Martín, S. and C. Sudriá Triay (1987) *El carbón en España 1770–1961: Una historia económica*. Madrid: Ediciones Turner SA

Díaz-Caneja Burgaleta, F. (1986) 'El potencial hidroeléctrico de España', *Papeles de Economía Española* 29, pp.163–180

El País (1990) *Anuario El País, 1990* Madrid

Estevan Bolea, T. (1983) 'Energía y medio ambiente', *Papeles de Economía Española* 14, pp.108–120

Fanjul, O. (1986) 'Los problemas de la industría petrolera', *Papeles de Economía Española* 29, pp.78–87

Fanjul, O. (1986) 'Proceso configurador del INH', *Economía Industrial* 248, pp.37–40.

Fernández, J. (1987) 'El sector petrolero español y la adhesión a la CEE', *Situación* 2, pp.16–31

Fernández-Cuesta, N. (1986) 'La liberalización del sector petrolero español', *Economía Industrial* 248, pp.41–56

Fernández Santamaría, F. and J. Leirado Campo (1987) 'Gas natural', *Situación* 2, pp.97–104

García Alonso, J. (1983) 'La energía en la economía española', *Papeles de Economía Española* 14, pp.2–13

García Alonso, J. (1986) 'La minería del carbón', *Papeles de Economía Española* 29, pp.110–140

García Alonso, J. (1987) 'El carbón en España', *Situación* 2, pp.32–53

Iranzo Martin, J. (1985) 'El sector energético español: realidades y posibilidades', *Papeles de Economía Española* 21, 271–90

Iranzo Martin, J. (1987) 'La energía nuclear en España' and 'Las energías renovables', *Situación* 2, pp.75–96 and pp.105–12

Luisa Huidobro, M. (1988) 'Sector eléctrico: deuda y financiación', *Economía Industrial* 261, pp.73–8

Marín Quemada, J. (1986) Política de energía, in Gamir *et al.*, *Política económica de España*. pp.321–348. Madrid: Alianza Editorial

Marín Quemada, J. (1987) 'El balance de energía' and 'Petróleo 1987', *Situacion* 2, pp.5–8 and 9–15

Martos Martínez, R. (1987) 'Consumo final de energía y de electricidad en España', *Situación* 2, pp.54–74

Ministerio de Industría y Energía (MINE) (1989a) *Estadística minera de España 1987.* Madrid

Ministerio de Industría y Energía (MINE) (1989b) *Informe anual sobre la industría española, 1988.* Madrid

Munoz del Barrio, C. (1983) 'Reconversión de la estructura refino', *Papeles de Economía Española* 14, pp.293–8

Nadal, F. (1989) 'Con la luz encendida', *El País* , 16 April, Sección Negocios p.10

Otero Moreno, J. (1983) 'Estructura del consumo energético en España', *Papeles de Economía Española* 14, pp.52–72

Paya, C. and B. Garcia-Sineriz (1986) 'Hispanoil en la hora actual', *Economía Industrial* 248, pp.73–9

Perez Cava, F. (1986) 'Estructura del sector de combustibles gaseosos en España', *Economía Industrial* 248, pp.57–72

Pozo-Portillo, J. (1983) 'La revisión del Plan Energético Nacional', *Papeles de Economía Española* 14, pp.21–51

Saez García, J. (1986) 'El papel de las compañías distribuidoras en el desarrollo del gas en España', *Economía Industrial* 248, pp.81–8

Sebastián Gascón, C. (1982) 'El sector energético y el crecimiento española', *Información Comercial Española* 581

Sudria, C. (1987) 'Un factor determinante: la energía', in J. Nadal *et al.*, *La economía española en el siglo XX*. pp.313–363. Barcelona: Editorial Ariel SA

Tamames, R. (1983) *Estructura económica de España, Vol.1*. Madrid: Alianza Editorial

Terán, M. (1978) 'La minería y las industrías extractivas', in M. Terán *et al.* (eds), *Geografía general de España*, pp.404-28. Barcelona: Editorial Ariel SA

Trincado, J. (1988) 'Algunos temas relevantes para el futuro del sector eléctrico', *Economía Industrial* 261, pp.33–5

♦ Chapter 6 ♦

Manufacturing industry

6.1 Manufacturing industry

Manufacturing has been shaped by a political economy in which the market mechanism was constrained by a high level of protectionism and state intervention; originating in the nineteenth century, elaborated in the period of autarchy, then modified during the years of the 'economic miracle' and the 'economic crisis'. The impact of the economic crisis, coupled with the shift towards a more open and liberal economy, introduced a more-competitive environment, bringing market pressures to bear on industrialists and prompting a process of market-led restructuring. Government policy has attempted to manage this process, adding a political dimension to the objective of placing manufacturing on a more competitive footing in preparation for full integration in the European Community. Restructuring has also brought increased integration into the international economy, especially through the corporate networks of multinational companies, which have themselves been reorganising on a European and often global basis. Six case studies covering iron and steel, fertilizers, textiles, food, motor vehicles and electronics exemplify the process of industrial change.

In comparison with Germany, France and Britain, the absolute size of the manufacturing sector is small, though its relative size (as a proportion of the economically active population and GDP) is broadly in line with that in other European Community countries. In 1990 the number of people working in industry (excluding construction but including energy, water and mining) was 2.98 million, twenty-four per cent of the total occupied population (INE, 1990), contributing about twenty-nine per cent of the GDP (Banco de España, 1989).

Spanish industry evolved in a peculiar political economy, which has left an indelible mark, hindering the emergence of full international competitiveness and leaving firms exposed to penetration by foreign capital. That mark is characterised by:

i) The small size of firms and plants: This characteristic has limited the opportunities for scale economies and made it difficult to raise long-term finance, to participate in research and development and to engage in exports. Further fragmentation has resulted from many firms being engaged in a diversity of product lines with little specialisation within one segment of the market (García Fernández, 1989). Ninety per cent of all the country's industrial companies have fewer than 100 employees, accounting for fifty per cent of industrial employment (Tamames, 1986). Only one Spanish company, the state holding company INI, was amongst the one hundred largest industrial companies in the world in 1988 (by value of sales), in sixty-first position. Even in Europe only two Spanish companies, INI and Repsol, in 1988 were amongst the top 100 European Community companies (measured by turnover).

ii) An industrial structure weighted towards traditional industry: In 1986 one third of all employment and one quarter of value added in manufacturing industry arose from the three sectors food, drink and tobacco; textiles and clothing; and wood, cork and furniture (Table 6.1).

Table 6.1 The structure of industry, 1986

CNAE Group*	Sector	Employment (occupied population)		Value added	
		Numbers	%	pta. million	%
11–15	Energy	125,178	6.0	1,544,965	20.0
16	Water	30,175	1.4	70,817	0.9
21	Metallic-minerals extraction	6,734	0.3	20,874	0.3
22	Primary processing of metals	78,565	3.8	311,794	4.0
23	Non-metallic-minerals extraction	21,863	1.0	64,649	0.8
24	Non-metallic-mineral products	120,244	5.7	420,858	5.4
25	Chemical industries	116,984	5.6	695,493	9.0
31	Metal products	214,968	10.3	547,146	7.1
32, 33, 39	Machinery and mechanical equipment	110,248	5.3	360,959	4.7
34, 35	Electrical and electronic goods	110,155	5.3	378,122	4.9
36–38	Transport equipment	196,417	9.4	578,911	7.5
41, 42	Food, drink and tobacco	340,536	16.3	1,171,051	15.1
43, 453–456	Textiles and clothing	212,605	10.2	445,433	5.8
452	Leather and shoes	52,878	2.5	124,639	1.6
46	Wood, cork and furniture	144,328	6.9	243,608	3.2
47	Paper and publishing	105,913	5.1	429,190	5.6
48	Rubber and plastic goods	85,845	4.1	264,054	3.4
49	Other manufacturing	19,984	1.0	52,418	0.7
	Total	2,093,620	100.0	7,732,981	100.0

* CNAE: Clasificación Nacional de Actividades Económicas, 1975

Source: INE, 1989

iii) A small defence sector: In 1987 defence represented less than ten per cent of the state budget (in 1984 the defence budget for Spain was less than one fifth that for the United Kingdom). There were an estimated 29,000 people employed in the sector in 1986 (*Economía Industrial*, 1987), of whom about 20,000 were in the public sector (essentially Bazan (ships), Casa (aircraft), Enasa (military vehicles), Inisel (electronics) and Empresa Nacional Santa Bárbara (weapons)).

iv) Geographical concentration: The province of Barcelona is the dominant focus of industry in Spain, with almost one quarter of all employment. Outside of Barcelona manufacturing is concentrated in Madrid, País Vasco, Valencia and Alicante (which together with Barcelona account for about sixty per cent of all employment in industry). The distribution of head offices is still more highly concentrated. Of the fifty largest industrial companies in 1983 (based on sales figures), forty-five per cent had their head office in Madrid, twenty per cent in Barcelona and ten per cent in Bilbao. The provinces most dependent on employment in industry in 1990 were Alava and Guipúzcoa in País Vasco, Barcelona and Navarra, all of which had between thirty and forty per cent of their economically active population in industry (INE, 1990). This spatial concentration of industry, and especially of those sectors in crisis, continues to have important regional development implications.

v) Lack of competitiveness: Low productivity, overstaffing, obsolescent technology and the inefficient use of energy have been common features of Spanish industry. There has been a lower level of technical efficiency in Spanish industry in comparison with industry in western Europe (Berges and Simarro, 1987). Spanish industry used semi-skilled labour and well-known production techniques (late stage of the production life-cycle) acquired through patents, resembling industry in Greece and Portugal more than that in France.

vi) State involvement: The state has exercised a direct involvement across the whole spectrum of manufacturing through the INI, INH and DGPE and through extensive portfolio holdings held by the Bank of Spain in most of the leading companies. On 1988 sales figures the state had a major presence in all the top five Spanish manufacturing companies (El País, 1990).

vii) Involvement of financial groups: The major financial groups in Spain have extensive direct involvement in industry. Most of the large private companies, which are not foreign owned, tend to be dependent on financial groups.

viii) Family ownership, interlocking directorships and diversification: Family ownership of companies has been widespread in Spain, as has been the presence of interlocking directorships. Relatively small companies are frequently engaged in a diversity of economic activities.

ix) Foreign penetration: Substantial foreign penetration of the economy dates back to the nineteenth century when foreign investment built up in mining, railways, some public services and basic chemicals. Foreign investment was renewed in the 1960s and 1970s, but has exploded in the 1980s to dominate most industry.

x) Dependence on foreign technology: 'Spanish industry is dependent on foreign technology' (Tamames, 1986). Many firms in Spain produce goods with foreign patents or under licence. Frequently these patents have allowed production in the domestic market only.

xi) The widespread existence of monopoly power. In contrast to the atomistic structure prevalent in many areas of industry (such as clothing and parts of the food industry), there is a very high degree of concentration in sectors such as oil refining, cement, glass and agricultural chemicals.

xii) Domestic market orientation: Spanish industry, unlike its foreign counterpart, has been concerned primarily with the domestic market, a reflection both of the protection afforded the domestic market and the lack of international competitiveness. The degree of internationalism can be measured by the percentage of sales and percentage of production in countries outside of that in which the parent company is based. Most of the major Spanish exporting companies are subsidiaries of foreign multinationals (Ford, General Motors, IBM, Michelin,

Seat). Only INI, Cepsa, ERT and Femsa have had substantial exports. Overseas production was still almost non existent in the late 1980s. Hence internationalism has been very limited and essentially confined to sales. For example in 1989 (first six months) Spanish companies were responsible for only 1.9 per cent (ECU 298.3 million) of the total value of European cross border acquisitions, while as a target nation it represented seven per cent (ECU 1,083.7 million) of the value of all such deals.

6.2 Industrial reconversion

From the mid 1970s Spain entered an economic crisis that saw a net loss of one million jobs in industry, from 3.6 million in 1975 to 2.6 million in 1985 (a twenty-seven per cent reduction in the occupied population in industry). The economic crisis centred on those industries in which Spain had specialised in the 1960s. For example, domestic steel demand decreased from 11.8 million tonnes in 1974 to 6.9 million tonnes in 1985 and the tonnage ordered in shipbuilding fell to less than one quarter of a million tonnes in 1986. Changes in the structure of costs and in demand, together with the rise of the Newly Industrialised Countries (NICs), removed the competitive advantage that Spain had enjoyed in these sectors (Nadal, 1987).

The response to the recession was slower than in many other countries, a result largely of the combination of a protected economy and more pressing political problems that dominated Spain in the late 1970s. Industry was partly sheltered from the first oil shock by a cut in taxation on oil products, rapid domestic inflation and the persistence of negative interest rates. Large investment programmes in sectors such as steel and shipbuilding continued to be encouraged until the late 1970s, although demand had fallen substantially worldwide. Moreover, a number of traditional industries, such as textiles, were suffering increasingly from the competition of NICs. The growth of labour costs was proceeding at a pace incompatible with the maintenance of competitiveness, profit margins and employment. The situation came to a head in 1980 when, following the second oil shock, the authorities finally allowed the price of oil to adjust to international conditions while real interest rates turned sharply positive. The crisis found large industrial sectors completely unprepared and burdened with acute problems of overstaffing, excess capacity and indebtedness.

On the industrial front, the principal government response to the economic crisis was to promote industrial reconversion (*reconversión industrial*), a term adopted to describe the wide-ranging process of industrial restructuring in Spain in the 1980s. During this period the government introduced a series of measures described as adapting industry to the changing economic environment, with the basic objective of increasing competitiveness (Ortún, 1988), thereby aiming to promote a more orderly pattern of industrial restructuring than that which would have resulted from market forces alone. In practice the measures amounted to cushioning traditional industries from the full impact of the industrial crisis.

The first efforts by the government to positively adjust the economy occurred in 1977 with the Moncloa Pacts. But not until 1979 did the government begin negotiations with specific companies over restructuring production. In 1980 'reconversion decrees' were introduced to restructure specific industrial sectors, and measures were introduced to provide encouragement for the merger of firms (Ley 76/1980 provided tax incentives to firms that merged). The process started with kitchen appliances and special steels in 1980 and was extended in 1981 to eleven sectors that were considered to have been especially badly hit by the recession (Real Decreto Ley 9/1981 on Industrial Reconversion). They covered integrated iron and steel, special steels, carbon steels, common steels, semi-manufactured products of copper and its alloys, shipbuilding, textiles, footwear, motor-vehicle parts, electronic components and kitchen appliances. In addition, five companies followed special reconversion programmes: General Electric, Westinghouse, Talbot Automóviles, Asturiana de Zinc and the Standard Group. The programme soon ran into political problems as the negative impact of the restructuring process began to be felt in certain regions. There were also technical problems associated with underestimation of the financial cost involved and problems over monitoring the programme. A large proportion of the state transfers for industrial reconversion between 1979 and 1982 went to absorb losses rather than to tackle the underlying disequilibria.

Reinforcing reconversion began with the introduction of a broad legal framework in 1982 and was completed by a comprehensive White Paper on reindustrialisation published in 1983, followed by a Decree in November 1983. (This was subsequently converted into a law in July 1984– Real Decreto Ley 8/1983 and Ley 27/1984, Ley de Reconversión y Reindustrialización– effective as from December 1984. Rapid action was now essential given the imminence of entry into the European Community, which meant both increased competition and adoption of EC regulations limiting further state assistance to industry.

Reconversion strategy was designed to reduce the rate of deindustrialisation and to establish an industrial base capable of meeting international competition. To achieve this it was imperative to both: i) improve productivity and restore company profitability (by cutting excess capacity and overstaffing and by restructuring the financial liabilities of excessively indebted companies; a process described as financial cleansing– 'saneamiento financiero') and ii) promote investment and technological innovation in those activities with good future profit potential within the sectors affected. Eleven sectors were involved under the 1984 legislation (Table 6.2), essentially the same as the ones identified in 1981. Together they made a significant contribution to employment and exports (they were also mostly covered by EC restructuring policies). In addition to this sectoral programme, specific geographical areas with intense problems of industrial decline were designated as Urgent Reindustrialisation Zones (Zonas de Urgente Reindustrialización, ZUR), within which additional state benefits were available.

Implementation of reconversion policies varied according to the sectors involved. In sectors that were atomistic in structure, assistance was generally available to all companies (for example in textiles, where a large proportion of assistance was provided for intangibles such as improving design, image and marketing). In some sectors, notably special steels and kitchen appliances, competition and recession had generated price wars. Co-ordination and rationalisation of these sectors was necessary to take advantage of scale economies and specialisation of production. Thus cartels or industrial groups were formed

Table 6.2 Reconversion programmes

Sector	Dates	Number of companies	Labour Force		
			A	B	C
Integrated iron and steel	1980–90	3	42,837	22,761	24,715
Special steels	1980–90	11	13,744	5,016	6,119
Semi-processed copper	1981–84	4	4,503	3,430	3,401
Heavy forgings	1981–84	2	1,277	970	915
Fertilizers†	1984–88	10	8,541	7,232	6,517
Shipbuilding (GA)	1984–90	2	21,920	9,972	11,249
Shipbuilding (PM)‡	1984–90	27	15,427	8,198	9,162
Textiles	1981–86	683	108,844	98,919	98,919
Domestic electrical appliances§	1980–88	18	23,869	11,258	12,272
Vehicle electrical equipment	1981–85	2	6,720	5,378	5,269
Electronic components	1981–85	17	3,744	2,200	2,314
Alcatel-Standard Eléctrica	1983–91	1	16,133	7,756	11,459
ERT Group	1983–87	10	10,304	7,811	7,811
Marconi Española	1983–91	1	2,548	450	1,283
Total		791	280,411	191,351	201,405
			(100%)	(68%)	(72%)

* Labour force: A Initial, B Planned, C Actual 31 December 1988

† The fusion of ERT and Cros has resulted in further reductions in employment

‡ GA are large shipyards, PM are small shipyards

§ Of the eighteen firms initially covered in the domestic electrical appliance (white goods) sector, six closed and one left the sector; The labour force refers to the whole sector, including two firms that were not part of the reconversion programme

Source: MINE, 1989

(*carteles de recesión* and *sociedades de reconversión*; in the period 1980 to 1982 the only *sociedad de reconversión* was in special steels, in which steel companies and central government formed a company to manage the industry). Finally, in sectors where a few producers dominated (integrated iron and steel and shipbuilding), they generally became the direct responsibility of the INI. These industries posed the greatest social and political problems, as often whole communities were dependent on one firm.

Reconversion programmes required strong measures to achieve rapid results. These measures covered modernisation and rationalisation, financial restructuring ('*saneamiento financiero*'– including debt write offs, rescheduling of debt, new lines of credit, public underwriting of loans, etc.); fiscal measures (tax rebates, extension or fractioning of the payment of tax and social security debts), labour (facilities for the modification, suspension or termination of labour relations and for geographical mobility; aid for early retirement and the possibility of fractioning indemnities for dismissal due to contractual cut-backs stemming from a reduction of employment); and technology (for example the creation of a centre for promoting research and development in companies – the

Centro de Desarrollo Tecnológico e Industrial). Further indirect assistance included protection of the national market (for example controls on steel imports), encouragement of firms to merge, and encouragement of unions and employers to work together (the latter especially in the early 1980s).

Substantial public expenditure (in addition to private sector investment) was involved in implementing the measures constituting the reconversion programmes during the 1980s. The cost of the reconversion plan over the three years 1984 to 1986 alone was estimated at pta 1,000 billion (Banco de Bilbao, 1984c). Investment in modernisation and rationalisation of installations between 1981 and 1989 amounted to more than pta. 650 billion, including some pta 50 billion for intangibles such as design (especially in textiles and shoes) and research (especially in information technology; Ortún, 1988). Larger sums went into financial restructuring and labour measures. By sectors, probably the largest public investment was in the iron and steel industry.

Labour measures were fundamentally concerned with the treatment of those made redundant and taking early retirement as part of the process of improving productivity and reducing labour costs. The 1984 Plan envisaged a reduction in employment of about 80,000 to 90,000: some one third of the labour force in the firms affected. About ninety per cent of the reduction was to come from iron and steel, shipbuilding, home appliances and textiles. These planned reductions in the labour force had largely been met by the end of 1988 (Table 6.2). About twenty-five per cent of the total employment loss was expected to come from early retirements (initially from the age of sixty, then reduced to fifty-five). The rest of the workers involved were given the choice of either a considerable redundancy indemnity and an unemployment allowance, or else surrendering this indemnity to join the Employment Promotion Fund (Fondo de Promoción de Empleo, FPE) for up to three years. In return the FPE paid them eighty per cent of their last wage, encouraged recruitment by offering a subsidy to would-be employers, and provided free retraining.

The policy of reconversion has been very important in promoting industrial restructuring in Spain. Whole industrial sectors have been reorganised and the latest plant installed (as in integrated iron and steel and domestic electrical appliances). Mergers have been successfully promoted to create larger, more competitive companies (as in the fertilizer industry), and productivity has generally been increased. Reconversion policy was a major government initiative and one that became unrepeatable under European Community regulations.

6.3 Industrial policy in the late 1980s

While the protectionism and extensive intervention that was characteristic of Spain in the past was being dismantled, an active industrial policy within a market framework (consistent with European Community requirements to increase competition) was still considered necessary in the mid 1980s to bring Spain into line with other western industrial nations and to promote the further development of industry. But the emphasis in industrial policy shifted away from support to traditional industries, towards producing an economic environment conducive to the emergence of new industry. Until then little public funds had been put into stimulating research and development in Spain, as tight public spending controls and political considerations ensured that a large proportion of public expenditure went into cushioning the effects of recession and the restructuring programme. To achieve the new emphasis, policies concentrated on increasing the flexibility of the labour force, providing new technologies, helping small and medium sized enterprises, and promoting industrial exports.

Thus public-policy makers sought to establish the coherence of a policy of liberalisation coupled with selective public-sector intervention centred on the promotion of new industry. The most important doubt that overhangs this process is whether the state will be able to resist pressures to adopt some form of protectionism should domestic industry be threatened by increasing import penetration. Any such action would have to be taken within the context of the European Community. The principal strategic risk is that Spain will be caught between competitiveness based on low-cost production and competitiveness based on new technologies (Maravall, 1987).

6.4 The iron and steel industry

The iron and steel industry was one of the first targets of government intervention to stem the tide of industrial decline. At the beginning of the 1980s the iron and steel industry was still characterised by over-capacity and obsolescence. Some 80,000 people were employed, of which about half were in the integrated iron and steel sector. Investment programmes implemented in the early 1970s had assumed demand growing to 20 million tonnes by the mid 1980s. This led to the construction of a fourth integrated iron and steel works in Sagunto (Valencia) and production capacity of around 18 million tonnes in 1985. In practice, recession reduced domestic demand to only about six million tonnes in 1985, additional production being channelled into exports (Table 6.3). Since then exports have

Table 6.3 Iron and steel production and trade (millions of tonnes)

| Year | Production | | Iron and Steel | |
	Iron	Steel	Exports	Imports
1946–50	0.6	0.7	—	—
1961–65	2.0	2.9	—	Over 2.0
1971	3.0	5.4	—	Over 2.0
1975	6.8	11.1	2.1	—
1980	6.4	12.7	4.5	1.3
1982	5.9	13.3	—	—
1985	5.5	14.2	7.8	1.4
1986	4.8	11.9	5.2	2.6
1987	*	11.7	4.8	2.4
1988	*	11.9	3.9	2.7
1989	*	12.8	3.6	3.2

* Iron production included in that for steel

Sources: La Industria Siderúrgica Española, 1986; MINE, 1987; *El País*, 1990

been squeezed, compensated partly by a recovery of domestic demand (apparent domestic steel consumption in 1989 was 10.9 million tonnes).

The industry, dominated by the state integrated iron and steel producer Ensidesa (Empresa Nacional Siderúrgica SA) and the private company AHV (Alto Hornos de Vizcaya), was slow to react to declining markets and increased competition from steel producers in the Newly Industrialised Countries. Uncoordinated action to rationalise the sector began in the late 1970s. In 1979 the major shareholders in the Sagunto complex relinquished their holdings to INI and Ensidesa began closing its plants in Mieres, La Felguera and later in Avilés. However, in comparison with many other countries employment contraction was small – only thirteen per cent between 1974 and 1982 – while steel consumption in Spain fell by one third to about 200 kg per capita. The first reconversion plan was issued in 1981, although little effective action was taken until new measures were introduced in 1984 that carried the rationalisation process through to the end of the 1980s.

From the mid 1980s one of the most costly reconversion programmes in Spain was initiated with the objectives of reducing capacity (for example with the closure of steel making at Alto Hornos del Mediterráneo (AHM) in Sagunto, owned from 1972 by Ensidesa), improving efficiency through modernisation, and rescuing the two integrated iron and steel producers AHV and Ensidesa. The programme cost about pta. 1,500 billion from 1984 and involved a planned reduction in jobs of some 25,000 in integrated iron and steel by 1990 (from about 43,000 in the early 1980s; Tizón, 1989). These reductions have been concentrated in the recently designated 'zones of industrial decline' (Salmon, 1990). About half of the programme cost was associated with refinancing the sector ('saneamiento financiero') and the social costs of redundancies, involving direct financial compensation to employees coupled with job creation programmes (for example in Sagunto the INI has participated in new firms such as an Italian/Spanish glass venture, a fertilizer factory and the addition of electroplating facilities to the cold rolling mill owned by Sidmed – the company formed from the remains of AHM).

Reconversion in the integrated iron and steel sector came to a close at the end of February 1989 with the inauguration by Ensidesa of a modern LD-oxygen (Linz and Donawitz) steelworks in Avilés with a capacity of 2.5 million tonnes. Ensidesa is now the largest integrated iron and steel group in Spain (labour force of 16,350 in 1988 and production of steel in 1990 of around 4 million tonnes), with plants in Avilés (Asturias) and Veriña (3 km from Gijón, Asturias). The private integrated iron and steel sector is represented by AHV with factories around Bilbao (especially along the river Nervión, for example in Baracaldo, Sestao, Ansio and Basauri) providing direct employment to about 7,200 in 1990. Although the company is a private one, substantial credit from the state (especially the Banco de Crédito Industrial) has left it virtually nationalised. Both Ensidesa and AHV (annual production of steel around 1.7 million tonnes) now have modern, integrated facilities and a continuous strip mill each. Technological change has also reduced the use of domestic raw materials, such that the industry now displays a high degree of import dependence and no longer forms a very important market for Spanish coal. Reconversion and the more buoyant demand for steel enabled the sector to return to profitability in 1989 (although both companies were carrying substantial debts).

In the special-steels sector, restructuring involved the creation of an organisation to oversee the restructuring programme (Aceriales: Sociedad Anónima para la Reconversión de Subsector de los Aceros Especiales). This in turn led to the formation of two groups: Aceros de Guipùzcoa (bringing together the firms Aceguisa, Acerías y Forja de Azcoitia, Aceros de Irura and Fundiciones Echevarría), and Aceros de Acenor (uniting the three firms Aceros de Llodio SA, Echevarría and Pedro Orbegozo, to which were later joined Aceros Olarra and Forjas Alavesas). Their goal was to trim capacity to just over one million tonnes with about sixty per cent destined for the domestic market and forty per cent for export. The restructuring plan was due to be completed at the end of 1987 (by which time employment was to have been reduced by 8,500, sixty per cent of the initial figure), but in 1989 the government were still attempting to complete the mergers. Acenor is now controlled by public capital and is seeking foreign participation.

In the more dispersed industry of common steels, the government has watched over a long process of concentration, reduction in capacity and strengthening of different industrial groups, resulting in a new map of common steel production in Spain. La Compañía Española de Laminación SA (Celsa), Aristraín and Marcial Ucín y Siderúrgica Sevillana (the latter controlled by the Italian group Riva) have emerged as strong groups along with the company Acerinox, which is located in the province of Cádiz in southern Spain.

Where a sector containing private companies was covered by a reconversion programme, as in the case of common steels, companies could request government assistance in restructuring programmes worked out between them and the government. An illustration of this process is provided by the Celsa group. Following the grouping of companies under the umbrella of Celsa (the companies included the parent company Celsa, Torras Herreras, Nueva Montaña Quijano and Sidegasa), assistance was requested from the Ministry of Industry and Energy to cover the intended closure of Sidegasa (Siderúrgica de Galicia, SA), the dismantling of a blast furnace of Celsa and an electric furnace of Torras Herreras, and for retirements (of those aged fifty-five and over) in Nueva Montaña.

From 1986 European Community regulations have covered the iron and steel industry in Spain, although a three-year transition period was allowed, during which the government was able to continue to subsidise steel and to provide substantial aid to the sector. During this time shipments of steel to the EC were limited by quotas (amounting to over 800,000 tonnes in 1986). The transition period ran out at the end of 1988, leaving the Spanish integrated iron and steel industry fully covered by the European Coal and Steel Community regime.

Despite the long and costly process of reconversion, further restructuring and investment in new facilities (for example to produce higher-value added products) will be necessary throughout the steel industry to ensure its long-term survival (for example Ensidesa has sought pta. 40,000 million for such actions over the three years 1990 to 1993). The integrated iron and steel sector remains relatively small in scale and split between two producers. The government should be able to foster restructuring given its position as a major shareholder and an institution to whom large debts are owed across much of the industry (indeed as a consequence of reconversion the steel industry in Spain has virtually been mortgaged to the public sector). But the process is unlikely to be easy and the danger is that rivalry within the industry will obscure the threat of foreign competition. Furthermore, in those companies where there are major public shareholdings (for example in AHV), there is the difficult problem of who should determine company strategy, the traditional management or the government. Equally there are significant differences in business culture between companies (for example between AHV and Ensidesa).

Further rationalisation and vertical integration will characterise the European steel industry in the early 1990s, with steel producers buying control of downstream distributors and processors (in part to secure market share and engage in 'just-in-time' delivery systems). In 1990 British Steel hoped to acquire the specialist steel producer Aristraín, despite a bid from a Spanish consortium led by Ensidesa. Thus alliances with foreign companies and foreign takeovers in areas of profitable production are as likely as domestic mergers.

6.5 Fertilizers

Like the iron and steel industry, fertilizer manufacturing is also energy intensive. Thus following rapid expansion in the 1960s and early 1970s, the industry was severely affected by increasing energy costs, which coincided with falling demand. The resulting market pressures brought rationalisation (including the withdrawal of the American multinationals Gulf and Esso, whose interests were acquired by Cros SA and ERT; Table 6.4), hastened in the late 1980s by a government-inspired reconversion plan. There is now only one major Spanish fertilizer company, that controlled by the private sector Ercros group. In 1988 the industry produced 5.7 million tonnes, but a growing trade gap has appeared, with imports having risen from 200,000 tonnes in 1986 to 1.7 million tonnes in 1989.

Table 6.4 Restructuring in the fertilizer sector, 1970–80

Original company	Acquiring company
Abonos Sevilla	ERT
Catalana de Abonos	ERT
Fertiberia (Gulf Oil)	ERT
Sociedad Ibérica del Nitrógeno	ERT
Amoniaco Español SA (Esso)	Cros SA
Inquitasa	Cros SA
Rumianca-Siasa	Cros SA
Encaso, Ensidesa, Repesa	Enfersa

Source: Robles Teigeiro, 1988

In the early 1980s the fertilizer industry was uncompetitive at the international level, having relied on government subsidies and protection in the domestic market. Production costs were generally higher than those of competitors and prices needed to be reduced to competitive levels (in 1986 urea prices in Spain were pta. 40 per kilo compared with pta. 30 per kilo for imports). An important problem remained that of the spatial distribution of plants, which required reorganisation to achieve a more efficient pattern of supply across the dispersed domestic market. In 1984 there were a dozen companies owning more than forty plants, many of them obsolete. The greatest problem was in nitrogenous fertilizers: the Spanish industry used naphtha as its main input (subsidised by the government) instead of the natural gas used in competitor countries. To address the problems the government introduced a reconversion plan for the sector in 1985. As this was still incomplete in 1987, the industry secured two further years of protection from the European Community on imports of urea (covering 1987 and 1988).

The reconversion plan for the fertilizer sector (Plan de Reconversión de Fertilizantes) embraced sweeping changes including a reorganisation of production through company mergers; financial restructuring; a reduction of the labour force; and rationalisation of the pattern of plants through selective investment, plant closures and a reduction in capacity (about eighty per cent of the Plan was concerned with the nitrogenous division of fertilizer production along with the adjustment of capacity to demand; Table 6.5). By March 1989 the number of plants had been reduced to thirty, capacity reduced by more than one million tonnes and the labour force cut by 1,500. The involvement of the Kuwait Investment Office in both of the two major private–sector companies, ERT and Cros, SA paved the way for the merger of these two companies under the name Ercros at the end of 1988, with the formation of Fesa (Fertilizantes Españolas SA) as its fertilizer division. Fesa then controlled about fifty-five per cent of the fertilizer market, a further twenty-five to thirty per cent being controlled by Enfersa (Empresa Nacional de Fertilizantes, a subsidiary of INI). As the final act of the Plan, the government sold Enfersa to Fesa in 1989, to leave one major private-sector fertilizer company. In 1990 Fesa–Enfersa still contained excess capacity and was carrying substantial debts. Ercros hoped to sell off some of its interests (those in potash to INI, Electro Metalúrgica to Enher and pharmaceuticals to a private company), using the money to reduce the debts of the fertilizer company, cut capacity (candidates for closure being the plants in Castellón, Lérida, Luchana– Baracaldo, Málaga and Santander) and invest in new equipment.

6.6 Textiles

In its broadest sense the textile sector embraces textiles *senso stricto* (cotton, wool, silk, etc.), synthetic fibres, clothing, carpets and shoes (Table 6.6). In 1986 official statistics put the number of people employed in this broadly defined sector at 274,000 people (thirteen per cent of all industrial employment– including that in energy and mining), contributing about seven per cent of the industrial product. However, its true size and importance is understated by official figures, which miss that part of the industry that operates in the submerged economy. In towns and villages across Spain, and especially in Cataluña, País Valenciana and Andalucía, the textile industry operates partly as a 'cottage industry' undisclosed to the authorities. The growth of the submerged economy was one response of textile producers to the economic crisis, and

Table 6.5 Proposed reductions in capacity in the fertilizer industry (Plan de Reconversión de Fertilizantes, 1985)

Product	Company	Location	Capacity (tonnes)
Ammonia	ERT	Huelva	100,000
	Cinsa	Las Palmas	33,000
	Nicas	Valladolid	75,000
	Cros	La Coruña	100,000
	Cros	Málaga	100,000
Sub total			408,000
Urea	Cros	Málaga	—
Ammonium sulphate	ERT	La Felguera	15,000
	ERT	Sevilla	42,000
	Cinsa	Las Palmas	115,000
	Enfersa	Cartagena	115,000
Sub total			287,000
Ammonium nitrate	ERT	La Felguera	120,000
	Enfersa	Puentes García Rodríguez	122,000
Sub total			242,000
Calcium superphosphates	Cros	Badalona	200,000
	ERT	Montgat	200,000
	Inabonos	Pamplona	60,000
	Mirat	Salamanca	40,000
Sub total			500,000
Complex fertilizers	Cros	Rentería	90,000
	Cros	Tarragona	120,000
	Cinsa	Las Palmas	100,000
	Induca	Bilbao	120,000
	Cros	Madrid†	30,000
	Cros	Mérida†	60,000
	Cros	La Coruña†	30,000
Sub total			550,000

Note: With the merger of ERT and Cros, the Plan has been revised to include the closure of the FESA plants at Montgat, La Felguera, Madrid, Valencia, La Coruña and Mérida with a total production of 780,000 tonnes; a new plant for Enfersa is planned at Sagunto and new installations in the Nicas plant in Valladolid; plants in Huelva and Cartagena have been adapted to natural gas

Total reduction in capacity from 3.4 million tonnes to 2.3 million tonnes in complex fertilizers

† Reductions in output

Source: *El País*, 26 March 1989

continues to be a means of survival in the face of increasing competition. Fragmentation is a problem throughout the industry (except in synthetic fibres), with small and medium-sized family firms predominating, especially in clothing and shoes (Table 6.6).

Many problems had their origin in the period of autarchic development, which left an industry with poor management, out-dated plant and low productivity, unable to face growing competition from Newly Industrialised Countries and from synthetic fibres. Expansion in the 1960s was based almost entirely on the small domestic market, resulting in slower growth than elsewhere in north-west Europe, hindering the development of specialisation. There were a series of restructuring plans (for wool in 1962 and particularly for the cotton industry in the 1960s) but they failed to produce a modern, internationally competitive industry, allowing imports to grow in spite of import protection. Falling demand in the domestic market during the 1970s forced manufacturers to look for export markets and to invest overseas.

Table 6.6 The textile sector, 1976 and 1986

Sector (CNAE)	Establishments		Employment		Value added (pta. billion)	
	1978	1986	1978	1986	1978	1986
Thread and cloth (431 to 434)	2,281	1,458	97,803	53,548	88	135.4
Knitted goods (435)	1,717	1,228	37,503	30,263	27.1	62.7
Finished goods (436)	510	379	21,141	13,078	19.2	34.3
Carpets, other textiles (437 to 439)	1,494	1,018	25,264	16,194	19.3	41.8
Sub total	6,002	4,083	181,711	113,083	153.8	274.2
Tanners (441)	445	335	12,675	10,527	14.6	35.1
Leather goods (442)	1,329	850	14,500	7,269	8.3	14.4
Shoes (451 and 452)	2,893	2,035	65,235	35,082	50.9	75.2
Mass-produced clothes (453, 455)	4,510	4,344	118,164	93,861	89.8	161.7
Made-to-measure clothes (454)	4,495	2,010	9,089	3,429	3.8	3.6
Fur (456)	326	249	3,774	2,232	2.9	5.8
Synthetic fibres (2516)	21	16	9,728	8,699	15.1	45.6
Sub total	14,019	9,839	233,165	161,099	185.4	341.4
Total	20,021	13,922	414,876	274,182	339.2	615.3

Sources: INE, 1984a; INE, 1989

Until the late 1970s foreign firms were of little importance (except in synthetic fibres), but their presence has slowly grown during the 1980s. For example Hilaturas de Fabra y Coats, SA are controlled by a British group; the Japanese company Kondobo opened a new factory in 1987 in Gerona, to produce cotton thread and textiles mainly for export; and in 1989 the state enterprise Intelhorce in Málaga was sold to the Italian Benetton group. Such developments pose a clear threat to Spanish producers, who have tended to be insular in outlook, having been protected from the outside world by a high tariff wall (with no more than five per cent of textile output exported and imports accounting for about ten per cent of consumption in the early 1980s). Since 1986 the industry has begun to face direct competition from other European Community producers (especially Portugal with its lower labour costs, estimated by the Werner Institute in 1985 to be one third of those in Spain, Italy and France) and from developing countries, which hope to be able to export larger quantities of goods to western Europe after the present Multifibre Arrangement runs out in July 1991. Imports have tripled since 1986 as a result of the reduction in import barriers and the appreciation of the peseta. In 1988 imports of textiles and clothing were valued at pta. 346 billion and exports at pta. 212 billion compared with a surplus of pta. 15 billion in 1986 (*El País*, 1990).

The textile industry is concentrated in Cataluña and País Valenciana (sixty per cent of all employment in textiles and clothing and fifty-four per cent of all employment in leather and shoes in 1986; INE, 1989), while specific sub-sectors display even greater concentration. In contrast, the finishing industries of clothing and footwear are more widespread. Madrid, Barcelona and Valencia are particularly important centres for clothing.

Ninety per cent of cotton spinning and eighty per cent of cotton weaving are located in Cataluña (Tamames,1983), predominantly in the province of Barcelona (which alone contains eighty-five per cent of the industry in the region). Many of the factories are along the Llobregat, Cardona, Besós and Tordera rivers and on the coast. There are also major factories in the urban areas of Barcelona, Manresa and in Gerona. The climate, port facilities, water power and a history of textile manufacturing have all contributed to the present importance of this region. Outside of Cataluña, there are isolated cotton textile centres in the Islas Baleares, the Levante, Andalucía and Extremadura. Production of cotton thread has been increasing, from 175,000 tonnes in 1980 to 211,000 tonnes in 1986.

The wool, silk and leather industries are similarly concentrated in Cataluña, especially in Barcelona. The wool industry flourished in medieval Spain in centres such as Béjar, Medina del Campo, Palencia, Medina de Rioseco, Segovia, Sabadell and Tarrasa. Now over half the industry is in Cataluña, especially in Barcelona where the main centres are in the city of Barcelona, in Sabadell and Tarrasa. Outside of Cataluña, Alcoy is an important centre in Alicante and Béjar in Salamanca (especially for rugs). Other woollen centres include Palencia, Logroño, Zaragoza, Burgos and León. The silk industry too has a long history (especially in Granada) but is now of less importance, pure silk having largely given way to other materials. Raw silk is mainly produced in Alicante and Murcia, while silk production is undertaken in Cataluña, Orihuela (Alicante), Almonacid, Burjasot (Valencia), Valencia, Granada and Palma de Mallorca. The most important centre for the leather industry is in Barcelona, where Igualada is the main centre for the preparation of skins. Outside of Cataluña other important leather centres are in Valencia, Castellón, La Coruña and Ubrique (Cádiz).

The main centres for shoe production are in the Levante (Alicante produces more than half the national output, important centres being Elda, Novelda and Villena) and the Islas Baleares (particularly in Mallorca, where the main centre is Inca). Other shoe-production areas are in Castellón (Valle de Uxó), Zaragoza, Logroño, Albacete and Barcelona. The shoe industry enjoyed spectacular growth in the 1960s and 1970s (from 30 million pairs at the beginning of the 1960s to 200 million at the end of the 1970s, of which about fifty per cent were exported), but as elsewhere in the textile industry it too now faces problems of growing labour costs, increased competition from Newly Industrialised Countries, marketing weaknesses and a fragmented structure.

The importance of the textile industry for employment, the extent of the problems that it faced, the prospect of greater competition on membership of the European Community, the assistance being given to the textile sector by other industrial countries and, arguably, the political weight of the main area of textile employment prompted the early emergence of a textile reconversion plan. The Plan de Reconversión del Sector Textil began to take shape in 1979 and was finally approved in 1981 (under Real Decreto 2010/1981). It attempted to foster the adaption of the industry to meet international competition through measures to promote the renewal of plant and equipment, to improve the financial structure of companies, and to improve 'intangibles' such as marketing, image, quality and design. Twenty-four per cent of investment went into 'intangibles', which were recognised as an important element in competitiveness in the 1984 Reconversion Law.

Under the Reconversion Plan programmes were approved for 691 firms (of which thirty failed to implement their programmes) embracing about twenty-five per cent of the labour force (including virtually all those in the synthetic fibre sector). Twenty-eight per cent of the reconversion programmes approved contained measures to reduce employment, while fifteen per cent contained proposals to expand employment. The net effect was to reduce employment by 9,929 (total losses were 11,156; twenty-eight per cent by early retirements). These relatively small labour force reductions covered by the Plan must be viewed against the very substantial losses that had occurred prior to the Plan, registered employment in the textile sector having fallen from 415,000 in 1978 to only 274,000 in 1986 (Table 6.6). Almost all the large firms in the industry were given financial assistance. Thus of the 661 firms that implemented reconversion plans, forty had more than 500 workers, 318 had 50–500 workers and 303 had less than fifty workers (MINE, 1987). Assistance went especially towards the capital intensive areas of production (for example synthetic fibres), with much of the equipment being imported. Most of the firms assisted (509) were in the textile sector *senso stricto* (for example 131 firms in cotton) and clothing (141 firms). As the textile industry displays a certain degree of spatial concentration, assistance too has been spatially concentrated, with over half of the firms and workers covered by the Plan located in Cataluña and twenty per cent of the firms in País Valenciana. The total investment realised by the firms in the Plan totalled pta. 184 billion of which pta. 111 billion in textiles, (including pta. 47 billion in cotton), pta. 42 billion in clothing and pta. 31 billion in man-made fibres. Twelve per cent of the total investment (pta. 22.6 billion) came from central-government assistance (grants) outside of the subsidised loans from the industrial credit bank (Banco de Crédito Industrial, BCI; MINE, 1987). The Plan expired at the end of 1986 (although in 1987 the programmes for some firms were still incomplete).

Rationalisation in the industry is still incomplete and further contraction is certain. Employment losses will also occur from the submerged economy if this is exposed by tighter controls. Large firms need to continue policies aimed at introducing more flexible labour relations, increasing research and development, improving design and marketing, and stepping up trade promotion.

6.7 Food, drink and tobacco

The food, drink and tobacco industry (abbreviated here to the food industry) is the most important manufacturing sector in Spain as measured by employment and value added (with an estimated gross value of production in 1989 of pta. 5,900 billion). Approximately 350,000 to 400,000 people are employed in the sector (together with others in the underground economy), representing some sixteen per cent of all industrial employment and value added (including that in energy and mining) and close to twenty per cent of all manufacturing industrial employment and value added. The industry also provides a major intermediate market for the agricultural sector. Over 40,000 food-industry establishments range in size from the sole trader semi-subsistence business to some of the largest businesses in Spain and multinational companies. In 1988 about one quarter of the 200 largest Spanish companies were in the food sector, including Unilever España, Ebro, Elosúa, Danone, Conservera Campofrio, Pascual Hermanos, El Aguila, Osborne y Compañía and La Cruz del Campo (*El País*, 1990). In terms of employment the largest sub-sector is bread, cakes and biscuits, employing about 90,000 people, followed by meat (employing some 46,000), then dairy products and conserves and fruit (Table 6.7). In brewing Spain is the third largest producer in Europe, with beer production in 1989 of 2.73 billion litres (*El País*, 4 March 1990).

Table 6.7 Food, drink and tobacco by sector, 1986

Sector	Occupied population	Establishments
413 Meat products	46,835	3,905
414 Milk products	26,100	870
415 Juices and conserves	23,279	695
419 Bread, cakes and biscuits	89,994	22,516
420 Sugar	5,687	36
425 Wine industry	22,439	3,951
429 Tobacco	10,213	28
Other	115,989	—
Food, drink and tobacco	340,536	—

Note: The whole food sector covers sectors 411 to 429. Hence the table excludes the manufacture of spirits, beer, cider, mineral water, animal foods, sweets, coffee, chocolate, pasta, flour, fish products, olive oil and oil products

Source: INE, 1989

The food industry is dispersed across the country, broadly echoing the distribution of population and reflecting the pattern of agricultural production. Andalucía and Cataluña are the two most important regions. Barcelona (eleven per cent) and Madrid (nine per cent) are the two most important provinces, others being Valencia (with six per cent), Murcia and Sevilla (with five per cent each).

Food manufacturing is also particularly important to the regional economy of Murcia and to the local economies of many Andalucian cities such as Málaga, Granada and Sevilla.

Within this overall pattern of dispersal there are many examples of geographical specialisation in particular sub-sectors, related to the distribution of raw materials and the evolution of particular production techniques. Examples include the sherry industry in Jerez de la Frontera, dairy products in Asturias, *turrón* in Valencia and practically fifty per cent of firms registered to the meat sector concentrated in Castilla–León and Cataluña. There are also numerous examples of food industries that dominate local economies such as the biscuit industry of Estepa (Sevilla), the distilleries of Rute and Montilla (Córdoba), and the mineral-water industry of Lanjarón (Granada).

As in many other sectors of manufacturing industry, the food industry too is characterised by the small size of plants and firms, which remain as limitations to competitiveness despite numerous amalgamations. In 1978 the average size of establishment was seven employees. Small plants are characteristic of the pastry and cakes industry, in which in 1985 there were 22,050 plants with less than twenty persons and only five with over 500 persons (Rodriguez, 1989). In contrast, brewing is characterised by large plants. In 1987 the fifty largest food companies in Spain accounted for only thirty-five per cent of the total turnover of the sector. None of the sugar groups in Spain are in the top ten in the European Community. The sugar company Ebro was eleventh in 1989 with a quota of 326,000 tonnes, compared with the largest company, British Sugar, with a quota of 1.14 million tonnes.

The organisation of the industry varies between sub-sectors, but the most common form of market structure is that of a few large companies (often foreign multinationals) serving national, and sometimes international, markets, and a multitude of small ones serving local markets. Direct state involvement has been small, except in the case of the tobacco industry, which has been the monopoly of the state owned group Tabacalera, SA. In some sub-sectors control of production is confined to a few companies, this being the case in tobacco, in sugar, in which four companies (Ebro, Sociedad General Azucarera, Compañía de Industrias Agrícolas, and Cooperativa Onésimo Redondo de Valladolid, Acor) share over ninety per cent of the market, and in brewing, where the six largest groups control over ninety per cent of the market (Table 6.8). In other sub-sectors the market is shared by small and medium sized companies. For example in the meat industry, the four largest firms (Oscar Mayer, Revilla, Campofrio and Estellés) accounted for only 19.4 per cent of the market in 1988 and the eight largest firms for only 28.5 per cent. Outside of these large and medium-sized companies, the multitude of small family firms, with very localised markets, face increasing competition from national and multinational producers. Many of these small firms will disappear in the wake of increased competition. Equally there will be further concentration among the larger companies.

Some companies are quoted on the Stock Exchange, but many remain in the hands of families. For example the manufacture of meat products has traditionally been a family business: Campofrio is owned by the Ballvé and Yartú families, Estellés and Fuertes are owned by families of the same names. Other examples of large family-owned companies are Larios (the distillers based in

Table 6.8 The major brewing groups, 1989

Group	Parent-company production in 1989		Whole-group production in 1989
	million litres	%	%
El Aguila, SA	485	17.7	17.7
Mahou, SA	440	16.1	16.1
San Miguel, SA	380	13.9	13.9
La Cruz del Campo, SA	335	12.3	21.6
Damm, SA	340	12.4	16.9
Unión Cervecera, SA	150	5.5	6.5
All six Major Brewers	2,130	77.9	92.7
Others	604	22.1	7.3
Total	2,734	100.0	100.0

Note: Other groups include Grupo Cia Cervecera Canarias with 2.18 per cent of the market, Hijos de Rivera SA with 2.0 per cent, Sical SA with 1.41, La Zaragozana SA with 1.24 and El Aguila Negra SA with 0.66 per cent.

Sources: *El País*, 4 March 1990 and 24 June 1990; Pozo, 1989

Málaga) and Vall Companys SA (a vertically integrated meat and cereals group) based in Lérida.

Restructuring in the food industry has been market led, there having been no reconversion programme in this sector. Restructuring has involved a complex process of spatial, structural and organisational change resulting in a realignment of production (sometimes involving greater specialisation and sometimes greater diversification), concentration and internationalisation. In the food industry added complications have resulted from exposure to the Common Agricultural Policy and the food harmonisation measures necessary for a single market in food in 1992.

Diversification has been one response to increasing market pressures, although many companies are already part of diversified groups (Kas and Savin are controlled by Banco Bilbao Vizcaya, Ebro by the Kuwait Investment Office through the holding company Torras Hostench). In sugar refining the company Ebro has developed backward links to agriculture (with its own farms), horizontal links into other forms of food production and forward links into food distribution. Sociedad General Azucarera markets sugar, alcohol and yeast and has a holding in the meat company Corporación Alimentaria Ibérica (CAI). Acor was solely dedicated to sugar-beet refining but then diversified into cereals and vegetables. The big meat companies have also diversified into other food products: Navidul into cheese and Campofrio into fish and dairy products. The increasing importance of distribution has also led to the strengthening of distribution systems and vertical integration.

The most publicised feature of restructuring has involved company mergers and concentration as companies endeavour to rationalise their operations. In so doing, many formally local or regionally based companies have become national or even international in outlook. In dairy products the four dairies of Gurlesa, Inlena-Copeleche, Bayena and Urbia, which operate in País Vasco and Navarra, amalgamated in 1988. The new company will be able to take advantage of the economies of scale enjoyed by the major companies in the sector: Lactaria Montañesa SAM-RAM, Pascual, Central Lechera Asturiana and Puleva (the Granada based firm that in 1988 took over Colema, a dairy product firm in Málaga). In sugar the three companies Ebro Compañía de Azucares y Alimentación, Compañía de Industrias Agrícolas and Sociedad Azucarera Ibérica planned to merge in 1990 to form the company Ebro Agrícolas Compañía de Alimentación, SA, which would have over fifty per cent of the market (a merger prompted by the Kuwait Investment Office). Although mergers have led to larger companies, these remain relatively small by international standards. For example, the average size of company in the brewing industry increased from 50 million litres per year in 1980 to 78 million litres per year in 1988, but even the largest Spanish company was not among the top ten in the European Community.

Restructuring in the tobacco industry has resulted from the break-up of the tobacco monopoly following membership of the European Community. The state has exercised a monopoly (dating back to the seventeenth century) over the production, processing and distribution of tobacco in Spain (except in the Islas Canarias where a multinational industry exists) through the company Tabacalera SA (Compañía Arrendataria Tabacalera, SA). The company, which was established in 1945, employs over 8,000 people with factories in Alicante, Cádiz, La Coruña, Gijón, Logroño, Madrid, Málaga, San Sebastián, Santander, Sevilla, Tarragona and Valencia. Diversification into other food industries has turned Tabacalera into one of the major food companies in Spain, in addition to having interests in property and tourism. It is a shareholder with RJR Reynolds (USA) in the Spanish activities of Nabisco Brands, having absorbed at the end of 1988 a large part of the activities in this business of the other public food sector company Endiasa (Empresa Nacional para el Desarrollo Alimentario).

Greater concentration of production has been accompanied by selective investment and numerous plant closures. For example in flour milling, there were 1,600 mills in Spain in 1978, most of which were small, family-owned concerns. In 1990 there were only about 420 remaining, with further significant reduction essential to allow for new, more efficient plant (such as that of Vall Company in Arévalo (Avila) with a milling capacity of 500 tonnes daily) and a reduction in the current overcapacity in the industry (capacity for milling 10 million tonnes but only 4.5 million tonnes required by the domestic market; Maté, 1989). In sugar refining there has been a reduction in the number of refineries from thirty-two at the beginning of the 1980s to twenty-four in 1988, with closures of La Vega, El Carmen and San Isidro in Granada, Antequerana in Málaga, Luceni in Zaragoza, Santa Eulalia in Teruel, Aranjuez in Madrid, and Rosales in Sevilla. Apart from the direct employment effect of plant closures (leading to a reduction of the industry labour force from 9,500 in 1978 to 6,300 in 1988), the indirect impact has fallen on the farmers engaged in sugar cultivation (some 50,000 in 1988).

Concentration is inhibited by strong company loyalties and conflicts of personalities. As a result, precipitous company concentrations have sometimes been unsuccessful. An illustration of a failed merger is provided by the history of the two Spanish family-owned olive-oil firms Elosúa (based in Asturias) and Pont (based in Lérida). These two companies joined in 1985 to form the company

Aceites Españoles, SA with the intention of buying the second-largest olive-oil company Carbonell, SA (seventy-eight per cent Elosúa and twenty two per cent Pont). It was an action encouraged by the government, which sought to ensure Spanish control over an important market segment. However, rivalry between the two firms resulted in each of them trying to increase their capital so as to buy the other out and thereby separate once more (*El País*, 11 June 1989).

Along with concentration, the other major feature of industrial restructuring has been increased foreign penetration, with multinational companies strategically positioning themselves for 1992. In so doing, foreign capital is coming to dominate the food industry, as it increasingly dominates other areas of Spanish industry. The antecedents of foreign ownership date back to previous centuries (for example with the development of the sherry industry in Jerez de la Frontera), and some companies established plants in Spain in the 1950s and 1960s (for example Coca Cola established a bottling plant in Barcelona in 1953). However, foreign penetration has risen sharply in the 1980s, giving most major food industry multinationals a presence. Of the ten largest food groups operating in Spain in 1987, only in four was Spanish capital in the majority, and two of these were public companies: Endiasa (today practically absorbed by Tabacalera and Merca) and Guissona (a co-operative of agricultural producers). The situation may not be untypical of some other European countries, but it is a significant change for Spain.

Foreign multinationals are now found throughout the food industry. They have control over the two major companies in the mass-produced bread market, Bimbo (owned by the American drinks company Anhauser Busch, which also uses Bimbo to distribute its drinks products in Spain) and Panrico (owned by Allied Lyons of the UK). The meat sector is dominated by three multinationals: Unilever (which in 1986 acquired the meat company Revilla), Nestlé and Oscar Mayer of Germany. The poultry sector is dominated by about four or five multinationals following a wave of acquisitions that have included those by the French firm Doux and the American firm Tyson Foods. In the drinks sector, more than half of the Spanish coffee market is divided between the Swiss company Nestlé, the Dutch company Douwe Egberts and General Foods of the United States. In conserves the company Chistu has passed into the hands of Pillsbury (the USA food manufacturer, itself now owned by Grand Metropolitan), and Orlando has gone to Heinz. In sugar the company Ebro (with over one third of the Spanish sugar market) has fallen into the hands of Torras Hostench (controlled by the Kuwait Investment Office). In the soft-drinks market over sixty per cent is taken by the products of the multinational companies Coca Cola, Pepsi-Cola and Cadbury–Schweppes (although many multinational brands are manufactured or distributed under license by Spanish firms). In brewing the six major groups control over ninety per cent of production, and all are either foreign owned or have significant foreign penetration (for example El Aguila is owned by the Dutch company Heineken and Unión Cervecera by United Breweries). Even in the traditional family wine-making business, multinational companies are gradually increasing their presence; thus Guiness had a major holding in the largest wine producer AGE (with brands such as Romeral and Siglo) before selling it to Banco Banesto.

While the dominant flow of foreign investment has been inward, some Spanish companies have been expanding abroad, predominantly through increasing exports and seeking contracts with foreign distributors rather than through direct investment. For example the drinks company Freixnet (the manufacturer of Cava champagne) has significant markets in the United States and Japan, and Nutrexpa (the manufacturer of the chocolate drink Cola Cao) also has an important export business. But generally Spanish food companies have not been oriented towards exports. At the beginning of the 1990s they were more concerned with defending their domestic markets. Where foreign investment has occurred it has been concentrated in southern Europe (especially Portugal). The sugar refiner Ebro has a forty-five per cent holding in the Portuguese company Vasco de Gama (which produces fish and oil). Sociedad General Azucarera has a twenty-five per cent holding in Unión Sacárica Emiliana de Italia and a sixty-six per cent holding in the Turkish yeast company Ozmayyas.

Growth in demand and changes in consumer tastes have characterised the food market. Demand has expanded on the back of rising disposable incomes and increasing consumer spending. The industry grew by about eight per cent per annum in the three years 1987 to 1989 (growing from pta. 5,930 billion in 1988 to pta 6,400 billion in 1989 compared with the five per cent growth in GDP; a market size approximately the same as the UK). Alongside this growth has been a shift in consumer tastes away from traditional products towards higher-value added processed foods and higher quality products, and those products considered to be more healthy and environmentally friendly. Meat and meat products account for about one quarter of expenditure, followed by fish and fish products (eleven per cent). These trends also demonstrate an element of consumer convergence, changes in demand that are gradually aligning consumer behaviour in different European countries.

On the supply side there have been fundamental and far-reaching shifts in the pattern of distribution, with the rapid growth since the 1970s of supermarkets and hypermarkets and the decline of the traditional small store. As distribution has become more concentrated, so power to determine the path of the food industry has passed from manufacturers to the distributors, of which many of the largest are foreign companies. Distributors, selling an increasing range of their own brand products, are able to promote imported products. They also provide a much closer interface with the consumer and can quickly respond to (and shape) shifts in consumer tastes.

Traditionally Spain has had a net surplus on food trade, but that surplus has rapidly dwindled as the domestic market has been opened up to competition, especially from other European Community countries. In 1989 there was a deficit of pta. 71 billion on agricultural and food-product trade (exports of pta. 813 billion and imports of pta. 884 billion).

Spanish food exports remain concentrated on relatively unprocessed products (with the main increases in primary agricultural products), while imports tend to have a higher-value added content. Other EC countries have pursued a strategy of entering the Spanish market, with good results, but Spain has been less successful in exports. For example in 1988 food products exported from France to Spain increased by 22.4 per cent (on 1987) to reach pta. 114,000 million. Such success may be partly attributed to the aggressive action of the private sector in other countries and better foreign-government promotion of products. In Spain the private sector has been less active and government agencies (such as the Trade Agency, Instituto de Comercio Exterior) may have been less efficient. Part of the problem is image, Spanish products often being shipped to France or Italy for final packaging before sale to final consumers.

On the import side changing tastes have fuelled imports. For example, imports of fruit from the southern hemisphere have increased spectacularly. Import quotas on these products disappeared in 1990. In 1983 almost all the fruit and vegetables passing through the Mercabarna (wholesale market for Barcelona) were Spanish; in 1988 twelve per cent of the vegetables and three per cent of the fruit was imported (*El País*, 11 June 1989). Fresh-fruit imports especially are on the increase, although the major import items are fish, crustaceans and molluscs, which rose from pta. 64,280 in 1985 to pta. 174,694 in 1988; drinks, from pta. 15,425 to pta. 45,851, meat and fish products, from pta. 8,388 to pta. 19,668; and sugar and sweets, from pta. 3,625 to pta. 19,640.

The major weaknesses of the Spanish food industry are its small size and limited product research. It also lacks experience of international markets, suffers from a low-quality product image and generally displays insufficient management and workforce training. Competitiveness in the 1990s will depend on improving distribution networks, professional training and, perhaps most importantly, improving the image of products.

6.8 Motor vehicles

The motor-vehicle industry has been a leading sector in Spanish industrial development. It now symbolises the modern, international face of industry, incorporating the latest automated and robotised production techniques in factories linked to multinational production systems, presaging the changes now taking place elsewhere in the economy. Some 70,000 people are employed in car assembly (1986), but if the number employed in other motor-vehicle production and parts and components is added, the figure is closer to 350,000; adding the number in related activities may take the total closer to half a million (Economía y Finanzas Españolas, 1987). It is one of the major manufacturing industries in Spain, and with a car- manufacturing capacity of over one and a half million units per year, it is one of the leading car producers in the world. The motor-vehicle industry also makes a significant contribution towards exports, with six of the leading ten Spanish export companies in 1988 (*El País*, 1990).

Cars were being produced in Barcelona at the end of the nineteenth century. In the first quarter of the twentieth century, production spread to other centres in Spain but remained small in scale.

In Barcelona the companies of Hispano-Suiza and Elizalde were particularly important. The Civil War diverted production to military equipment. Following the war the policy of import substitution and autarchic development isolated the industry, directing output to the domestic market. Enasa was established by INI in 1946 and Seat in 1949, both initially in Barcelona. Components factories grew around an existing engineering base. During the 1950s the domestic industry expanded and some French manufacturers managed to secure production facilities. In the 1960s the industry was opened up to a larger number of mainly

European motor-vehicle manufacturers, attracted by the low labour costs and protected domestic market. The industry was still largely nationalised but had a high degree of technological dependence on foreign companies.

In the 1970s and early 1980s the giant American and Japanese manufacturers Ford, General Motors and Nissan arrived and the emphasis in production switched to exports. The agreement reached with Ford was important in opening up car production in Spain, as it involved important concessions in terms of state involvement and the national content of cars produced. Through the 1970s and early 1980s there was a gradual reduction of duties on imported components, especially after 1979.

In the decade from the mid 1970s to the mid 1980s there were major losses in motor-vehicle manufacturing world-wide, as reduction in demand coincided with increasing production costs and overcapacity. Global restructuring followed, involving substantial investment in new plant and equipment as well as structural, technological and spatial reorganisation of the industry. Cars have become lighter in weight (involving a switch in materials) and are marketed world-wide. During the period of restructuring, Spain continued to attract investment for reasons of relatively low labour costs, a protected domestic market, access to the European Community, economies of scale, government assistance and trading potential with South American markets (Table 6.9). Labour costs have been lower in Spain than in north-west European countries and trade union organisation generally weaker.

Table 6.9 Saloon-car production, 1960 – 89

Year	Production	Year	Production
1960	39,732	1983	1,141,581
1965	145,460	1984	1,176,893
1970	450,426	1985	1,230,071
1975	696,124	1986	1,281,899
1980	1,028,813	1987	1,402,574
1981	855,325	1988	1,497,967
1982	927,500	1989	1,638,615

Note: Saloon-car exports in 1989 were 925,143

Source: *El País*, 1990

Entry into the European Community opened up the potential for integration in the European motor-vehicle industry, leading to a specialisation in small vehicles and a reorientation towards exports. Production in Spain offered a degree of continuing protectionism until the early 1990s. Access to the European Community market, coupled with expanding demand in the late 1980s, attracted further American, Japanese and other non-Community investment (for example that by the Swedish company Scania). Scale economies have been possible as a result of the large, established motor-vehicle industry in Spain, including a substantial components industry. Finally, various forms of assistance have been available from the government for motor-vehicle manufacturers and foreign investment.

The motor-vehicle industry is now wholly within the hands of foreign multinational companies (Table 6.10), following the sale of Seat in 1986 and Enasa in 1990. Five foreign multinational companies are involved in saloon-car manufacture, the largest volume of cars being produced by the Seat company, now a subsidiary of Volkswagen. The Seat company (Sociedad Española de Automóviles de Turismo) was set up by INI in 1949 with the participation of Fiat (which provided the patents) and other private capital. In 1967 Fiat took a thirty-six per cent holding in the company, but after sustaining substantial losses pulled out of the company in 1981, leaving INI to find a new partner. An agreement was reached with Volkswagen (VW) in 1983, which finally led to a majority shareholding in 1986. Initially production of Seat cars was centred in Barcelona, then in 1974 Seat took over the former British Leyland plant in Pamplona, which became its second major production centre. Following the take-over by Volkswagen a major investment programme was begun, aimed at raising capacity to 400,000 units a year in 1990 and incorporating the Spanish plants in the Volkswagen organisation (concentrating on the production of the small VW Polo).

Table 6.10 Motor-vehicle firms in Spain

Company	Employment (1988)	Production (saloon-car units, 1989)	Sales value (pta. billion, 1988)	Export value (pta. billion, 1988)
Seat Volkswagen	23,777	449,904	384	160
Fasa-Renault	18,904	274,334	382	90
General Motors	9,763	369,727	352	175
Ford España	9,548	293,927	291	140
Citroen Hispañia	8,831	119,298	188	53
Peugeot Talbot	6,760	131,425	177	30
Motor Ibérica	6,771	47,000★	134	28
Suzuki-Land Rover	3,853	—	33	17
Enasa	5,930	11,777★	116	25
Mercedes-Benz	3,641	10,005†	101	22
Michelin	11,959	—	137	63
Firestone Hispania	6,017	—	55	22
Femsa	5,178	—	56	28
Pirelli	4,594	—	57	8

★ The sale of all automobile units in 1986

† The production of all automobile units in 1986

Source: El País, 1990

The French companies Renault and Peugeot Citroen were established in the 1950s. The Fasa-Renault company (Fabricación de Automóviles SA) was established in 1955 with factories in Valladolid and technical collaboration and patents from Renault. A factory producing transmission systems in Sevilla was acquired in 1966 and in 1977 a further assembly plant began production in

Palencia. Production has been directed at the domestic market. Peugeot Citroen was established in 1957 as Citroen Hispañia, based in the duty-free zone at Vigo. This site enabled it to import fully assembled cars as well as kits from France for final assembly. The other part of the company's activities in Spain grew out of the take-over of Chrysler's operations in 1978. In 1963 Chrysler had developed an association with the then independent truck producer Barrieros Diesel, producing vehicles under the Simca and Dodge marks at the company's plant in Villaverde, Madrid. Following the take-over by Citroen, vehicles were sold under the Talbot name (the Talbot truck factory was later sold to Renault Industrial Vehicles).

The arrival of Ford in the early 1970s marked the beginning of a new wave of motor-vehicle investment in Spain, directed towards developing an export base within an integrated multinational organisation. Authorisation for a factory at Almusafes (Valencia) was given in 1973 on the basis of the level of investment involved and the guarantee of exporting a specified quantity. The factory began producing engines in 1975 and cars in 1976. In 1989 the Ford plant was producing 1,460 car units a day and had a capacity to produce about 1,935 engine units per day. In 1988 the plant produced 293,927 cars and 401,315 engines. Production is concentrated on small cars (Fiestas, Escorts and Orions) and engines (below 1300cc). Exports (essentially to other European countries) form a major component of output. The company has been extending its plant in Valencia and has built a new motor vehicle electronics factory near Cádiz.

General Motors followed Ford into Spain at the end of the 1970s. Agreement was reached in 1979 for a car-assembly plant on the industrial estate at Figueruelas (24 km from Zaragoza), plus component factories at Logroño (bodywork) and Puerto Real (Cádiz; suspensions); the latter provided valuable employment in an area suffering from serious unemployment problems resulting from the decline of the shipbuilding industry. The project represented the largest-ever foreign investment in Spain and involved a package of development incentives. From the outset, the plant was built as an export base for small-car production (initially the Corsa model) in Europe, producing on average 365,000 cars a year. The company is one of Spain's largest exporters.

Japanese manufacturers have concentrated on the production of light vans and all-terrain vehicles. Nissan entered Spain in 1977 through participation in Motor Ibérica. Motor Ibérica had emerged in 1954 with a factory in Barcelona producing trucks (Ebro) and tractors under licence from Ford. Massey Ferguson took a thirty six per cent holding in 1965, which was sold to Nissan in 1980. Nissan has since increased its holding in Nissan Motor Ibérica to seventy-five per cent (1987). The company is centred in Barcelona, where it has produced the Nissan Patrol since 1983. In addition it produces heavy trucks and an increasing number of light vans (fifty-four per cent of the light-industrial-vehicle market 3.5–4.9 tonnes). Suzuki–Land Rover Santana was formed from Metalúrgica de Santa Ana in Linares (Jaén), which had been established in 1959 building vehicles under licence from British Leyland and Willys Overland of the USA. In 1980 the company formed an agreement with Suzuki to build a number of Suzuki Santanas. Then in 1984 Suzuki acquired an eight per cent equity holding, increasing it to seventeen per cent in 1986 (while the Land Rover holding fell to thirty-three per cent).

Apart from the companies mentioned above, industrial vehicles are also produced by the former public enterprise Enasa (the sale of a majority holding in which was finally agreed with Fiat in 1990), Mercedes Benz de España and Renault Vehículos Industriales. Enasa (Empresa Nacional de Autocamiónes) was fully owned by INI, having been established in 1946 with factories in Barajas (Madrid) and Barcelona (where it occupied the old factory of Hispano-Suiza). In 1966 it took over the Sava truck plant (established in 1957) in Valladolid. Enasa also has a plant in Mataro. Initially Enasa received technical assistance from Leyland, but now builds original vehicles, buses and trucks under the trade name Pegaso. In the 1980s the company developed collaborative links with other European manufacturers, notably MAN (now part of Volkswagen) and DAF. Sales are concentrated in the domestic market where it has thirty-one per cent of the heavy vehicle market (sixteen tonnes and more). Mercedes-Benz began making light industrial vehicles with Enmasa (an INI company) in 1960. From 1969 this operation became Mercedes Benz de España with plants in Barcelona and Vitoria. Then in 1981 Daimler Benz took a majority holding in Mevosa (a company established in 1950 with German capital) in Vitoria, where it builds vans. In 1986 the bulk of production was still oriented to the domestic market but export of light vans was increasing. Renault Vehículos Industriales has a plant at Villaverde, Madrid (formally belonging to Talbot), producing trucks, coaches, buses and vans mostly for the domestic market (twenty-three per cent of the heavy vehicle market, sixteen tonnes and over).

The two-wheeled motor vehicle market is divided into mopeds/scooters (*ciclomotores*) and motorbikes (*motocicletas*). Like the other parts of the motor-vehicle industry, it too has been engulfed by foreign multinational companies, especially the Italian and Japanese, and is being reoriented towards exports. Vespa, Derbi, Yamaha, Puch (now controlled by Suzuki) and GAC (Mobilettes) are the main companies producing mopeds and scooters. The Japanese have taken complete control of the motorbike market, absorbing the relatively small Spanish manufacturers such as Sanglas, Butaco, Ossa and Montesa. Yamaha began commercial collaboration with Sanglas in 1977 and later became the major shareholder. Production is concentrated in Barcelona (a new site having been acquired on an industrial estate in the Urgent Reindustrialisation Zone of Cataluña).

Spain has a well-established components industry, dominated by European and American multinational companies. Valeo España SA is the Spanish subsidiary of the French group Valeo. It includes the companies Faespa SA, Ferodo España SA (which acquired Fraymon tyres in the 1970s) and Valeo Distribucion SA. Femsa is a major electrical-equipment manufacturer, acquired by the German company Bosch in the 1970s. Grupo Tudor is one of Europe's leading battery manufacturers. Fiat has extensive parts-manufacturing facilities in Spain including Weber España (with headquarters in Guadalajara) and Taisa (Tecnología de la Automación y de la Industria), a rear-view-mirror manufacturer. Bendix España, SA is the major supplier of brakes and hydraulic equipment in the Spanish car market. The company has its headquarters and three factories in Barcelona, two factories in Santander, one in Pamplona and one in Bilbao. Amongst the tyre manufacturers, Michelin has been established in Arranda del Duero since 1970 and is the largest in terms of sales as well as being a major exporter. Bridgestone (Firestone) and Pirelli also have major production facilities in Spain.

The Spanish motor-vehicle market expanded rapidly after 1986, following a collapse in the late 1970s and slow growth in the early 1980s. Motor vehicles are supplied to the market through production in Spain, imports and the sale of second-hand vehicles. The car market absorbed 638,000 units in 1977, then fell to around 500,000 in the early 1980s. The slump also affected the second-hand market, in which the number of car transfers remained static at around 650,000 to 700,000 per year. As the purchase of new vehicles fell, so the average age of vehicles increased (postponement of new purchases). In 1985 more than thirty-five per cent of cars in Spain were over ten years old (Economía y Finanzas, 1987). Demand recovered to 648,000 in 1986 before exploding to over a million in 1988 and 1989 (Table 6.11). There was a similar boom in motorcycles, with 133 per cent more motorcycles being registered in 1989 than in 1986 (more than 107,000 units; El País, 1990).

Table 6.11 The car market in Spain (saloon cars and derivatives)

Year	Number of cars in Spain	Domestic sales	Registrations	Imports	Import penetration	Exports
1960	290,500	—	—	—	—	—
1970	2,377,726	414,702	399,171	12,103	3.0	40,882
1975	4,806,833	534,067	572,188	9,126	2.0	156,354
1980	7,556,511	504,051	538,989	60,545	11.2	525,845
1985	9,273,710	480,081	542,975	64,609	11.9	865,304
1986	9,761,968	538,654	647,717	106,531	16.4	809,001
1987	10,218,526	796,483	927,805	248,666	26.8	706,705
1988	10,788,975	910,685	1,056,711	349,278	33.1	786,795
1989	11,434,363	976,084	1,149,373	425,032	37.0	925,143

Sources: Banco de España, (1990) *El País*, 1990; Farré Terre, 1986

Although Spain is an important vehicle exporter, its position within the spatial division-of-labour of multinational companies means that it is also exhibits specialisation in the small car and van market. Hence many types of vehicle (generally higher-value added ones) must be imported. Furthermore, imports are becoming increasingly competitive (especially Japanese cars, which have been virtually excluded) as the tariff protection around the Spanish market is reduced (import duties on EC and EFTA vehicles falling from thirty-three per cent in 1986 to zero in 1993 and for third country imports from forty-five per cent in 1986 to ten per cent in 1993). In the 1980s Spain operated a reduced duty allocation (32,000 units in 1985, 36,000 in 1987 and 40,000 in 1988), attracting only 17.4 per cent duty. This quota system disappeared in 1989 as tariffs were dismantled. From being a negligible part of the market in 1975 and only eleven per cent of the market in 1980, imports now represent almost forty per cent of the new-car market and there is a deficit on the balance of trade in 'vehicles and tractors'. The picture is worse in motorcycles where imports now represent over one half of new registrations (from twenty-four per cent in 1984; El País, 1990). Further import penetration must be expected, especially from Japanese cars, leading to a continuing deterioration in the balance of trade.

Both central and regional government have assisted investment by foreign motor-vehicle companies. For example the central government has sought to consolidate the position of the motor-vehicle industry in Spain through the Plan General de Promoción Industrial y Tecnológica del Sector Fabricante de Automóviles, set up in 1985 (under the Ley de Reconversión y Reindustrialización 1984). This recognised the importance of the motor-vehicle industry in Spain and provided for assistance to motor-vehicle manufacturers to modernise their plants. Despite substantial re-equipment in the late 1970s and early 1980s, assisted by reduced duties on the imported plant and equipment necessary for modernising factories, in the mid 1980s some production plants still needed to tackle the problems of obsolescence, dated technology and overstaffing. All companies negotiated state aid to cover the cost of modernisation and training labour. Talbot, Fasa Renault, Ford and Citroen were helped by these measures. Both Citroen and General Motors have also benefited from being in assisted areas: Citroen in the Large Area of Industrial Expansion (GAEI) of Galicia and General Motors in the Industrial Zone (PPLI) of Figueruelas, Zaragoza. Special measures were taken to ensure the survival of Seat and its successful takeover by VW. In 1988 Ford was given substantial government assistance to build a new auto-electronics plant in Cádiz. In 1990 the regional government of Navarra offered a significant package of inducements to attract the Swedish truck manufacturer Scania to a site in Pamplona.

6.9 Electronics

The electronics industry forms part of the high-technology base of contemporary economic development. Spanish involvement in this sector has always been closely linked with foreign multinational companies (notably Telefónica with ATT), there being relatively little indigenous development. Liberalisation of the Spanish market has brought a wave of further foreign investment, actively encouraged by the government. As a result, with the one exception of Telefónica, foreign multinational companies completely dominate production in Spain, while consumption of personal computers and software is largely met through imports.

Industrial policy has sought to expand the high-technology base in Spain, both through specific sectoral policies and through broader industrial promotion schemes (for example substantial national and local government assistance was provided for the ATT-Microelectrónica plant in Madrid– $60 million in grants out of total investment of $200 million– and similar substantial assistance is being provided for the GEC plastics plant in Cartagena). One important sectoral policy was the National Electronics and Information Technology Plan (PEIN, 1984–7), providing assistance covering microelectronics, telecommunications and advanced automation. Industrial promotion schemes are illustrated by the recent development of science parks which, outside of those in Madrid and Barcelona, represent part of the drive by regional governments to attract high-technology industry. Despite these initiatives, investment in research-and-development facilities (predominantly concentrated in Madrid and Barcelona) still lags behind that in production plant, reflecting a skills shortage that the government is attempting to overcome through promoting technological education and training and closer scientific collaboration with European research institutes.

The principal telecommunications company is Telefónica (La Compañía Telefónica Nacional de España, CTNE), which had a monopoly over telecommunications in Spain until European Community regulations required the monopoly to be broken up. This was set in motion through the Telecommunications Law (Ley de Ordenación de las Telecomunicaciones, LOT), under which Telefónica lost its monopoly in all areas of telecommunications services (for example in the sale of terminals and value-added services such as information technology and telecommunications accessories) with the exception of the basic telephone service. The company is one of the largest in Spain, with international Stock Market quotations. Flotation on these international markets has been accompanied by an increase in foreign participation in the company from three per cent in 1982 to twenty-three per cent in 1987 (nearing the legal limit of twenty-five per cent), the state retaining a thirty-three per cent holding through the DGPE. In 1988 the value added by the company was three times that of any other Spanish company; it had the largest labour force, and the largest sales outside the oil sector (El País, 1990).

Beyond the provision of telephone services, other market segments are being divided between the major foreign multinationals. For example Alcatel-Standard Eléctrica (a subsidiary of Compagnie Generale d'Electricite of France) was joined in 1990 by ATT-Network Systems and LM Ericsson-Intelsa in the supply of telecommunications equipment and services, while in heavy electrical engineering GEC-Alsthom, Siemens and Asea Brown Boveri dominate. Many major foreign multinational electronics companies, including Fujitsu, IBM, Olivetti, Rank Xerox and Siemens, now have plants in Spain. IBM has factories at Fuente del Jarro and Puebla de Vallbona (Valencia) and a research facility in Madrid. During the 1980s it was the only significant export company in this sector, being one of the top ten exporting companies in Spain (El País, 1990).

Amongst the other multinational companies, most have chosen Madrid or Barcelona for the centre of their operations, especially for research and development (coinciding with an estimated two thirds of the market for information-technology equipment and being the centres of decision making for company development strategies involving electronics provision, especially the banks). Examples include the ATT-Microelectrónica plant, Siemens, Marconi and IBM research in Madrid. In Barcelona, Sharp opened a new factory in 1987 in San Cugat del Valles designed to produce televisions and hi-fi equipment. Outside of these two centres, IBM have a manufacturing plant in Valencia; Nixdorf Computers (now part of Siemens) have a plant in Toledo; Alcatel, Siemens and Fujitsu have plants in Málaga. Fujitsu entered Spain in 1975 through a joint venture with Telefónica and INI in the company Secoinsa. In 1985 Fujitsu became the major shareholder, forming Fujitsu España, SA in 1986 (which includes a forty per cent holding by Telefónica). The company also has research, development and production facilities in Madrid and Barcelona. General Electric (General Electric España) is building a silicon-and-plastics complex at Cartagena (Murcia) oriented towards exports (to begin operation in 1991).

The electronics and electrical-engineering sector illustrates the reorganisation policy being pursued by the government in an endeavour to establish more-competitive Spanish companies, safeguard employment and reduce government support to industry. Within INI the electronics companies have been grouped into the sub-holding company Inisel. Some companies have been exchanged between public enterprises. For example the INI holding in Fujitsu was transferred to Telefónica, Inisel shed its military telecommunications interests (the company Pesa) to Amper (a subsidiary of Telefónica) and the INI software subsidiary Eria is likely to be merged with Entel (a subsidiary of Telefónica). Other public companies are being sold to the private sector, many of them having been acquired in the late 1970s and early 1980s. For example Intelsa was sold by Telefónica to Ericsson. In industrial electrical engineering La Maquinista Terrestre y Marítima (MTM), Ateinsa and Macosa (subsidiaries of INI) were sold to GEC-Alsthom, which may also acquire the other major group in the industrial-electrical-equipment industry Cenemesa (formally Westinghouse España). Reorganisation of the defence electronics sector is being promoted by INI, involving an exchange of activities by which each company will specialise in a particular activity, or by merger. In the public sector Inisel is the major Spanish electronics group in the defence sector, although the aircraft group Casa also have defence interests. However, attempts to merge Inisel with the major private-sector company Ceselsa had proved unsuccessful by mid 1990.

Telefónica has also been undergoing rationalisation, hastened by the break-up of its monopoly. The company had already embarked on a programme of restructuring, involving the sale of some companies in the group, while participating in new ones. For example, Intelsa was sold to Ericsson while Telefónica formed ATT-Microelectrónica de España as a joint venture with the American company ATT. The joint venture is centred on a new factory at Tres Cantos (north of Madrid, opened in November 1987) designed to produce 1.75 micras custom-integrated circuits (semi-conductors) especially for export. Apart from joint investment in production, the Spanish government provided sixty per cent of the investment in grants and loans, plus the cost of technicians trained in the USA. Further restructuring led Telefónica to sell its holding in ATT Microelectrónica de España to ATT (leaving the American company as a substantial beneficiary of public assistance), to specialise in telecommunication services by taking a holding in ATT-Network Services.

6.10 Industrial restructuring

Three key features have characterised the industrial restructuring process: concentration of production (especially where entry is difficult for small firms and where the state or foreign capital have had significant interests); a slimming down of the public sector; and the growing penetration and domination of foreign capital, linked to an increased integration into multinational production systems within which Spanish companies occupy a peripheral position.

The most potent force for restructuring has been that of international competition and foreign capital. Where foreign companies have acquired Spanish companies or where Spanish companies have had major foreign shareholdings, rationalisation has followed. Equally, the pressure of foreign competition has itself forced restructuring.

The government's role is more debatable. On the one hand, direct state involvement in public enterprises and encouragement to the private sector, especially through the reconversion programmes, has brought about some radical restructuring. On the other hand, rationalisation of the public sector has been impeded by inter-ministry rivalry, and much of the government's effort under the banner of reconversion was clearly linked to political goals (particularly to the bargaining process with the trade unions). This resulted in an emphasis on salvaging selected traditional manufacturing industries and cushioning the social impact of recession, rather than on promoting new industry. As a result, reconversion may have been left too late to adequately prepare industry for a more competitive environment. Only a few industries have been completely overhauled; traditional manufacturing industry remains vulnerable to competition from the Newly Industrialised Countries, and Spain still lacks an indigenous high-technology base.

It is perhaps unrealistic to expect industrial restructuring to have kept pace with the speed and magnitude of change in the political economy. It may be possible to adopt new technologies quickly, but reforming business practices and educating and training a new labour force takes time. Restructuring has also been impeded by intense personal rivalries – exemplified by the conflicts between the banks, which exercise control over large swathes of manufacturing industry. Frequently private companies have preferred alliances with foreign companies rather than with other Spanish companies. Finally, the threat of competition has generally provoked a defensive reaction, with companies seeking to secure their existing domestic markets rather than seek new markets outside Spain.

A more open and flexible economy entails a number of strategic risks. The principal risk is that, shorn of market protection and exposed to tighter company control, large areas of Spanish industry will be be insufficiently competitive to survive, caught between competitiveness based on low-cost production and competitiveness based on new technologies (Nadal, Carreras and Sudria,1987). Foreign multinationals will dominate industrial production, leaving the country exposed to remote decision-making centres, peripheral to multinational empires and peripheral to the European market. Balanced against these risks is the possibility that Spanish industry will grow more vigorously within a competitive environment than it did within the framework of extensive intervention.

References and Bibliography

Banco de Bilbao (1984a) 'Geografía de la inversión industrial', *Situación* 3, pp.5–64
Banco de Bilbao (1984b) 'Los sectores industriales preferidos por la inversión', *Situación* 2, pp.5–75
Banco de Bilbao (1984c) 'Industrial reconversion', *Situacion* 1, pp.15–16
Banco de Bilbao (1987) *Informe Económico, 1986*. Bilbao
Banco de España (1989) *Informe anual*. Madrid

Berges, A. and R. Simarro (1987) in F. Maravall (ed.), *Eficiencia Tecnica en las grandes empresas industriates de España y Europe*, p.40–58

Carlota, S. (1985) 'El sistema asociativo empresarial en el sector textil español', *Papeles de Economía Española* 22, pp.187–200

Castano Collado, C. (1986) 'Nuevas tecnologías en el automovil: el caso español', *Economía Industrial* 252, pp.67–78

Donges, J. (1976) *La industrialización en España*. Barcelona: Oikos-Tau

Economía Industrial (1987) La industria de defensa en España, No. 253, pp.31–124

Economía y Finanzas (1987) Numero extraordinario dedicado al Salon Internacional del Automovil, No. 91, March.

El País (1990) *Anuario El País, 1990*. Madrid

Fabregat, V. *et al.* (1980) 'Problemas actuales y perspectivas futuras del sector textil-confección', *Papeles de Economía Española* 5, pp.168–83

Farré Terre, A. (1986) 'La regulación de la industría de automoción en España y sus relaciones con el desarrollo del sector', *Economía Industrial* 252, pp.27–43

García Fernández, J. (1989) 'La teoría de Stigler sobre la regulación como marco de la política empresarial pública 1973–1988', *Papeles de Economía Española* 38, pp.224–42

Hawkesworth, R. (1981) 'The Rise of Spain's automobile industry', *National Westminster Bank Review*, February, pp.37-48

Hernández Delgado, J. (1987) 'La Industria española en el primer año de adhesion de la CEE', *Economía Española* 2,095, pp.2781–5

Herrero, R. and F. Pallardo (1988) 'Aproximación a las fuentes de información de la economía Española', *Economía Industrial* 260, pp.123–37

Instituto Nacional de Estadística (INE) (1984a) *Censo Industrial 1978*. Madrid

Instituto Nacional de Estadística (INE) (1984b) *Encuesta Industrial 1978 a 1981*. Madrid

Instituto Nacional de Estadística (INE) (1989) *Encuesta Industrial 1983 a 1986*. Madrid

Instituto Nacional de Estadística (INE) (1990) *Encuesta de la Población Activa, primera trimestre*. Madrid

Jiménez-Alfaro, F. (1984) 'Panorámica de la industría de los fertilizantes en España', *Economía Industrial*, January No.235, pp.93–109

Maravall, F. (ed) (1987) *Economía y política industrial en España*. Madrid: Ediciones Pirámide SA

Maté, V. (1989) 'Sálvesa quien pueda', *El País*, (Sección Negocios, p.8) 10 September, p.8

Ministerio de Industria y Energía (MINE) (1987) *Informe anual sobre la industria española, 1986*. Madrid

Ministerio de Industria y Energía (MINE) (1989) *Informe anual sobre la industria española, 1988*. Madrid

Muñoz, J. et al. (1979) 'The growing dependence of Spain's industrialization on foreign investment', pp.161–175 in D. Seers et al (eds) *Underdeveloped Europe*. Hassocks: Harvester Press

Nadal, J., A. Carreras and C. Sudria (1987) *La economía española en el siglo XX*. Barcelona: Editorial Ariel SA

Ortún, P. (1988) 'Las ayudas e intervenciones públicas en los procesos de reconversión industrial', *Economía Industrial* 259, pp.103–12

Pérez Simarro, R. (1986) 'Situación comparativa de la industria española', *Economía Industrial* No.246, pp.21–31

Pozo, W. (1989) 'The brewing industry', *Aral* 1016, pp.29–36

Pujadas Forgas, J. (1985) 'Plan de reconversión del sector industrial', *Boletín de Estudios Económicos* XL, No.124, pp.33–42

Rivilla Barreno, I. (1986) 'Perspectivas estrategicas de la fabricación de automoviles de turismo en España', *Economía Industrial* 252, pp.45–66

Robles Teigeiro, L. (1988) 'La concentración en la industría española de fertilizantes en España', *Boletín de Estudios Económicos* XLIII, August, No.134, pp.307–29

Rodriguez, M. (1989) 'Los productos de bollera y pastelería en alza', *Aral* 1011, pp.56–9

Salmon, K. (1990) 'Regional policy and incentives', *in Spain: Trade and investment opportunities*, pp.59–68 London: Caversham Press

Tamames, R. (18th ed. 1989) *Estructura Económica de España 1*, Madrid: Alianza Editorial

Tamames, R. (1986) *The Spanish Economy*. London: C. Hurst & Company

Tizón, A. (1989) 'La salida del túnel', *El País*, 19 March Seccion Negocios p.7

♦ Chapter 7 ♦

The service sector

7.1 The service sector

Services constitute the largest and most diverse sector in the Spanish economy, with about fifty-four per cent of the occupied population and a further nine per cent in construction. Although there are significant spatial variations in the importance of services (dominating the economies of Madrid and the Mediterranean regions), the steady accumulation of employment in the service sector marks the most general characteristic of restructuring in the Spanish economy. Public administration, distribution (wholesaling and retailing), education, health, commercial services, communications, transport and tourism all fall within this sector. Construction too, with its close links to property development, may be dealt with alongside this sector. Each of the sub sectors mentioned above deserves its own chapter, but space alone must limit examples of structure and restructuring to financial services and retailing. Construction is included briefly to emphasise its importance in the economy. Tourism, as the most important industry in Spain, is dealt with in the final chapter.

7.2 Reforming the financial services-sector

Reforms, prompted by membership of the European Community, have brought liberalisation and the adoption of European Community standards to financial services: to banking, insurance, the Stock Exchange and accountancy. At least as much as in other sectors, financial services evolved in an isolated environment, focused on the domestic market, protected from foreign competition and regulated by government controls. This unique environment protected inefficient practices and allowed a multitude of small companies to survive. A more open and liberal regime has spurred competition, leading to a wave of restructuring covering the merger of domestic institutions, alliances with foreign companies, expansion abroad and the increased penetration of markets by foreign firms. In the public sector the state has generally been loosening its control and allowing public enterprises to broaden their capital base and adopt more market-oriented practices.

7.3 Banking

The banking system comprises the state banks, the commercial banks, savings banks and foreign banks. Within the private banking system, commercial banks retain a slightly larger share of all deposits than the savings banks (Table 7.1). Banks have been faced with change in the services that they perform and in the technological and economic environment in which they operate. For example, many banking activities now operate on a truly global basis, requiring global representation. Liberalisation in financial markets has created competition between banks and insurance companies in the field of policies that combine savings with insurance. Automation has opened the door to staff reductions in many traditional areas of retail banking, allowing staff to be redeployed in other areas of financial services.

Table 7.1 Distribution of deposits within the private banking system

Sector	Deposits	%
Spanish commercial banks	19,970	47
Spanish industrial banks	2,464	6
Foreign banks	440	1
Sub total	22,874	54
Savings banks†	17,042	40
Caja Postal	804	2
Co-operatives (rural and non-rural)	1,460	3
Sub Total	19,306	46
Total	42,180	100

* Figures for deposits are *recursos ajenos* at 31 January 1990, in pta. billion

† Savings banks includes all the Cajas de Ahorro Confederades
Source: *Ahorro*, 1990

7.3.1 Government intervention

Government policy has been directed at unifying the treatment of all banking institutions, liberalising the financial markets and reinforcing the system of regulation. Overseeing this process is the Spanish central bank, the Bank of Spain (Ontiveros and Valero, 1988). This institution was established in 1856 and nationalised in 1962 as an autonomous organisation within the Ministry of Economy and Finance (Ministerio de Economía y Hacienda). The Bank has been a significant influence in determining the leadership of the major commercial banks.

An example of the process of liberalisation is provided by the package of measures for deregulating the banking industry that were introduced in March 1987. This scrapped ceilings on interest rates on sight and short-term deposits (previously set by the Ministry of Economy and Finance), which had provided a source of cheap funds. Commissions for banking services were also freed. These measures followed a sharp reduction in the share of deposits (*coeficientes*), which banks were obliged to channel into government directed-investments. The system of '*coeficientes*' (due to be phased out in the early 1990s) involved a complex system of ratios whereby the government directed a large part (up to fifty per cent) of bank deposits into privileged sources of finance for the Treasury and other sectors. This privileged finance was available at below-market rates of interest, providing both a source of budget finance and a means of monetary control. Although the Bank of Spain can still require compulsory deposits to be retained with it (allowing control over monetary growth), the measures signified the virtual disappearance of privileged credit channels in Spain and will gradually liberate bank funds (as current bonds reach maturity).

7.3.2 The state sector

The state sector of banking covers the Bank of Spain and the Official Credit Institute (Instituto de Crédito Oficial; ICO). The latter supplies about ten per cent of the total credit to the private sector and manages development funds related to the European Community. Historically the ICO has received money from the Bank of Spain (via the *coeficientes*) and its major finance through the Treasury from ICO bonds. Loans from the ICO were made at about two per cent below market rates of interest. However, the ICO is being shifted into the private-sector banking environment. Under the Budget Law of 1988 (Ley de Presupuestos Generales del Estado, 1988) the ICO was converted from an autonomous organisation to a state company. This change of status enables the ICO to operate in much the same way as any private bank. Simultaneously, reductions in public sector expenditure and the '*coeficientes*' are obliging the state banks to seek an increasing proportion of their funds on the open market and to become more competitive.

The state banking institutions (Entidades Oficiales de Crédito, EOCs) are dependencies of the ICO. These state banks are:
i) Banco de Crédito Agrícola (BCA) was founded in 1925 as the Servicio Nacional de Crédito Agrícola, dependent on the Ministry of Agriculture. It was transferred to the Ministry of Economy and Finance in 1962.
ii) Banco de Crédito Industrial (BCI) was established in 1920 to provides finance to the industrial sector. In 1982 it absorbed the failed Banco de Crédito para la Construcción (established in 1939 to finance reconstruction after the Civil War), which had the largest volume of lending amongst the EOCs and had a major involvement in shipbuilding. The BCI has been one of the main recipients of loans from the European Investment Bank.
iii) Banco de Crédito Local was established in 1925 to provides loans (mostly long-term ones) to town councils, provincial councils and local firms.
iv) Banco Exterior de España (BEE) was established in 1923, operating as a private bank until it was nationalised in 1971. The bank became the agency for channelling export credits from official funds (Crédito Oficial a la Exportación). Its virtual monopoly of export finance came to an end when the market was liberalised in 1985.
v) Banco Hipotecario de España (BHE) was established in 1872. It is responsible for providing the largest proportion of all official credit (thirty-two per cent in

1988). The bank specialises in housing and construction finance. Traditionally it has provided finance for the purchase of 'protected' dwellings (Viviendas de Protección Oficial), but it has gradually been extending its lending to finance the construction, purchase and improvement of all housing.

Shifting the state banking sector into the private banking environment has required a determined drive to increase efficiency and to broaden the capital base of constituent banks. Their ability to compete in the private banking system is restricted by management used to working within the state sector, their centralisation and limited branch networks; the latter is a particular problem for the BHE (with about forty branches at the beginning of the 1990s, intending to expand to one in each province) and the BCA (with just a head office and four branches (two in the Islas Canarias)). Thus in order to provide a better service these banks must either establish new branches (as in the case of the BHE) or try to acquire an existing branch network (as in the case of BCA).

7.3.3 Commercial banks

Most of the commercial banks were established in the middle and late nineteenth century. In 1857 the Banco de Bilbao was established by the Chamber of Commerce in Bilbao. In 1901 the Banco de Vizcaya and Banco Hispano Americano were established. In 1902 Banco Español de Crédito was established in Madrid, followed by Banco Central in 1919. Banking reforms in 1962 (Ley de Ordenación Bancaria, which is no longer in force) forced specialisation into industrial or retail banking. In fact the new banks that were created were merely appendages of existing banks.

Restructuring was forced on the sector following the collapse of fifty banking institutions (including twenty in the Rumasa group) during the banking crisis between 1978 and 1982. In response to the crisis, the Deposit Guarantee Fund (Fondo de Garantía de Depósitos) was set up to ensure the security of deposits, and the major banks were obliged to assist in rescue operations. For example the industrial banks Banca Unión and Banca Urquijo merged to become Banco Urquijo Unión and were taken over by Banco Hispano Americano, then sold in 1988 to Banco March. Banca Catalana, which collapsed in 1982, is now a subsidiary of Banco Bilbao Vizcaya. The period was also marked by an expansion in bank branches. Between 1974 and 1985 the number of branches increased by 10,957.

Liberalisation and modernisation (especially the adoption of new technology) gradually penetrated the sector during the early 1980s, bringing the system into line with the norms and practices of the banking nations of Europe. The time frame for adaption was set by the seven-year transition period (from January 1986) granted to Spain under its European Community entry agreement.

Spanish commercial banks are small by world banking standards; they have extensive branch networks and have tended to be less efficient than banks in north-west Europe. In the late 1980s there were thirty-eight national banks, twelve regional banks and fifty-five local banks (a classification that is now only used for statistical purposes). No Spanish bank was ranked in the top fifty banks in the world in 1989, and only Banco Bilbao Vizcaya in the top one hundred. At the beginning of 1990 Banco Bilbao Vizcaya had deposits of about pta. 3,200 billion (Table 7.2). The leading five banks accounted for about fifty-six per cent of all deposits in the commercial-bank system, leaving scope for consolidation. Yet while the government has encouraged consolidation, rivalries between banks have hindered such development (for example the failed merger between Banco Central and Banco Banesto in 1989 and the management problems faced by the Bilbao Vizcaya group). There is a dense network of commercial-bank branches, numbering 16,697 on 31 December 1985 (one office to every 2,332 inhabitants, compared with 1:3,791 in Britain and 1:9,000 in West Germany; in 1988 there was a bank or savings bank office for every 1,303 people in Spain compared with 1:1,540 in France and 1:3,125 in Italy). The average of credits per bank worker was barely half the level of other European Community countries in 1985, and there were few employees per branch (less than ten employees per branch compared with about eighteen in France; Lerena, 1989). These characteristics contribute towards high costs (although the large number of branches also provides an excellent distribution system for selling financial products), which in the past were offset by the higher price of services. Competition is forcing these prices down and necessitating cost reductions: reductions that are being found in increased automation, in staff reductions (although staff are also being freed to

Table 7.2 Spanish commercial banks

Commercial banks	Deposits (pta. billion)*	Branches	Employment
Banco Bilbao Vizcaya	3,224	3,216†	32,941†
Banco Español de Crédito (Banesto)	2,445	2,236‡	16,900‡
Banco Central	2,347	—	—
Banco de Santander	1,988	—	—
Banco Hispano Americano	1,845	—	—
Banco Popular Español	989	—	—
Banco Exterior de España	885	—	—
Banco Intercontinental Español	746	—	—
Banco de Sabadell	637	258§	3,577§
Banco Atlantico	599	—	—
Banco Pastor	506	—	—
Banca Catalana	465	—	—
Barclays Bank	414	—	—
Banco Urquijo-Unión	353	—	—
Other	3,692	—	—
Total all banks	21,135	16,697‖	163,752‖

* Figures for deposits are *recursos ajenos* as of 31 December 1989

† The number of branches and employment at 31 December 1987

‡ The number of branches and employment at the end of 1987

§ Branches and employment in March 1989

‖ The total number of branches and of employment in December 1985

Sources: *Ahorro*, 1990; *Papeles de Economía Española* 32, 1987

market a broad range of financial services) and through branch rationalisation. Thus from 1986 through to 1989, employment in commercial banks decreased by an average of one per cent per year from 159,000 to 155,000 (these figures include foreign banks which increased their employment).

In many cases Spanish commercial banks control substantial commercial and industrial interests, giving them a significant role in restructuring outside the banking sector. Banco Banesto and Banco Central probably control the largest industrial empires (in May 1990 Banesto announced that it would float off its industrial holdings in a new holding company– La Corporación Banesto– which it claimed accounts for more than one per cent of Spain's economy). For example, Banco Banesto has major shareholdings in the construction company Agromán (seventy-one per cent in April 1989), the cement company Valenciana de Cementos, the mining and metals company Asturiana de Zinc and the engineering company Mecanizaciones y Fabricaciones (Mefasa). In the late 1980s Banco Central controlled the industrial companies Cepsa, Dragados y Construcciones, Unión Fenosa, Iberpistas, Autopistas del Mare Nostrum, Española de Zinc and Minas de Aznalcóllar, in addition to other banks and financial services (such as Banco de Granada, Banco Fomento, Banco Crédito y Inversiones, Banco Internacional de Comercio and Banco de Valencia), insurance and property companies. Banco Bilbao Vizcaya has major interests in numerous financial services and property companies along with large holdings in the industrial companies Kas and Metalquímica dei Nervión.

Traditionally Spanish banks have not been internationally oriented. For example, in 1989 the assets of the overseas branch network of the Banco Bilbao Vizcaya represented only 0.5 per cent of the value of its Spanish banking network, and eighty per cent of overseas assets were in Europe (Banco Bilbao Vizcaya, 1990). However, internationalisation has been a strategy favoured in the late 1980s, with many Spanish banks opting to form alliances with foreign banks rather than with other Spanish banks. Expansion into foreign markets is gradually gaining ground, with Portugal having been an early target. For example, Banco Banesto acquired a stake in the Portuguese Banco Totta e Acores during the latter's privatisation. Outside of Portugal Banco Bilbao Vizcaya (BBV) was planning an exchange of bank branches with Banque Nationale de Paris (BNP) under which BBV would swap forty of its branches and the Banco de Crédito y Ahorro (with forty-five branches) for BNP's Crédit Universel subsidiary (a bank specialised in consumer-credit facilities with 85 branches in France). This would be the first time a profitable mainstream bank has sold off a subsidiary. The deal would give BBV an important beach-head in Europe and allow BNP to expand its branch network in Spain. Other examples of overseas expansion and foreign alliances include the ten per cent holding of Banco Santander in the Royal Bank of Scotland (RBS), acquired in 1989; RBS has a reciprocal holding in Banco Santander. Banco Santander has also acquired a German subsidiary (CC Bank) and a Belgium subsidiary (Crédit du Norge Belge). Outside of Europe, Banco Santander has agreements with Japanese and United States companies. Similarly, foreign investment in Spanish commercial banks has been slowly increasing, amounting to between nine and sixteen per cent of the holdings of the five largest banks in March 1990.

Apart from structural changes and internationalisation, banks have also been diversifying into a broader range of financial services and have set up investment-banking divisions as part of the world wide move towards securitisation (for example Banco Santander de Negocios and Banco Hispano Industrial). Banks have evolved to become the financial intermediary between investors and borrowers, as well as being responsible for the payment systems and for liquidity in the economy generally.

7.3.4 Savings banks (cajas de ahorros)

The savings banks have expanded rapidly in the 1980s, following liberalisation in 1977 that allowed them to operate on a similar footing to commercial banks (although twenty-one per cent of profits were still channelled into charitable activities). The number of savings-bank branches increased by 4,000 between 1975 and 1985. Their share of total deposits increased from thirty-three per cent to nearly forty-six per cent in the period 1979 to 1989, making big inroads into mortgages, leasing, life insurance and a number of traditional banking services. In 1990 there were seventy-seven savings banks grouped into the Confederación Española de Cajas de Ahorros (CECA, which excludes the rural savings banks), with 12,350 branches; in addition to these there are the branches of the Post Office Savings Bank (Caja Postal, controlled by the Ministry of Transport, Tourism and Communications). The largest savings banks are La Caixa (the Caja de Pensiones para la Vejez y de Ahorros de Catalunya y Baleares; it was founded in 1904, and is also a pensions and insurance company), the Caja Postal (with 246 branches and access to 1,382 post offices across the country) and the Cajamadrid (Table 7.3).

Table 7.3 The savings banks

Savings bank	Deposits (pta. billion)*	Branches (Dec. 1986)	Employment (Dec. 1985)
La Caíxa	2,901	951	—
Madrid	1,637	700	—
Barcelona	1,105	441	—
Postal	814	246	—
Cataluña	734	—	—
Zaragoza, Aragón y Rioja	604	—	—
Galicia	587	—	—
Valencia	548	—	—
Mediterráneo (Alicante y Murcia)	467	—	—
Vizcaya	401	—	—
Other	9,738	—	—
Total all savings banks	19,536	12,610†	65,819

* Figures for deposits are *recursos ajenos* as of 31 December 1989

† Total number of branches in December 1985

Sources: *Ahorro*, 1990; Chislett and Vitzthum, 1987; *Papeles de Economía Española* 32, 1987

There are two types of savings banks, general savings banks and rural savings banks. They can be privately or publicly owned (state, provincial or municipal ownership). Many general savings banks were initially founded by the Church in the eighteenth century as non-profit-making institutions, and a small number are still owned by the Church. Roughly a third were founded by local governments (especially *diputaciones provinciales*).

Savings banks are run as foundations (there being no shareholders) through councils consisting of a prescribed mix of savers, employees and representatives of local authorities. Government legislation has required these councils to become more democratic and 'visible' (the majority of management boards in ordinary savings banks were renewed in elections in 1977). The governing councils then elect a president. The composition of these governing councils, on which political parties have seats, has been one of the major constraints on mergers between savings banks. Profits must be ploughed back into operations (thus ensuring that conditions of employment in savings banks are very favourable) or else put into public works benefiting the community (in June 1987 there was pta. 695 million in the Community Welfare Fund of the CECA).

Savings banks were tightly controlled by the state until the 1980s, predominantly concerned with private savings, and have been seen in the past as mechanisms for transferring capital from the less-developed to the more-developed regions. All savings banks were required to invest a substantial proportion of their deposits (targeted by compulsory investment coefficients) in fixed-interest securities and a slightly smaller proportion of their deposits in credits at privileged rates for specialised companies and projects (e.g. INI or subsidised housing schemes). Until 1951 they had to invest at least sixty per cent of their money in public funds. Since then the level of investment in official funds has been steadily reduced, reaching forty-one per cent of deposits in 1977 and then thirty-five per cent in early 1984. These investments were never evenly distributed. The principal recipients, both during the economic boom and since the crisis, were the more advanced and industrialised regions in the north. In Andalucía in 1982 it was estimated that roughly fifty-five per cent of the savings banks' obligatory deposits were invested in the north. There were also imbalance in those investments that were free, even though seventy-five per cent of them were meant to be distributed in the regions in which the banks operated. Regionalism has directed attention towards this territorial dimension of savings banks investments, prompting pressure for a greater level of investment in the home region.

Restrictions limiting the savings banks to their home regions were lifted in 1989 in return for restrictions on insurance activities (the decree concerning the expansion of savings banks was announced in June 1988 and published in the *Boletín Oficial del Estado* (BOE) in January 1989). Savings banks can now open offices outside of their region of origin (they were previously limited mainly to taking over rural savings banks in crisis outside of their home region), although La Caixa and Caja Postal had already developed a nation-wide branch network. Liberalisation has paved the way for sweeping mergers (Table 7.4). However, while mergers have constantly been discussed, they have been slow to materialise due to intense personality conflicts and local rivalries.

Table 7.4 Mergers and proposed mergers amongst the savings banks in the late 1980s

Proposed savings bank	Former savings banks
Caja de Castilla–La Mancha	Cajas de Toledo, Cuenca, Guadalajara, Ciudad Real and Albacete
Caja España	Cajas de Palencia, León, Zamora, Popular and Provincial de Valladolid (agreed in 1990)
Caja Mediterráneo	Cajas de Alicante, Murcia and Valencia
Unicaja	Cajas de Almería, Antequera, Málaga and Ronda
Ibercaja	Cajas de Aragón, Rioja and Zaragoza (in operation 1990)
La Caixa (Caja de Pensiones de Barcelona)	La Caixa and Caja de Ahorros de Barcelona (implemented in July 1990)

Note: Other proposed mergers: Caja de Cáceres and Caja de Plasencia; Caja de Monte de Piedad de Sevilla and Caja de Huelva (merger completed); Caja de Salamanca and Caja de Soria (agreed in June 1990); The *cajas* in País Vasco

Lifting of geographical restrictions followed a lengthy debate dating back to the late 1970s. Until 1977 all savings banks were restricted to the region in which they originated. Then in 1977 the largest were allowed to open branches in the five largest cities in Spain. The large Cajas (notably La Caixa and the Cajamadrid) favoured liberalisation to allow branch networks throughout Spain (branching), with at least fifty per cent of their offices outside of their region of origin by the end of 1992. They argued that this would allow them to compete on equal terms with the commercial banks and with any foreign savings banks that became established in Spain. They were supported in their proposals by the government and the Bank of Spain (which also wanted the large savings banks to absorb some of the ailing rural savings banks).

In contrast, the smaller and medium sized savings banks sought strict limits on territorial expansion, with no more than twelve branches of a savings bank outside its region of origin by the end of 1992. They argued that nation-wide expansion would result in a drain of savings away from poor regions to be invested in more prosperous ones, that foreign savings banks had not been inclined to expand outside their country of origin, and that there was the implicit threat of greater competition and a reduction in the number of savings banks. They were supported by the regional and local governments and by the commercial banks. A commission failed to reach an agreement on this issue in 1987, but the prospect of a single European market left little alternative to liberalisation.

Regional governments have been promoting mergers within their areas to ensure banks large enough to remain based in their region (Table 7.4). For example, in Castilla y León five savings banks merged in 1990 to form Caja España. In Andalucía there is a proposal to have one savings bank for eastern Andalucía and one for western Andalucía. In western Andalucía the savings banks Monte de Piedad de Sevilla and Caja de Huelva have merged. In the east, Unicaja will group the savings banks of Ronda, Málaga, Antequera and Almería.

This will make it the sixth largest in Spain, with over 3,000 employees and about 450 branches.

However, by far the most important merger has been that between La Caixa and Caixa de Barcelona (proposed in June 1989 and implemented in July 1990), creating the largest financial entity in Spain and the second largest savings bank in Europe (by deposits) after la Cassa di Risparmio delle Provincie Lombarde (Cariplo). The new group has a network of over 2,000 branches and over 11,000 employees; it had a combined balance sheet of more than $30 billion in 1989, and owns a broad portfolio of commercial and industrial interests (including important stakes in Autopista Concesionaria Española (forty-nine per cent), Autopista del Garraf (twenty-five per cent), Autopista Terrassa-Manresa (ten per cent), Catalana de Gas (thirty-one per cent), Fecsa, Tabacalera (two per cent), Telefónica (three per cent) and Túnel de Cadí (fifty-seven per cent).

Domestic rivalries have tended to divert attention away from policies designed to internationalise the savings banks. Nevertheless some of the larger ones have moved in this direction. The Caixa de Cataluña reached an agreement in 1989 with la Cassa di Risparmio di Genova y Imperia (Carige) to share services, thereby establishing a network extending from Rome to Málaga. The Caja Canarias was the first to expand into the Americas in 1987 with an office in Caracas, Venezuela.

The rural savings banks (*cajas rurales*) were co-operative ventures set up at the beginning of the twentieth century (numbering 501 in 1926). In 1941 they were integrated into the Organización Sindical, with the provincial rural savings banks forming the Caja Rural Nacional (CRUNA) in 1957. Smaller local rural savings banks (*cajas rurales locales*) were grouped into the Central de Cajas Rurales (CECAR) which had balances equal to about ten per cent of CRUNA. In 1971 they became the direct responsibility of the Bank of Spain. Rural savings banks only provided official credit and became characterised by poor loan management. CRUNA did not operate effectively as a supervisory body, becoming directly involved with the banks it was supervising (through, for example, common directorships). By the early 1980s the CRUNA group was in serious financial difficulties, threatening the stability of the financial system.

Severe economic problems among the rural savings banks led the government to seek reforms (including greater transparency in operation and tighter financial controls), rescue operations from other banks, and mergers (Table 7.5). Among the mergers proposed was that between the rural savings banks and the state agricultural bank the Banco de Crédito Agrícola (BCA). In 1983 all the rural savings banks made a global agreement with the BCA, followed in 1984 by individual agreements (between fifty rural savings banks and the BCA) made for three years. Thus in 1984 the Grupo Asociado Banco de Crédito Agrícola–Cajas Rurales (BCA–CR) was formed. If this grouping had solidified, it would have become the eleventh largest bank in Spain, and the largest in terms of the number of branches. The group specialised in finance for agriculture, fishing and related industries (including lines of official credit and short-term loans) and technical assistance to agriculture. The bank also channelled funds into agricultural projects from the Agricultural Fund of the European Community and from the BCI.

In the late 1980s many rural savings banks rejected the arrangements with the BCA and began to look for a foreign partner when ICO insisted that its subsidiary

Table 7.5 Expansion of the savings banks by absorption of rural savings banks in crisis

Savings bank	Rural savings banks absorbed
Cajamadrid	Caja de Crédito Mutual, Caja de Inversiones, Caja Rural de Madrid, Caja Rural de Gerona, Caja Rural de Reus, Caja Rural de Palencia (50% of branches), Caja Rural de Cantabria (50% of branches), Caja de Crédito de Granollers, Caja de Crédito de Mediterráneo, Caja de Crédito Industrial
La Caixa	Caja Rural de Talavera, Caja Rural de Palencia (50% of branches), Caja Rural de Cantabria (50% of branches)
Caixa de Barcelona	Caja Rural de Pirineo, Caja Rural de Almería, Caja Rural de Barcelona, Cooperativa de Alfarrás (part of finance), Cooperativa de Perelló (part of finance), Cooperativa de Calafell (part of finance)
Caixa Galicia	Caja Rural de La Coruña, Caja Rural de Pontevedra, Caja Rural de Orense
Caja de Ahorros de Salamanca	Caja Rural Provincial de Avila
Caja de Ahorros de Murcia	Caja Rural de Murcia
Caja de Ahorros de Aragón, Zaragoza y Rioja	Caja Rural de Segura-Cinca

Source: Hernández, 1989

should have a controlling interest in any merged group. Twenty-four rural savings banks (representing about seventy per cent of the pta. 1,000 billion of deposits held by the ninety-odd rural savings banks) joined with Deutsche Genossenschaftsbank (DG Bank, the umbrella organisation for West Germany's co-operative banks and the sixth-largest bank in Germany) to apply to open a new bank called Banco Cooperativo Español (BCE) eighty-six per cent owned by Cajas Rurales and fifteen per cent DG Bank. The new bank will centralise information and establish overall policy for its members, who will retain their existing branch networks.

7.3.5 Foreign banks

Foreign banks have gradually built up their presence in Spain after they were allowed to open full branches in 1978, although some foreign banks had established a much earlier presence (for example Crédit Lyonnais, Société Generale, Banco Nazionale del Lavoro, Bank of London and South America – the last opened in Spain in 1916). Bank of America went to Spain in 1965 to form a joint venture with Banco Santander, subsequently buying out its Spanish partner. In March 1987 there were forty foreign banks in Spain (twenty from the European Community) and ten Spanish banks were foreign controlled. In 1987 the share of total credit held by foreign banks (including Spanish banks controlled by foreign interests) had levelled off at around fifteen per cent.

During the 1980s foreign banks were limited to three branches (which required authorisation from the Ministry of Economy and Finance and the Bank of Spain) and there were limits on access to peseta savings. This meant that the only way to gain access to the full retail-banking system was through the acquisition of lame Spanish banks. Following the 1978 banking crisis and the first liberalisation, Banque Nationale de Paris, Barclays Bank, Arab Banking Corporation, Citibank and Bank of Credit and Commerce International bought networks from the Deposit Guarantee Fund. For example Barclays acquired thirty-eight branches from its acquisition of Banco Valladolid (in 1986 it had a total of fifty-five branches) and Citibank acquired Banco de Levante. In 1985 Chase Manhattan took over a small industrial bank (Banco Finanzas) and National Westminster Bank formed a joint venture (Nat West March) with the Mallorca-based Banca March (which had eighty-one Spanish mainland branches). In 1988 Nat West March acquired a Basque-based banking group and took a holding in Banco Hispano Americano and Banco Popular Español. In 1989 National Westminster Bank raised its participation in the joint venture to eighty-three per cent (from forty per cent), the group controlling 161 branches. Even after the beginning of 1993, when European Community banks will have full access to the Spanish market, it will be difficult for them to compete with the extensive branch networks of Spanish banks. Thus more acquisitions of Spanish banks are likely.

7.4 Insurance

Within Europe a widespread restructuring of the the insurance market has been taking place, stimulated by the prospect of a single European financial-services market in 1992. Insurance companies can already sell their products on the strength of a single license granted in the country of their head office. Fragmentation in the European industry has brought alliances in domestic markets and a search for foreign outlets. Banking and insurance interests have converged; the growth of life insurance business has attracted banks, while the distribution networks of banks has attracted insurance companies. As with banks, deregulation, competition and technology are converting insurance companies into international all-purpose financial institutions. One-stop financial shopping has become an increasingly attractive proposition.

Many European companies have been increasing their capital base to expand. For example the state owned French insurer Union des Assurances de Paris (UAP), Europe's second-largest insurance group, announced plans in 1990 to raise £1 billion in preparation for expansion and the Single European Market. The deal also sealed the alliance with Banque Nationale de Paris (BNP). The other two French state insurers (Assurances Generales de France (AGF) and Groupement des Assurances Nationales (GAN)) have been allowed to sell stakes to banks and foreign investors since February 1990.

In Spain the insurance industry has been characterised by a large number of small companies (Tables 7.6 and 7.7) and ownership by banks. The insurance market has been relatively small, reflecting a degree of under-insurance compared with other industrialised nations (total premiums being only 2.2 per cent of GDP in 1986 compared to over eight per cent in the United States and the United Kingdom). By far the largest volume of business in 1985 was in vehicle insurance, more than two and a half times larger than life insurance (Table 7.8). As a consequence of the initially small market and the high growth of the economy, most forms of non-life income grew rapidly in the late 1980s (Table 7.8), making it attractive to foreign investment. Net income from life premiums experienced exceptional growth as a result of the introduction in 1986 of 'single premium life policies' (*seguros de prima única*). Thus net premium income from life policies increased from pta. 417.1 billion in 1986 to pta. 571.6 billion in 1987, thence escalating to about pta. 1,400 billion in 1988. Over half of this income arose from single-premium policies, ninety per cent of which were sold by a dozen companies.

Table 7.6 Size structure of the insurance industry, 1985

Volume of premiums (pta. millions)	Number of companies
Less than 500	386
500–1,000	45
1,000–2,500	52
2,500–5,000	41
More than 5,000	27
Total	551

Source: *Economía y Finanzas Españolas 183–185*, 1986

Table 7.7 Major Spanish insurance companies, 1988

Net premium income (pta. billion)			
Life		Non-life	
Euroseguros	260.0	Mapfre Mutualidad	43.4
Rentcaixa	229.9	La Unión y El Fénix	39.8
Vidacaixa	225.1	Mutua Madrilena Automovilista	34.7
Plus Ultra	172.0	Winterthur	25.5
Caixa de Barcelona	72.4	Santa Lucia	22.9
Others	461.9	Others	284.9
Total	1,421.3	Total	451.3

Note: Leading insurance companies by sector in 1988 were: Vehicles Mapfre Mutualidad; Fire Catalano Occidente and La Unión y el Fénix; Health Sanitas; Personal Accident La Unión y el Fénix; Transport Musini
Source: *El País*, 1990

No Spanish insurance company is amongst the top ten in Europe (the largest, Mapfre, had a gross premium income in 1989 of less than ten per cent of the largest European group, Allianz). In 1988 there were about 450 insurance companies, many of them operating only in health and death benefits. Market fragmentation has been highest in personal accident, fire and vehicle insurance (in personal accident the five largest companies controlled only thirty-two per cent of the volume of business in 1988), while the greatest degree of concentration has been in health (the top five companies controlling seventy-one per cent of business in 1988; Table 7.8). In 1988 the top five non-life companies, had a combined market share of about thirty-seven per cent, compared with the top five life companies which had sixty-eight per cent of the life market. Foreign insurers had a combined market share of about thirty-five per cent.

Table 7.8 Volume of business and degree of concentration in the insurance industry

Sector	Percentage of business				Volume of business (pta. billion)	
	Largest company		Five largest companies			
	1985	1988	1985	1988	1985	1988
Vehicle	9.5	15.9	28.5	48.4	186.2	257.7
Health	17.1	26.0	50.5	71.2	62.4	73.6
Fire	8.5	11.9	23.0	41.9	46.6	70.1
Personal accident	4.6	8.2	17.4	31.9	—	33.3
Transport	17.7	15.5	48.9	49.1	—	30.4
Total non-life	—	9.6	—	36.9	—	451.3
Life	9.6	18.3	30.5	67.5	73.4	1,421.3
Total	—	—	—	—	575.70	1,872.6

Sources: Economía y Finanzas Españolas 183–5, 1986; El País, 1990

Since the mid 1980s a process of consolidation has been working through the industry, encouraged by the government and given a time frame by the seven-year transition period for financial services and the Single European Market in 1992. The insurance law of 1984 (Ley de Ordenación del Seguro Privado) was very important in providing the basis for the adaption of the insurance industry to an open market in insurance. Tighter capital regulations introduced in 1985 have also contributed to consolidation, as many companies were forced to close down (in 1987 alone, ninety-four companies were forced to close by the official regulatory body, the CLEA).

Many of the insurance companies in Spain are controlled by the banks, providing an extensive distribution system for selling insurance. For example La Unión y el Fénix is controlled by Banco Banesto, Vitalicio by Banco Central, La Estrella by Banco Hispano Americano, Hercules Español by Banco Exterior de España, Cénit by Banco Santander, Euroseguros and Aurora Polar by Banco Bilbao Vizcaya, Rentcaixa and Vidacaixa by La Caixa. Conversely the Mapfre group have diversified into banking, creating Banco Mapfre in 1990.

Apart from consolidation, Spanish insurance companies have been looking for foreign outlets. Many have opened offices in Portugal, while Mapfre has bought the Belgian reinsurance company Compagnie Internationale d'Assurances et Reassurances (CIAR) and has pursued a policy of expansion into Latin America, for example taking control of the South American reinsurance company Caja Reaseguradora de Chile.

Foreign penetration of the insurance industry has existed for some time (in the form for example of the Swiss companies Winterthur and Zurich), but increased notably in the late 1980s (in 1989 it was estimated that one half of the industry was in the hands of foreigners), not just through overseas offices but also through foreign participation in Spanish companies. Thus Allianz owns the company Cresa, BUPA owns Sanitas and in 1990 Norwich Union acquired Plus Ultra from Banco Bilbao Vizcaya.

7.5 Other financial services

The Spanish stock market has played only a very limited role in providing funds to the private sector. There are four markets, in Madrid (established in 1831), Bilbao (established in 1890), Barcelona (established in 1915) and Valencia (established in 1981). Overall, the stock market has been characterised by a narrow range of companies traded, limited trading times and excessively restrictive practices. Trading in shares, bonds and debentures was exclusively controlled by eighty-seven 'agentes', and insider dealing was rife. In 1987 only 312 companies were quoted on the Madrid market, with trading concentrated mainly on banks, public utilities and Telefónica, lacking a broad representation of the corporate sector. In fact the number of companies quoted had fallen from about 500 in 1978 as a result of the economic crisis. The crisis led many investors to withdraw their savings, with the consequent collapse of share prices and trading volumes. The share of stock markets in providing funds for the private sector fell from 19.6 per cent in 1975 to 4.2 per cent in 1981.

A new law governing the Stock Exchange in Spain was introduced in 1989. This set up a national stock exchange commission (Comisión Nacional del Mercado de Valores, CNMV) made up of five members appointed by the government plus the deputy governor of the Bank of Spain and the director general of the Treasury. Continuous trading was introduced and greater transparency in the market was sought. From 1989 any European Community company has been able to buy up to thirty per cent of a stock market firm; this rose to fifty per cent in 1991 and by 1992 any non-Community company will be entitled to do the same.

Accountancy has been another area dominated by practices uncommon elsewhere in Europe. As companies have sought stock-market quotations and a more public profile, so more transparent and internationally acceptable company accounts have had to be produced. Reform of accountancy practices and the need for many companies to present a reliable image (especially on the international scene) have allowed the major multinational accountancy firms to penetrate the Spanish market.

7.6 Retailing

Distribution in Spain (retailing and wholesaling) represents about twelve per cent of the GDP and employs directly about 1.7 million people (15 per cent of the labour force, larger than in many other European Community countries). Following a long period of inertia, distribution has been undergoing rapid change, involving increased concentration (overseen by the banks, public-sector companies such as Mercasa and Tabacalera, and foreign investment), greater foreign penetration and the wider application of new technologies.

The structure of retailing falls into two sectors: a traditional sector made up of a dense pattern of small, family-owned businesses, and a modern sector covering large stores, supermarkets, hypermarkets, shopping centres and small specialist shops. This dual distribution system is reflected in the density of distribution outlets, lack of concentration and a highly skewed pattern of sales. In the late 1980s there were three points of sale for every 1,000 inhabitants; the largest Spanish distributor accounted for only 2.7 per cent of total distribution (and the thirty leading companies for only thirty per cent of distribution); ninety-five per cent of the points of sale represented only fifty-four per cent of sales, while five per cent of points of sale (the modern sector) accounted for forty-six per cent of sales (Barrio, et al. 1990).

Changes in retailing have been associated with changes in consumer behaviour and work patterns, increasing consumer demand and more-efficient distribution systems. Traditional shops and street markets are yielding to supermarkets and hypermarkets, and routine shopping is shifting to edge-of-town and out of town shopping centres. Given the number of small stores in Spain, this trend presages a significant change in both the pattern of employment and, more broadly, in the pattern of life. In addition, the traditional mixture of land use across urban areas is changing to a pattern of greater spatial specialisation and concentration of functions, with city centres becoming dominated by office activities and the sale of luxury goods.

The traditional shop has been an integral part of Spanish society, frequently part of the family home and providing little more than a small supplement to household income. These small shops were often supplied through a lengthy chain of agents (a distribution system that added significantly to prices). Such shops are still important but are on the decline in the face of increased competition from modern shopping facilities. For example, one survey estimated that traditional shops declined from seventy-one per cent of food sales in 1975 to only thirty per cent in 1987 (Barrio et al., 1990), with a forecast further decline to only sixteen per cent in 1995. Another survey put the share of food sales from traditional shops in 1990 at about twenty-five per cent (Nielson Company, 1990). The Ministry of Agriculture estimate that the share of traditional shops in all food sales to households fell from 53.3 per cent in 1987 to 49.2 per cent in 1989, while food sales to households from supermarkets increased from 30 to 31.4 per cent and from hypermarkets from 3.5 to 5.8 per cent (Maté, 1990). Strategies for the survival of small shops have been specialisation and niche marketing (boutiques and delicatessens), the provision of value-added services, or the formation of associations for bulk purchasing.

The modern sector arrived very late in Spain (the first large department store opened in 1956, the first supermarket in 1960 and the first hypermarket in 1973) and its development was further retarded by the economic crisis of the late 1970s and early 1980s. However, from the mid 1980s there has been rapid growth, driven by rising consumer expenditure and fuelled in part by foreign investment, adding the names of an increasing number of multinational stores (including C&A and Marks and Spencer) to well-established ones such as El Corte Inglés, Galerías Preciados and Cortefiel.

Since the mid 1980s there has been an explosion of supermarkets, hypermarkets and shopping centres. Supermarkets have grown from nineteen per cent of all food sales in 1980 to thirty-one per cent in 1989, and are set to dominate food sales in the future. The first hypermarket was opened in Barcelona in 1973. Development was slow during the 1970s, making them a phenomenon of the 1980s, with more than eighty being built during the decade. In 1990 there were about 130 such establishments, with further stores being projected by 1992. The majority of the stores belong to one of four companies (accounting for about seventy-five per cent of hypermarket sales), three of which – Pryca, Continente and Alcampo – are owned by French groups, only Hipercor (a subsidiary of El Corte Inglés; Table 7.9) being Spanish.

Table 7.9 Leading retailers in 1988

	Sales (pta. billion)	Employment	Stores	Shareholders
Hypermarkets				
Pryca	212.5	—	27	Carrefour and Grupo March
Saudisa-Continente	147.0	7,840	16	Promodes, Banco Bilbao-Vizcaya
Alcampo	121.5	5,200	12	Auchamps
Hipercor	75.0	2,677	6	El Corte Inglés
Supermarkets				
Mercadona-Superette Group	81.0	5,900	103	
Eroski	47.2	1,592	116	
Diasa	39.8	1,100	309	
Digsa	33.1	775	163	
Sabeco	20.8	1,029	38	
Jobac	19.0	1,300	95	
Department stores				
El Corte Inglés	475.3	33,953	—	
Galerías Preciados	85.4	8,733	—	
Specialist clothes stores				
Cortefiel	28.0	2,500	70	
Zara	44.0	—	95	
C&A	6.0	450	6	

Source: Adapted from Barrio *et al.*, 1990.

Shopping centres too have mushroomed in the late 1980s. For example, between the summer of 1988 and November 1989 a dozen new shopping centres were opened, including Colombia, Galéria del Prado and Arturo Soría Plaza in Madrid, Boulevard Rosa Diagonal in Barcelona, Las Huertas in Palencia and the Kuo

Centre in Santander. Parquesur opened at the end of 1989 to become the largest shopping centre in Madrid, embracing 140,000 square metres, overtaking in size the 125,000 square metres of La Vanguada (opened in 1985). Parquesur contains 320 shops (and 6,000 parking spaces) including the hypermarket Alcampo, the department store Galerías Preciados, and C&A.

Foreign penetration of retailing is gradually building, although hypermarkets have from the outset been dominated by foreign businesses. Galerías Preciados was bought from the government by a South American group after the collapse of the Rumasa empire, and was sold on to the British Mountleigh group in 1988. C&A have developed a significant number of outlets in the 1980s and in early 1990 the first branch of Marks and Spencer opened in Madrid as a joint venture with Cortefiel (Marks and Spencer España is sixty-seven per cent owned by Marks and Spencer and thirty-three per cent by Cortefiel). The company envisaged opening a further ten stores throughout Spain by 1995.

7.7 Construction

The construction industry has been one of the largest sectors of the Spanish economy, accounting for between five and ten per cent of all employment (some one million people) and GDP, depending on cyclical and seasonal factors. The industry is set within a complex ownership structure embracing interlocking links with other construction companies, construction materials, financial institutions and property-development companies. For example, Banco Central has an important holding in Dragados y Construcciones; Banco Banesto has a majority holding in the construction company Agroman and also in the cement company Valenciana de Cementos; Grupo Construcciones y Contratas (Grucycsa, chaired by the Albertos) owns Portland Valderrivas (which in turn has the majority holding in the Torre Picasso in Madrid). The family-run Entrecanales y Tavora, SA has moved into the finance business with a merchant bank, Baninvest SA, and Grucycsa has a major shareholding in the construction company Focsa. Furthermore, spiralling property prices and property-tax loopholes (currently being closed through a detailed national catastral survey and changes in tax and property laws) have attracted a substantial property services industry, drawing finance from across the whole spectrum of the Spanish economy.

Ease of entry into the less sophisticated areas of construction has enabled a multitude of small businesses to develop (many operating in the submerged economy), although the majority of public sector works and a large part of all construction activity is undertaken by members of SEOPAN (Empresas de Obras Públicas de Ambito Nacional), comprising about 100 medium-sized companies. Even the largest company, Dragados y Construcciones (Table 7.10), is only of medium size by world standards. Thus unless there are mergers to create larger and more competitive companies, it is likely that the national construction companies will disappear.

The economic miracle brought an enormous volume of work for the construction industry, as the coastline was urbanised, the urban areas expanded and some of the infrastructure necessary for a modern industrial nation was established. Economic crisis brought contraction in the late 1970s and early

Table 7.10 Major Spanish construction companies, 1988

Company	Sales (pta. billion)	Employment
Dragados y Construcciones	156.0	11,692
Focsa	101.2	13,300
Cubiertas y MZOV	97.1	6,843
Entrecanales y Tavora	95.0	7,500
Ferrovial	86.2	3,660
Hasa-Huarte	73.0	4,406
Agromán	69.4	5,623
Construcciones y Contratas	47.3	6,339
Ocisa	35.9	2,484
Auxini	17.2	1,784

Source: *El País*, 1990

1980s, followed by a renewed boom in the second half of the 1980s. The construction industry grew by ten per cent per year in 1987 and 1988 and by thirteen per cent in 1989, with construction activity in 1989 (worth an estimated pta. 4.2 billion) exceeding the previous record year in 1974. According to various analysts, Spain will be the country in the European Community with the greatest demand for public works in the early 1990s; notable projects include the 1992 Olympic Games in Barcelona, the World Fair in Seville and a major communications infrastructure programme including the construction of new European-gauge, high-speed rail links. Added to this is the projected continuing growth of housing, leisure and tourism facilities.

The complexity of company ownership structures and the peculiar environment within which Spanish construction firms have operated (with contractors financing their own work for up to six months in advance of payment), have made it difficult for foreign firms to gain access to the Spanish market and to gain control of Spanish construction companies. Nevertheless, pressure from foreign firms built up in the late 1980s, especially as many major multinational construction companies pulled back from the Third World to establish cross border acquisitions and joint ventures in Europe. For example, in 1989 the German company Phillipp Holzmann (one of the largest construction firms in Europe) acquired a fifty per cent holding in Jotsa, having previously signed an agreement with Agroman; the French company Bouygues has several Spanish holdings, Heron International acquired forty per cent of the construction company Torcovir in 1989; and Hasa-Huarte was taken over in 1987 by a group headed by the Fiat civil-engineering subsidiary Impresit. In response, the larger construction companies have been expanding abroad (for example both Huarte and Dragados have acquired companies in Portugal and Ferrovial has acquired an Italian construction company).

7.8 Restructuring of the service sector

The service sector has emerged in the late twentieth century as the main source of employment and income in Spain; in this it is similar to other western industrialised countries. What distinguishes the service sector in Spain is the dominance of tourism, the scale of employment in distribution and construction, and the lack of exports apart from tourism (Cuadrado Roura, 1990): features of a peripheral economy.

Restructuring in the service sector is as widespread as in other sectors of the economy, impacting directly on the daily lives of Spanish people. In the past it has been precipitated by economic crises that have forced some companies into liquidation and others to rationalise their operations. In the late 1980s restructuring was driven by increased competition and technological change, and overseen by the banks, the government and foreign investment. Throughout the sector, excessive atomisation is giving way to concentration, domestic orientation to internationalisation, and semi-subsistence operation to greater commercialisation.

Considerable further restructuring is yet to come, resulting from integration in the Single European Market, changes in the political economy and broader currents of social change. In banking, defensive alliances, product diversification and domestic consolidation have been characteristic rather than international mergers, which may yet come. In the public sector there is still scope for rationalisation in financial services. For example, the problem of bank branch networks could be partly overcome by utilising the branches of the post office savings bank (Caja Postal); the competing services being offered by the Banco Hipotecario and the Caja Postal could be rationalised; and the state banks could embrace the insurance activities of the INI insurance subsidiary, Musini. Restructuring in the service sector will become increasingly visible as new forms of retailing spread and an increasing number of foreign company names appear on the street.

References and Bibliography

Ahorro, May 1990

Banco Bilbao Vizcaya (1990) *Annual Report 1989*. Bilbao

Barrio, J. *et al.* (1990) 'La distribución comercial en España', *El País*, 22 April

Berges, A. *et al.* (1990) *Internacionalización de la banca: el caso español*. Madrid: Espasa-Calpe SA

Casares, J. (ed.) (1987) *La economía de la distribución comercial*. Barcelona: Editorial Ariel SA

Chislett, W and C. Vitzthum (1987) 'Winds of change in Spain', *The Banker* 137, No.734, pp.103–13

Cuadrado Roura, J. (1988) 'El sector servicios: evolución, características y perspectivas de futuro', in J. García Delgado (ed.), *España: Tomo II, Economía*. pp.231–70. Madrid: Espasa-Calpe SA

Cuadrado Roura, J. (1990) 'La expansión de los servicios en el contexto del cambio estructural de la economía española', *Papeles de Economía Española* 42, pp.98–120

Cuadrado Roura, J. and M. González Moreno (1988) *El sector servicios en España.* Barcelona: Ediciones Orbis

Cuervo, A. *et al.* (1987) *Manual del sistema financiero: instituciones, mercados y medios en España.* Barcelona: Editorial Ariel SA

Cuervo, A. (1988) *La crisis bancaria en España 1977-1985.* Barcelona: Editorial Ariel SA

Economía y Finanzas (1986) Extraordinario sobre el seguro en España, Nos. 183–5

Economía y Finanzas Españolas 183–85 (1986) July–September. Madrid

Economia y Finanzas Españolas 188, (1986) December. Madrid

Economist (1990) 'European insurance', *Economist*, 24 February, pp.1–22

El País (1990) *Anuario El País 1990* Madrid

Financial Times (1986) 'Spanish banking and finance', *Financial Times*, 16 June

Hernández, S. (1989) 'La resaca de las fusiones', *El País* 23 April, Seccíon Negocios p.18

Lerena, L. (1989) 'La estrategía de la banca española ante el reto del mercado unico', *Situación* 1, pp.5–17

Maté, V. (1990) 'Con pan y vino', and 'Adiós, tendero, adiós', *El País* (Seccíon Negocios p.20) 11 March

Ministerio de Economía y Hacienda (1986) *Memoria del crédito oficial, 1985* Madrid.

Nielsen Company (1990) *Anuario/ Evolución Nielsen 1990.* Madrid.

Ontiveros, E. and F. Valero (1988) 'El sistema financiero. Instituciones y funcionamiento', in J. García Delgado (ed.), *España: Tomo II, Economía*, pp.367–430 Madrid: Espasa-Calpe SA

Papeles de Economía Española 32 (1987) *Sistema financiero: situación actual.* Madrid

Papeles de Economía Española 42 (1990) *España: una economía de servicios.* Madrid

Papeles de Economía Española 43 (1990) *Transformación financiera en España.* Madrid

Pelegri y Giron, J. (1985) 'El sector de seguros', *Papeles de Economía Española* 25 pp.173–88

Roldán Jiménez, A. (1989) 'Banca y seguro', *Situación* 2, pp.83–91

Sánchez Asiaín, J. (1988) 'Reflections on banking. Evolving parameters and new horizons', *Situacion*, March, No.16, pp.23–34

Tamames, R. (18th ed. 1989) *Estructura económica de España.* Madrid: Alianza Editorial

Torrero, A. (1982) *Tendencias del sistema financiero.* Madrid: H. Blume Ediciones

Torrero, A. (1989) *Estudios sobre el sistema financiero.* Madrid: Espasa-Calpe SA

White, D. (1985) 'Spanish banks gear up for EEC entry', *The Banker*, October, pp.25–9

♦ Chapter 8 ♦

Tourism

8.1 The tourist industry

The popular image of Spain is the one created by tourism. While this may be a distorted image, it nevertheless focuses on what is Spain's most important industry. With 54 million foreign visitors in 1989, bringing in $16 billion in foreign exchange, the industry is a key propulsive force in the economy. Apart from generating growth, tourism has been at the centre of both structural and spatial change, attracting investment into services, providing many of the new jobs in the service sector, and stimulating development around the coast.

Activities related to tourism permeate the economy, so increasing the difficulties of defining the sector. In major tourist areas almost all activities are either directly or indirectly linked to tourism, and yet few activities provide goods or services exclusively for tourists. Across the economy the hotel and catering industry is central to the sector (economic-activity group Hostelería y Restaurantes), but transport, the food-and-drink industry and construction are among the many closely linked sectors.

8.2 The growth of tourism

Tourism began to grow steadily during the 1950s, with annual growth rates in the number of foreign visitors averaging about fifteen per cent and the number of hotel beds increasing from 78,771 in 1951 to 150,821 in 1960 (Table 8.1). The momentum for growth was reinforced in 1959 by devaluation of the peseta and the opening up of the economy to foreign investment occasioned by the Stabilisation Act. The following year, the number of visitors increased by forty-six per cent over 1959, and thereafter continued to grow strongly throughout the 1960s and into the early 1970s. Growth was fed by an increasingly affluent population in north-west Europe, who were offered guaranteed sun in a country with a low cost of living, a stable society and government-controlled prices. The number of foreign visitors escalated from 4.2 million in 1959 to 34.6 million in 1973 and the number of beds in hotels from 142,000 to almost 700,000 (Table 8.1). Simultaneously the Spanish economic miracle of the 1960s increased disposable incomes within Spain, thereby stimulating domestic tourism.

The burgeoning tourist industry transformed fishing villages such as

Torremolinos into international tourist playgrounds. It engulfed regional economies, fuelled land speculation, spawned a multitude of service-sector activities, stimulated demand for agricultural and manufactured products, contributed to the high level of activity in the construction industry, and was a significant force behind cultural change. These developments, together with industrialisation in País Vasco, Cataluña and Madrid, were accompanied by a redistribution of the population: away from the agricultural regions of the interior towards the expanding industrial areas and the emerging urban tourist complexes around the coast. By 1981, seventy-five per cent of the population of Spain lived either in Madrid or in one of the provinces with a coastline. In the province of Málaga the population living in coastal municipalities increased from fifty per cent in 1950 to seventy-three per cent in 1986, swelling the resident population of Marbella, for example, from 9,629 to 74,807.

Table 8.1 Growth of tourism in Spain, 1950–89

Year	Visitors (million)	Hotel accommodation (number of beds)*	Current income (pta. million)	Index	Constant income (pta. million)	Index
1950	0.7	78,771‡	—	—	—	—
1960	6.1	150,821	—	—	—	—
1970	24.1	545,798	130,328	100	130,328	100
1975	30.1	785,339	230,682	177	130,476	100
1976	30.0	798,985	207,073	159	99,602	76
1977	34.3	803,747	313,163	240	121,006	93
1978	40.0	808,015	416,497	320	134,354	103
1979	38.9	806,552	—	—	—	—
1980	38.0	814,394	500,649	384	120,813	93
1981	40.1	811,700	—	—	—	—
1982	42.0	825,959	787,650	604	144,975	111
1983	41.3	834,536	990,000	760	162,562	125
1984	42.9	835,200	1,247,798	957	184,095	141
1985	43.2	843,337	1,374,700	1,055	186,425	143
1986	47.4	864,834	1,671,900	1,283	208,388	160
1987	50.5	886,699	1,826,400	1,401	216,193	166
1988	54.2	907,921	1,961,200	1,505	221,529	170
1989	54.1	918,649	1,924,000	1,476	203,490	156

* Hotel accommodation includes that in *hostales*

† Constant values based on the 1970 value of the peseta given in *Anuario El País*, 1990

‡ 1951

Sources: Banco Bilbao Vizcaya 1988, Banco de España, 1990; Secretaría General de Turismo

Faced with escalating demand, the private sector saw highly profitable opportunities in land speculation and development. The Spanish planning system was both unequipped and unwilling to control this sudden tide of development, offering as it did the opportunity of personal gain and both local and national economic growth. For the Franco regime it provided an invaluable economic support (especially as a source of foreign exchange) as well as tacit approval of the government (Valenzuela Rubio, 1985). During this period, tourist facilities grew like Topsy, leaving it for another generation to count the cost of disorderly urbanisation, much of which lacked an adequate infrastructure.

The boom in tourism faltered in 1974 with the onset of recession in the world economy. The number of visitors fell sharply and then stagnated for three years until 1977 (Table 8.1). Provision of new hotel accommodation was drastically cut back and many developments were left unfinished; thus the 798,985 beds in hotels in 1976 increased only to 806,552 in 1979. Similarly, income from tourism fell in the mid 1970s from its peak in 1973, real income not fully recovering until the 1980s (Table 8.1). This period of crisis prompted restructuring in the tourist industry, including the formation of larger hotel groups, a reduction in labour intensity (for example through the more widespread use of self-service facilities in hotels) and a switch towards the provision of apartment rather than hotel accommodation.

The late 1970s saw a recovery in the number of visitors but growth was once more interrupted by economic problems at the turn of the decade. Spectacular rates of growth resumed in the mid 1980s, reflecting the consumer boom in north-west Europe (especially in Britain, which accounted for over thirty per cent of the growth in foreign visitors between 1982 and 1987). Domestic tourism has also been growing rapidly within a buoyant Spanish economy. Optimism in the mid 1980s prompted significant further expansion of tourist accommodation, taking the number of hotel beds up to 907,921 in 1988. But this most recent upsurge in growth faltered again in 1989, catching many unprepared. Thus tourism in the Islas Canarias was forecast to grow by thirty per cent in 1989, but in fact the growth was negative. In 1990 further reductions in foreign inbound tourism have sent shivers through the whole tourism industry.

Just as over-optimism characterises periods of buoyant demand, so more pessimistic scenarios dominate troughs. A number of short-term factors could easily explain the interruption in growth in 1989: high interest rates reducing disposable incomes in north-west Europe (especially in Britain); exceptionally good weather in north-west Europe; a strong peseta, coupled with domestic inflation, and air-transport difficulties. Of more serious long-term concern is that growth may also have been halted by changing patterns of consumer demand (affected by a poor public image of Spanish tourism), new forms of tourism, long-haul holidays and more competitive alternative destinations (for example Morocco, Tunisia, Turkey and, most recently, eastern Europe).

These changes require strategic shifts in tourism development, especially the promotion of new tourism areas and new forms of tourism, coupled with improvements and remodelling of existing major tourist areas. The crucial problem is that an enormous supply of accommodation now exists that can only be filled through retaining a mass tourism market (the package-holiday market is estimated to represent about forty to forty-five per cent of the total foreign-tourism market), in which price competition is acute. The importance of this mass market will inhibit an Italianisation of the industry, that is, moving the industry away from the mass market and the mass-market image towards a higher-value added product.

8.3 The distribution of tourist accommodation

Tourist accommodation is provided in a variety of guises, from hotels to campsites and private accommodation (the term hotel is used here to refer to both 'hoteles' and 'hostales'). The total number of beds available for the use of tourists runs into many millions. Of this total only some 907,000 are in hotels and a further million in other forms of registered tourist accommodation; the remainder are unregistered and escape the official statistics. In 1989 forty-eight per cent of registered accommodation was in hotels, eighteen per cent in apartments, nine per cent in guest houses and twenty-five per cent on campsites. As a proportion of all tourist accommodation, that in hotels may represent about twenty per cent (anon.,1987a). Hotels are graded into five gold-star (hoteles), and three silver-star categories (hostales). About three quarters of hotel accommodation is provided in gold-star hotels (the largest proportion of this in the three-star category; Table 8.2). In 1989 there were 455 five and four gold-star hotels, 3,463 three, two and one gold-star hotels, and 6,592 silver-star hotels. There are also tourist apartments (96,270 in 1989), guest houses (casas de huéspedes), inns (fondas; 13,447 guest houses and inns in 1989), farm houses (casas de labranza), apartments and campsites. Unregistered accommodation includes second homes (which have increased in number from 800,000 in 1970 to over two million, an increasing number of them in the rural areas from which many present Spanish urbanites have migrated), apartments, rooms let in family houses, and unofficial campsites. Such facilities provide a flexible reservoir of accommodation against which registered accommodation must compete.

Table 8.2 Number of beds and bednights in hotels by type of accommodation, 1988

Accommodation	Number of beds	%	Number of bednights	%
Hotel 5 star	26,570	2.9	4,515,215	3.3
Hotel 4 star	123,974	13.7	26,135,232	19.0
Hotel 3 star	285,866	31.5	51,088,771	37.2
Hotel 2 star	143,660	15.8	22,664,699	16.5
Hotel 1 star	103,082	11.4	12,549,073	9.1
Hostal 3 star	11,375	1.3	1,483,555	1.1
Hostal 2 star	89,832	9.9	8,138,219	5.9
Hostal 1 star	123,562	13.6	10,763,531	7.8
Total	907,921	100.0	137,338,295	100.0

Source: Secretaría General de Turismo, 1989a

Registered accommodation is concentrated around the Mediterranean coast and in the major cities (Table 8.3). About three quarters of all accommodation is provided around the coast of the Mediterranean (including the Atlantic coast in the south), over one quarter of the total in the Islas Baleares and Islas Canarias. Urbanisation sprawls out around this coast, coalescing in high-density, high-rise agglomerations such as Torremolinos, Benidorm and Arenal: monuments to the tourist boom of the 1960s. Away from the Mediterranean coast, a further eight per cent of accommodation is provided in Santander and in Galicia, and five per cent in Madrid. Outside of these areas, pockets of accommodation are provided in the winter-sports resorts of the Pyrenees and across Spain in line with the distribution of population.

Table 8.3 Distribution of registered tourist accommodation (beds), 1988

Province	Hotel*	%	Guest house†	Apartment	Campsite	Total	%
Baleares	237,440	26.2	5,521	77,364	2,083	322,408	17.3
Gerona	76,351	8.4	10,126	18,714	73,089	178,280	9.5
Barcelona	62,841	6.9	24,374	6,053	44,924	138,192	7.4
Tarragona	29,573	3.3	4,062	27,453	64,356	125,444	6.7
Las Palmas	36,040	4.0	1,834	85,831	1,550	125,255	6.7
Málaga	51,825	5.7	4,510	35,213	10,764	102,312	5.5
Tenerife	50,421	5.6	2,404	39,053	700	92,578	5.0
Madrid	49,559	5.5	16,007	4,239	15,494	85,299	4.6
Alicante	50,545	5.6	3,401	7,431	21,343	82,720	4.4
Santander	11,387	1.3	2,696	1,025	26,878	41,986	2.2
Valencia	15,033	1.7	4,164	1,456	17,848	38,501	2.1
Castellón	11,075	1.2	1,975	7,640	16,095	36,785	2.0
Other	225,831	24.9	92,229	16,882	162,245	497,187	26.6
Total	907,921	100.0	173,303	328,354	457,369	1,866,947	100.0

* Hotels include *hoteles* and *hostales;*

† Guest houses include *fondas* and *casas de huéspedes*

Note: In 1989 there were 918,649 beds in hotels, 174,982 in guest houses, 335,803 in apartments and 470,358 on campsites; a total of 1,899,792

Source: Secretaría General de Turismo, 1989a

The spatial concentration of tourism has brought a form of saturated development to some areas (Torremolinos for example) together with substantial capacity, forcing fiercely competitive pricing and frequently allowing profitable operation only during the summer months. Some of this accommodation could be converted to residential use, should tourism demand evaporate (Salmon, 1985; such a measure was proposed by the regional government of the Islas Canarias in 1990). By contrast the majority of the interior has remained relatively undeveloped. Many sites of notable scenic and cultural interest, including the many national parks and nature reserves (such as Cazorla in the province of Jaén and Covadonga in Oviedo) have only recently been provided with modern tourism facilities.

Although the promotion of tourism away from the Mediterranean coast would help to raise regional incomes, the lessons of earlier development must be learnt, and tighter planning control enforced. Throughout the length of the coastline, lack of effective planning control has allowed many attractive landscapes to be blighted (Morris and Dickenson, 1987). In major resorts, visual pollution has been compounded by noise and water pollution. Additional public-service provision can go some way towards reducing these environmental problems, but they can only be installed at substantial public costs. Yet without such investment, tourists may begin to look elsewhere. The bulk of major tourist resorts are less than thirty years old; further investment in infrastructure and maintenance will be necessary if they are not to deteriorate rapidly into slums.

8.4 Foreign tourism

Foreign tourists take up more than half of all registered tourist accommodation. They are particularly important in the hotel sector, where in 1986 they accounted for sixty-eight per cent of 129.5 million bednights (INE, 1987a). The magnitude of the foreign-tourist market can be gauged in terms of the number of foreign visitors. In 1989 there were 54 million such visitors to Spain (including about three million Spanish people who are resident abroad), of which 35 million (sixty-five per cent) stayed for longer than twenty-four hours (0.2 per cent less tourists than in 1988). Ninety per cent of all foreign visitors are Europeans (Table 8.4), with about half of the Europeans coming from the neighbouring countries of France and Portugal (a large proportion of these are excursionists). The most important groups in terms of consumption are the British, the Germans and the French (about fifty per cent of all visitors). The former two nationalities dominate the official bednight statistics and are especially important for the hotel sector. In 1988 for example, visitors from Britain and West Germany represented only thirteen and fourteen per cent respectively of all foreign visitors, yet they accounted for twenty-three and eighteen per cent of all bednights recorded in hotels (SGT, 1989a). The dominance of these two nationalities in terms of hotel bookings is especially marked in the Islas Baleares and Islas Canarias (where over half of the visitors have tended to come from Britain and Germany). The British have also been particularly important for hotel bookings along the Costa del Sol. Such a concentration of demand indicates the sensitivity of Spanish tourism to variations in market conditions in European countries, especially Britain and Germany. They emphasise both the need to diversify the geographical pattern of demand and the need to extend the appeal of Spain to new market segments within established national markets.

Since 1974 growth in numbers of foreign visitors has come primarily from France, Portugal, Britain and West Germany in Europe, and from Morocco in Africa. Many factors affect the foreign demand for tourism, including the growth of disposable incomes in tourism source regions, holiday costs (affected by exchange-rate variations), exchange-control regulations, consumer tastes (influenced by publicity) and the organisation of marketing. Thus the miners' strike in Britain was a factor contributing to lower bookings from Britain in 1985, as was the bad publicity relating to bombing campaigns, crime and pollution in Spain. The French restrictions on foreign exchange reduced the numbers of French visitors in 1983. Mass tourism to Spain is recognised as being very price sensitive and thus vulnerable to price increases (which might come through either appreciation of the peseta or domestic inflation, both of which were affecting the industry at the beginning of the 1990s). However, given the volume of accommodation offered in Spain compared with that elsewhere in the Mediterranean, it is unlikely that a significant proportion of demand could be switched in the short term to other Mediterranean regions.

Table 8.4 Nationality of foreign visitors to Spain, 1976–89

Nationality	1976	%	1978	1980	1982	1984	1986	1988	1989	%
European
French	9.5	31.7	12.0	10.1	10.9	9.9	11.3	12.1	12.0	22.2
Portuguese	4.9	16.3	7.8	9.1	9.2	8.4	9.5	10.1	10.0	18.6
British	3.0	10.0	3.4	3.6	4.9	6.0	6.4	7.6	7.3	13.6
W. German	3.9	13.0	5.1	4.7	4.8	5.3	5.9	6.9	6.8	12.6
Scandinavian	1.2	4.0	1.6	1.1	1.3	1.5	1.8	2.4	2.2	4.1
Dutch	1.0	3.3	1.5	1.4	1.4	1.4	1.6	2.0	2.0	3.8
Belgian	0.9	3.0	1.2	1.0	1.0	1.0	1.1	1.4	1.4	2.5
Italian	0.4	1.3	0.5	0.5	0.7	0.8	1.1	1.3	1.5	2.8
Other European	1.1	3.7	1.6	1.7	1.6	1.9	2.1	2.4	2.6	4.8
Sub total	25.9	86.3	34.7	33.2	35.8	36.2	40.8	46.2	45.8	84.8
Non-European
American	1.3	4.3	1.6	1.5	1.5	1.6	1.5	1.6	1.7	3.1
African	0.9	3.0	1.6	1.5	2.2	2.7	2.7	3.0	2.9	5.3
Asian	0.2	0.7	0.2	0.2	0.3	0.3	0.3	0.4	0.4	0.8
Oceanian	0.1	0.3	0.1	0.1	0.1	0.1	0.1	0.1	0.1	0.1
Total foreign	28.4	94.7	38.3	36.5	39.9	40.9	45.4	51.3	50.9	94.2
Spanish*	1.6	5.3	1.7	1.5	2.1	2.0	2.0	2.9	3.1	5.8
Total	30.0	100.0	40.0	38.0	42.0	42.9	47.4	54.2	54.1	100.0

Note: Number of visitors in millions

* Spanish residents abroad

Sources: *El País*, 1990; Secretaría General de Turismo, 1989a

8.5 Domestic tourism

The domestic market for tourism is drawn from a population of 39 million (1990), relatively more youthful and with a lower disposable income than that in north-west European countries. These characteristics are reflected in the extent to which Spanish people use unregistered tourist accommodation and the small size of the outbound foreign-tourism market.

Spanish domestic tourism has been increasing, but remains distinctive in character to that of foreign tourism. The majority of Spanish people organise their holiday independently, with less than ten per cent using the services of a travel agent. Less than ten per cent of all bednights spent by Spanish tourists are in hotels (anon., 1987a), most people preferring to use their own second home (an increasingly common characteristic; Salvá Tomas and Socias Fuster, 1985; Barke and France, 1988) or the house of a friend, which results, in relatively stable tourism patterns. Most of the others prefer alternative self-catering accommodation. As a result, less than one third of all bednights spent in hotels were attributable to Spanish residents in 1988. Their average length of stay in hotels is also less than for foreigners (in 1984, 2.5 nights compared to 7.2 nights). In contrast, over half of all bednights in campsites were taken by Spanish people.

Outbound foreign tourism has expanded rapidly from a very low base level in the mid 1980s. In 1983 only about 0.6 million adults spent their holiday exclusively or mainly abroad. By 1988 it was estimated that sixteen per cent of all Spanish holidays were spent abroad. The most popular destinations are in Europe, especially France, Portugal, Italy and the UK. Excursions to the neighbouring countries of Andorra, France and Portugal are frequent.

8.6 The provision of hotel accommodation

The supply of hotel accommodation is provided essentially through the private sector. This sector has been characterised by a few large companies and a multitude of small ones, with a high proportion of domestic ownership. In 1982 only six companies offered more than 10,000 beds (Gutiérrez Fernández, 1984), the Cadena Sol hotel chain (Hoteles Mallorquines Agrupados) being the dominant group. In 1985 this Mallorca based chain (specialising in beach hotels, mostly in the Islas Baleares and Islas Canarias) owned ninety-three hotels offering 43,000 beds. In 1986 it acquired the Meliá hotel chain (sixteen hotels on the Spanish mainland and one on Tenerife, offering 9,071 beds, together with hotels in Venezuela, Iraq, Colombia and Morocco) to form the Grupo Sol Meliá. In 1989 the group owned 127 hotels, providing 34,790 hotel rooms and employing some 26,000 people. Other major hotel groups include the Barcelona-based Hoteles Unidos SA (Husa), with 125 hotels offering 22,000 rooms (the group is the largest catering company in Spain, owning Entursa) and Iberhotel, based in Mallorca with thirty-seven hotels offering 7,900 rooms (owned since 1983 by Touristic Union International of West Germany and a Spanish construction company). Concentration in the hotel sector has been slow, although greater than elsewhere in the industry. Thus in 1989 only forty per cent of hotels (sixty-five per cent of five star hotels) were integrated in a hotel chain or central reservation system; the

Sol Meliá group was still the only company with more than 50,000 beds (SGT, 1989b); and the sixty-five hotel chains in Spain covered only 200,000 beds.

Increasing competition has tended to hold down prices in the hotel sector, while operating costs have steadily increased. This has resulted in rationalisation, lack of investment and more concerted action by hotel owners over purchasing and the pricing of accommodation. Even in marketing, which has been left largely to the tour operators in the past, there has been an attempt to market particular hotel groups directly in foreign countries. Competition has brought the same trends as elsewhere in the economy: the formation of largër companies, increasing collaboration with foreign companies, and diversification. In 1984 Cadena Sol, in conjunction with the Kuwait Investment Office, bought the thirty-two hotels of the Hotesa group (Hoteles Agrupados SA, part of Rumasa, which had been appropriated by the government in 1983). In 1990 the Husa group (a family-owned firm) sold a twenty-seven per cent holding to the Arab investment group Agico (Arabian General Investment Corporation) and planned to float the whole group on the stock market in 1992, both measures designed to expand the capital base to support further growth.

Part of the increased competition has come from the growing interest of large multinational hotel groups in the country, including Hyatt International, Ramada, Trusthouse Forte (THF) and Holiday Inn. Sheraton operates the five-Star Son Vida in Palma de Mallorca and the Las Salinas in Lanzarote. Hyatt manages the Villamagna in Madrid and THF the Ritz in Madrid. Holiday Inn opened its first hotel in Spain (Madrid) in 1985. It has also invested in the construction of hotels in Sevilla and Barcelona and on the Costa Blanca (three-star hotels aimed at the business traveller), and in another ten establishments called Holiday Inn Garden Court. The latter offer low-priced, functional accommodation in towns of over 100,000, competing directly with more traditional Spanish accommodation. The pace of inward investment has continued to expand. In 1990 THF concluded a joint-venture agreement with the oil company Repsol to develop one hundred Little Chefs and Travelodges in Spain, and the French hotel groups Accor and Air France were looking to create hotel chains in Spain (especially through franchising arrangements under which hotels will operate mainly under the Ibis and Meridiane names respectively: three-star hotels located on the edge of cities and aimed at the business-traveller market).

In the public sector the state owns a chain of hotels (*paradores* and *albergues*) embracing eighty-five establishments (1989). The first *parador* was inaugurated by King Alfonso XIII in 1928 in Sierra de Gredos to facilitate hunting. This one was followed in 1929 by the Hotel Atlantic in Cádiz. Between 1928 and 1960 thirty-five buildings were opened. During the 1960s the chain was expanded with the addition of fifty new installations. In 1986 the chain provided over 8,672 beds in eighty-three establishments dispersed throughout Spain, offering a high standard of accommodation in traditional surroundings (frequently old castles and palaces). Following a period of reorganisation in the early 1980s, during which five *paradores* were closed (at Villacastín in Segovia, Pajares in Asturias, Marín in Pontevedra, Ojén in Málaga and Santa María de Huerta in Soria), the investment budget in 1989 provided for renewed expansion, including the opening of the *parador* of Cáceres. In the early 1990s it is anticipated that new *paradores* will open in Cuenca, Ronda (Málaga) and Santiponce (Sevilla). These new locations owe much more to careful consideration of viability criteria than previous sites did.

8.7 Travel agency and charter airlines

Travel agency remained atomistic in structure at the close of the 1980s, with only a few major groups, notably Viajes Meliá, Viajes Ecuador and Pullmantur. Viajes Meliá is an international travel agency group with over 300 offices in thirty-seven countries (1990); Viajes Ecuador too has offices abroad. The boom in tourism in the late 1980s has drawn many other companies into the business, notably El Corte Inglés (Tourmundial), adding further to atomisation.

The air-charter market is dominated by foreign companies, although in the late 1980s there have been attempts by Spanish companies to increase their participation. It is a high-risk business in which there is strong competition (especially from the major charter companies such as Britannia, Monarch and Dan Air), and a downturn in the market can quickly result in casualties. Spantax ceased operations in 1987 and was transferred to the DGPE. Another charter company, Hispania, also ceased operations in 1989 (in Britain, British Island Airways ceased operation in early 1990). Aviaco has transferred its charter operations to the newly formed Vuelos Internacionales de Vacaciones SA (VIVA), owned jointly by Iberia and Lufthansa. Iberia is also creating regional companies such as Binter Canarias. In Spain there were nine companies in 1989, which carried about five million passengers. In granting licenses to companies, the Dirección General de Aviación Civil (DGAC), part of the Ministry of Transport, seeks assurance in respect of experience in the business and some security that the companies will be able to find customers. Thus many of the Spanish air-charter companies have been formed with participation of foreign capital (for example Viva Air with Lufthansa).

8.8 Tour operators

In contrast to the atomistic supply of accommodation, a substantial proportion of foreign demand for tourism is channelled through a few large, foreign tour operators, such as Tourlatik Union International (TUI) in Germany, Spies and Tjaereborg in Scandinavia, and International Leisure and Thomson in Britain. These groups have gained their strength through control over the marketing of Spanish tourism in Europe. But they have also increased their proportion of tourist revenues through internalising a large part of tourism activities (providing package holidays), for example through affiliated charter-flight companies. The oligopolistic power of the foreign tour operators has allowed them not only to dictate the prices and conditions under which accommodation is offered, but also to exercise a strong influence over the pattern of tourism development. Their influence has been especially strong in the Islas Baleares and Canarias, and on the 'Costas'. In contrast, the tour operators have shown less interest in the interior.

8.9 Foreign investment

Since the 1970s foreign companies have been investing in tourism development. There is now significant foreign penetration in Spanish hotel chains (for example the German company TUI has a major holding in Hoteles Riu and a majority holding in Ultramar Express); the Italian company Parretti owns the travel agency Viajes Meliá; and most of the air-charter companies have foreign participation (for example the Swedish company Vingresor has a holding in Spanair, the British company International Leisure in Air Europa and the German company TUI a majority holding in Iberojet).

Investment in property development has been a major component of overall foreign investment. In many cases tourism facilities are provided in conjunction with broader property-development schemes. An early example of a combined property and tourism development was Sotogrande (Cádiz). In the 1980s the leisure company Brent Walker developed the marina complex of Puerto Sherry (Puerto Santa Mariá). A 450-hectare site on the Costa del Sol (at Benahavis) is being developed as a theme park (Montaña Mágica), and Anhauser Busch has proposed a substantial mixed-development complex, including a theme park, on a 833-ha site in Villa-Seca in Salou (Tarragona).

8.10 Economic and social dimensions of tourism

The relative merits of tourism as an agent of socio-economic development have been widely discussed (Kadt, 1979; Pearce, 1981; Torres Bernier, 1979), revealing significant costs alongside demonstrable economic benefits. Nationally, the growth of tourism provided an underlying dynamic to the economic miracle of the 1960s (Tamames, 1989), while drawing the Spanish economy into a more dependent relationship with external centres of decision making and demand, especially in Europe.

In major tourist areas the benefits of increased incomes, tax revenues, consumption and employment must be weighed against the additional costs of infrastructure investment, pollution, congestion, loss of land to non-tourist uses, the distortion of the labour market and investment patterns, and the alienation of the local population. During the major phase of tourism expansion, local/regional development was subordinated to national economic-growth requirements, including the generation of income that was then reinvested in the industrial areas of northern Spain and Madrid (Torres Bernier, 1979).

The importance of tourism within the national economy is borne out by the value of tourist consumption, direct and indirect consumption having averaged about ten per cent of the GDP since 1970 (in some regions its contribution is much higher; for example both the Islas Baleares and Islas Canarias are heavily dependent on tourism, and even in Cataluña tourism is estimated to contribute some fifteen per cent of GDP). The foreign-exchange element of this consumption is also of fundamental importance to the balance of payments. The net balance on the tourism account has always been positive and has enabled the financing of deficits elsewhere. In the late 1980s income from foreign tourism represented between twenty and twenty-five per cent ($16 billion in 1989) of the total income on the balance of payments current account (Banco de España, (1990)). This figure translated into between forty and fifty per cent of the value of all merchandise exports (forty per cent in 1989) and was sufficient to cover the merchandise trade deficit and help ease Spain into current-account surpluses. However, this was no longer possible at the close of the 1980s; the net balance on the tourism account in 1989 (reduced by lower earnings and higher expenditure) was unable to cover the escalation of the merchandise trade deficit.

Although Spain has received substantial income from tourism, there has been concern over the level of this income in relation to the volume of tourists. Income has been reduced as a result of the structure and organisation of the tourism industry, especially the extent of mass tourism through package holidays. In the 1980s it was estimated that less than half the cost of a package holiday finds its way into the Spanish economy (anon., 1987b; SGT, 1989b). Research by the Tourism Institute (Instituto de Estudios Turísticos) in Spain has consistently shown that average earnings per tourist are low in comparison with the world average. Thus although Spain occupied second place in the world in terms of the number of foreign tourists and foreign-tourism earnings in 1987, it was only seventeenth in terms of foreign-tourist expenditure per head (Trigo Portela, 1988). Expenditure per head appears lower still when calculated on a tourist/day basis As a result, while Spain received over 117 per cent more foreign tourists than Britain in 1986, foreign receipts were only some fifty-two per cent higher (Trigo Portela, 1988). The multiplier effect in Spain of total holiday expenditure by foreign tourists is reduced through tour operators' commissions, through money paid to the foreign charter-flight companies (often owned by the tour operators), and through money repatriated from Spain by foreign-owned activities.

The volume of employment offered in the tourism sector is another measure of its economic importance (anon., 1987c). The diffuse nature of the tourism sector, together with seasonality and the volume of informal employment mean that only rough estimates are possible. For example, in the hotel sector total employment in 1987 varied from 130,249 in August to 73,736 in December (INE, 1988). In 1990 the total number employed in tourism was put at 1.34 million: 800,000 directly employed (mostly in the hotel and restaurant sector) and 540,000 indirectly employed (Moreno, 1990; see also earlier estimates by Alcaide Inchausti, 1984 and Guillermo Viñeta,1988). The figure for total employment represents about ten per cent of the total economically active population. In spite of measures to reduce labour inputs the tourist industry remains labour intensive, necessitating the use of casual labour as a means of holding down labour costs to retain competitiveness in the international market-place. While there are social pressures to increase wages, average wages in the sector are unlikely to rise much in the face of very high levels of unemployment and the substantial numbers of people who are still in the agricultural sector.

Seasonality is an endemic problem in tourist areas, especially those that rely on climatic attractions. Some inland spas have a season as short as two months, and ski-resorts tend only to have a four-month season. Even the Islas Canarias and the southern Mediterranean coast, which offer warmth and sunshine for most of the year, cannot avoid the mould that traditional holiday periods impose on the length of the season. About half of all foreign visits to Spain are made during the three months of July, August and September, although seasonality varies both between locations and types of holiday (for example resorts in the south tend to be less seasonal than those in the north, and hotels exhibit less seasonality than campsites).

This seasonal pattern of demand creates financial problems in the tourist industry, distorts the labour market, necessitates the provision of expensive additional capacity in public services and infrastructure, and creates an annual cycle of apoplexy in season and anaemia out of season. Many hotels and other tourist businesses find it uneconomic to remain open out of season, and those that do remain open tend to reduce their staffing levels. As a result, substantial seasonal unemployment is a common characteristic of tourist resorts. Public transport, roads, water supply and sewerage facilities must all be able to deal with peak levels of demand, but seasonal congestion is still inevitable. Out of season, services and facilities are substantially underused. Diversification and discriminatory pricing policies are used to ameliorate these problems. Lower prices are charged out of season and there has been a particular attempt to attract the retired, who are not tied to fixed holiday periods. Attempts have also been made to break away from the narrow appeal of the climate, to encourage activity and special-interest holidays as well as business conventions.

The spatial pattern of tourism development has resulted in shifts in the pattern of regional incomes. In 1985 the Islas Baleares recorded the highest per capita family disposable income of the fifty provinces in Spain, compared with fourth position in 1969; Tenerife moved up to thirty-first from forty-first and Málaga to thirty-fourth from fortieth (Banco de Bilbao, 1987b). These changes in regional income reflect the stimulus provided by tourism to local economic activities and the resulting increased levels of income, consumption and employment. However, significant costs accompany these benefits. Such costs cover infrastructure investment, pollution, congestion (costs that show up as growth in regional incomes; Friedmann, 1983), loss of land to non-tourist uses, land- and house-price inflation, the distortion of the labour market and investment patterns, as well as the alienation of the local population. Furthermore, dependence of regions on tourism leaves them vulnerable to fluctuations in the fortunes of this industry.

The social dimension of tourism is less easy to measure than the economic one. Many factors, as well as tourism, have affected the evolution of Spanish culture. Undoubtedly the increased mobility associated with domestic tourism, and cultural contact with foreign tourists, have served to reduce isolationism and contribute to an acculturation process that has drawn Spanish culture towards that of north-west Europe. On the positive side this may be viewed as a process of enrichment and liberalisation. Conversely, the weakening of traditional social bonds, coupled with conspicuous consumption by tourists in areas frequently characterised by high levels of unemployment, have contributed towards rising crime rates in major tourist areas. Similarly, there is a danger that traditional culture will be overwhelmed and reduced to another form of tourist entertainment.

Tourism has also had a dramatic impact on the physical environment: a combination of natural amenities that have been fundamental to the growth of the industry. Rapid growth in the past has overwhelmed the planning system, leading to the despoliation of large expanses of coastline and creating intense local pressure on natural resources and public infrastructure in the vicinity of urban tourism complexes. This may have been forgivable in the past as the price of economic development. But a more prosperous economy can no longer afford to destroy the very basis of its most important industry. In this it is supported by stronger planning controls, a more adequate planning system, new environmental legislation and a growing awareness of environmental issues (Salmon, 1989).

8.11 Government intervention

The government influences the development of tourism both through general policies shaping the economic environment and directly through its ownership of tourism activities, provision of credit facilities, tourism marketing, development and training policies, the promotion of development, and planning controls. Regional governments have assumed responsibilities for regional structure planning and regional tourism development, while municipal governments are responsible for their own detailed planning, development control and promotion.

Amongst general policies, that on the foreign exchange rate has directly influenced competitiveness, while the policy of liberalising foreign investment in Spain has quickened the pace of private-sector tourism developments and increased foreign participation in the tourist industry. In the transport sector, government policy also plays a crucial role, for example in changing the accessibility characteristics of regions through spending patterns on transport infrastructure (for example expansion of the airport in Sevilla, the high-speed rail system linking Barcelona, Madrid and Sevilla, and the new motorway systems linking Madrid with Sevilla and Sevilla with the east-coast motorway), and in encouraging off-peak travel through transport pricing policy.

Within the central government, the Tourism Secretariat (Secretaría General de Turismo, SGT) of the Ministry of Transport, Tourism and Communications retains responsibility for national tourism policy and the co-ordination of tourism developments, although most responsibilities for tourism development have been devolved to the regions. The main agencies under the authority of the SGT are the National Tourism Institute (Instituto Nacional de Promoción del Turismo), which is responsible for research, and the promotion agency Turespaña (which also manages the exhibition halls in Madrid and Torremolinos). National overseas promotional activities are channelled through a network of national tourism offices in foreign countries, although individual regions, resorts and tourism organisations have increasingly adopted their own direct foreign marketing.

A chain of hotels (*paradores* and *albergues*), together with a number of official tourism and hotel schools (for example the hotel school in Marbella), are owned by the central government. A large proportion of the transport system falls within the public sector: the national airline Iberia, its subsidiary Aviaco and the charter airline Viva (in conjunction with Lufthansa); the railway system RENFE (which also runs an inter-city coach subsidiary, Enatcar) and FEVE; the shipping companies Transmediterránea, CTE and Elcano. In addition, municipalities own and operate their own urban transport.

State credit, involving lower rates of interest and longer repayment periods than generally available through commercial channels, has been used extensively to stimulate private initiative; however, the majority of funding for tourism development has come from the private sector, either internally financed or from private-sector finance houses (anon., 1987d). Grants have been available from the early 1970s within the context of a series of Hotel Modernisation Plans, with the main emphasis being on re-equipment, repair and refurbishment of existing hotels. Funds from the public sector have been available through the official credit agencies since 1942, and since 1965 specifically through the Banco Hipotecario de España (which now works in conjunction with the regional governments in channelling funds). However, to put the scale of recent public-sector finance in perspective, in the three years 1985 to 1987 tourist credit (*crédito turístico*) represented less than three per cent (pta. 3,273 million in 1987) of all annual credit provided under the policy of preferential credit (the majority being allocated to Viviendas de Protección Oficial); a small amount of other credit was also offered to the tourist sector under market conditions. In 1987 the tourist sector accounted for only 0.5 per cent (pta. 19,107 million) of all official credit (Banco Hipotecario, 1987).

Central-government policy in the 1980s has been directed at encouraging the continued growth of tourism (consolidating Spain's market leadership in the Mediterranean), while attempting to correct distortions and constraints on further development. The most serious problems have been perceived as over-reliance on a narrow market segment and the spatial and temporal concentration of tourism.

In confronting these problems the government has relied on measures to stimulate the private sector, on advertising campaigns during the 1980s directed at more 'up-market' tourism and aimed at promoting the interior (unknown Spain), and on diversifying the appeal of Spain ('*diversidad bajo el sol*'). However, these campaigns have been completely overshadowed by the literature supplied by tour operators. Apart from encouraging hotel improvements, emphasis is also being placed on camping sites, spas, golf courses and exhibition centres. Cultural facilities are being improved and new leisure parks built (with private capital). Diversification in the age structure of tourists is being sought, especially through promoting holidays for the elderly (Bardón Fernández, 1986). This group also offer the opportunity of extending the tourist season. Diversification of tourist sources is reflected in the marketing emphasis given to North America and Japan.

Regional, provincial and municipal administrations also sponsor tourism organisations and are increasingly promoting themselves (outside of Spain this promotion is normally channelled through the national tourism offices). In most regions grants have been available to municipalities to establish tourism offices (in Cataluña there were 109 offices in 1987) and there is public investment in tourism promotion (for example in the Consorcio de Promoción Turística de Cataluña (public/private body; anon., 1988). In the province of Málaga the Patronato de Turismo de la Costa del Sol is responsible for marketing the Costa del Sol both nationally and internationally. At the municipality level, Almuñécar (Granada) has promoted itself at international exhibitions outside of Spain as 'a tropical valley on the Mediterranean shore'.

8.12 Improving the coastal environment and promoting inland tourism

The pattern of tourism development has left coastal areas in need of renovation and protection while neglecting inland areas. The most important recent legislation affecting coastal tourism is that concerning the Law of the Coasts (Ley de Costas: Osorio Páramo and López Paláez 1988; Teixidor Roca, 1988). Under this law the coast has been placed under state authority (Zona de Dominio Público Estatal) in an attempt to improve current tourism provision, ensure public access to the coast (avoiding the privatisation of the coast), and prevent further deterioration of (and land speculation in) the coastal environment.

The new regulations confer much wider powers on the state in respect of the coast than existed before (Salmon, 1989). They also raise constitutional questions in relation to the treatment of private property (Article 33) and create potential conflict with the authority of the regional governments in relation to matters affecting the coast, ports, waste disposal and urban development. As a result the implementation of the law has been slow.

The promotion of rural tourism is seen as one of the means of revitalising rural areas and extending conservation, while diverting growth away from the congested coast and diversifying the tourism product (Salmon, 1989). Most regional governments have adopted appropriate policy measures. A variety of locations (historic towns, places of landscape quality, spas) and activities (climbing, fishing, horse-riding, hunting, winter sports) lend themselves to potential development, especially those areas in the vicinity of large towns and cities that can cater for the growing demand for excursions and weekend breaks. All these open up new sources of local employment and income.

A number of initiatives have emerged, including the development of family farms for tourism use and the improvement of information. Farm houses (*casas de labranza*) were introduced by the Ministry of Agriculture and the Ministry of Transport, Tourism and Communications in 1967. In 1983 the government of Cataluña began providing incentives to promote the establishment of similar rural tourist accommodation (*casa pagés*) to complement the income of farm families; by 1987 the first guide to these had been produced, listing forty-eight establishments. Better information has included improved signposting and the establishment of tourist routes such as the Route of the White Villages (La Ruta de Los Pueblos Blancos) in Andalucía. In 1983 the Consejo Superior de Investigaciones Científicas (CSIC) began to look for measures to manage and promote the rural areas. It undertook pilot studies in Vera (Cáceres) and Taramundi (Asturias) – both with natural tourism attractions – designed to identify and implement a series of tourism projects compatible with conservation and integrated with local life. The projects involved improved information and promotion, refurbishment of old buildings for accommodation, the improvement of recreational facilities (sports facilities, museums), commercialisation of local crafts and improved signposting. By 1984 a rural tourism policy had emerged (*Boletín Oficial del Estado*, 1984), involving small-scale, non-standardised, dispersed facilities, adapted to the natural and human environment (e.g. restoration of local architecture) within small units of space, with their own mini infrastructure (an example of such a programme being PRODINTUR,

Programas de Desarrollo Integrado de Turismo Rural en Andalucía). Developments should involve the local community, with the public sector providing funds for stimulating further private investment. A special programme exists providing assistance to spas anywhere in the country.

These initiatives provide the opportunity for diversifying economic activity, improving the provision of services and infrastructure, raising rural incomes and helping the rural areas to retain their populations. However, in many rural areas, although tourism may help to complement income from other sources, it is unlikely to form a commercially viable activity in itself. For this reason it may be difficult to attract private finance. Even where potentially viable projects exist, it may be difficult to find local entrepreneurs. Where larger-scale projects are identified, the challenge will be in enabling a form of development that does not destroy the rural environment, that ensures environmental conservation and the maintenance of indigenous culture.

8.13 The European Community and tourism development

European Community policies provide the context within which Spanish tourism policy is now framed: legislation, criteria for assessing the eligibility of tourism projects for Community funding and policy initiatives are echoed in Spain. This European context extends from general Community policies to specific tourism policy, rural development policy and financial assistance for regional development. In terms of general policy for example, the objective of a Single European Market has important implications for tourism, with the consequent freedom to establish tourism services anywhere within the Community and greater freedom of movement for people and capital.

Tourism policy in the European Community is designed to: i) foster the development of tourism within the European Community, ii) spread tourism more evenly through time and space, iii) provide a better integration of financial assistance through the various Structural Funds (Agriculture, Regional Development and Social Funds) and other financial instruments (New Community Instrument and European Investment Bank, EIB), iv) provide better information and protection for the tourist, v) improve the working environment in the tourist industry, vi) improve understanding of the sector through research, and vii) integrate conservation of the natural environment into development (Molina del Pozo and Pedernal Peces, 1987; Official Journal of the European Communities, 1986).

European regional-development policy has provided assistance for many tourism and tourism-related projects (including infrastructure projects such as improvements at Málaga airport). This is because a large proportion of Spain is classified as relatively less prosperous and therefore eligible for financial assistance in the form of both grants from the Structural Funds and loans from the EIB (from 1980–6 the EIB lent ECU 350 million for tourism projects throughout the European Community; e.g. marinas, hotels, small tourism firms; Regional Studies Association, 1988). Old industrial areas facing decline are specifically eligible for assistance, including that for tourism projects. In rural areas, assistance for tourism projects is also available from the European Agricultural

Guidance and Guarantee Fund (EAGGF), designed to broaden economic activity away from agriculture and to promote environmental conservation.

8.14 Restructuring tourism

In contrast to most other sectors of the Spanish economy, tourism has developed within the context of an international industry, in which Spain has found itself in a peripheral relationship to the core centres of demand and decision making in north-west Europe. Foreign companies have controlled marketing and many components of the tourism product, leading to a substantial 'leakage' of income from foreign inbound tourism. This, together with the small domestic foreign outbound tourism market and the character of domestic tourism, has prevented the development of an international Spanish tourism industry. What has emerged is a very competitive domestic industry, characterised by insufficient size and lack of vertical integration. Only in the hotel sector, and to a lesser extent in travel agency, has some degree of concentration appeared. In the next few years market pressures will induce further concentration in the industry (especially in the hotel sector) and further penetration by foreign capital. Only the larger Spanish hotel groups are likely to expand into foreign markets.

Unquestionably tourism is a vital ingredient of the Spanish economy. Restructuring the industry away from its dependence on low-cost foreign inbound package summer sun-and-sand holidays will be essential for its continued success. Whether or not this is successful will depend on changing popular perceptions of the tourism product (an image problem echoed elsewhere in the Spanish economy). Unfortunately the industry may be locked into the supply of a low-value added product (again a familiar scenario) by its peripheral position in the international tourism industry. It is also possible that without the formation of stronger Spanish companies, foreign companies will capture an increasing share of foreign outbound tourism. As the rest of the economy will come to realise, integration in the international economy can stimulate rapid growth, but only a form of growth that fits within an international division of labour.

References and Bibliography

Alcaide Inchausti, A. (1984) 'La importancia de nuestra economía turística', *Situación* 1, pp.26–49

anon. (1987a) 'Estudio de la demanda extrahotelera en España (informe resumen)', *Estudios Turísticos* 96, pp.19–53

anon. (1987b) 'El gasto turístico', *Estudios Turísticos* 93, pp.3–26

anon. (1987c) 'El empleo en el sector hotelero', *Estudios Turísticos* 94, pp.3–37

anon. (1987d) 'La financiación interior del turismo en España', *Estudios Turísticos* 95, pp.49–72

anon. (1988) 'Evolucion de los principales indicadores y macro magnitudes del turismo en Cataluña', *Horizonte Empresarial*, No.1,981, pp.18–22

Banco Bilbao Vizcaya (1988) Informe económico 1987. Bilbao

Banco de Bilbao (1987a) *Informe económico*. Bilbao

Banco de Bilbao (1987b) *Renta Nacional de España 1985*. Bilbao

Banco de España (1990) Boletín Estadístico, Abril. Madrid

Banco Hipotecario (1988) *Memoria 1987*. Madrid

Bardón Fernández, E. (1986) 'Viajes de vacaciones de la tercera edad en Europa', *Estudios Turísticos*, No.92, pp.77–94

Bardón Fernandez, E. (1987) 'El turismo rural en España', *Estudios Turísticos* 94, pp.63–76

Barke, M. and L. France (1988) 'Second homes in the Balearic Islands', *Geography*, Vol.73, pp.143–145

Boletín Oficial del Estado (1984) *Tourism policy*, 2 August, Madrid

Bote Gómez, V. (1987) 'Importancia de la demanda turística en espacio rural en España', *Estudios Turísticos* 93, pp.79–91

Clark, J. (1988) 'Spain and the Balearic Islands: National Report No.146', *International Tourism Reports* 1 (Economist Intelligence Unit), pp.5–28

Díaz Alvarez, J. (1988) *Geografía del Turismo*. Madrid: Editorial Síntesis

Esteve Secall, R. (1982) *Ocio, Turismo y Hoteles en la Costa del Sol*. Málaga: Diputación Provincial de Málaga

Figuerola Palomo, M. (1984) 'Instrumentos de política económica aplicados al turismo', *Situación* 1, pp.68–96

Figuerola Palomo, M. (1986) 'El sector hotelero en España', *Estudios Turísticos*, No. 91, pp.3–22

Figuerola Palomo, M. (1987) 'Las agencias de viajes en la comercialización turística', *Agent Travel* 1,No.4, p.18

Friedmann, J. (1983) 'Life space and economic space: contradictions in regional development', in D. Seers (ed.) *The crisis of the European regions*,Chapter 8. pp.148–162 London: Macmillan

Greenwood, D. (1972) 'Tourism as an agent of change', *Ethnology* 9, No.1, pp.80–91

Guillermo Viñeta, S. (1988) 'Política económica del turismo', *Horizonte Empresarial* 1,981, pp.10–13

Gutiérrez Fernández, D. (1984) 'Los problemas de las empresas turísticas en la actual coyuntura económica', *Situación* 1, pp.50–67

Instituto Nacional de Estadística (INE) (1986) *Encuesta de la población activa*. Madrid

Instituto Nacional de Estadística (INE) (1987a) *Movimiento de viajeros en establecimientos turísticos, Resumen Anual 1986*. Madrid

Instituto Nacional de Estadística (INE) (1987b) *Viajes de vacaciones, 1983*. Madrid

Instituto Nacional de Estadística (INE) (1988) *Movimiento de viajeros en establecimientos turísticos, Resumen Anual 1988*. Madrid

Jurdao Arrones, F. (1979) *España en venta: Compra de suelos por extranjeros y colonización de campesinos en la Costa del Sol*. Madrid: Editorial Ayuso

Kadt, E. (1979) *Tourism: passport to development?* Oxford: OUP

Marchena Gómez, M. (1987) *Territorio y turismo en Andalucía*. Sevilla: Junta de Andalucía

Marchena Gómez, M. (1988) 'La estrategia territorial de la nueva política turística en Andalucía', *Urbanismo* 4, pp.55–64

Miguelsanz Arnalot, A. (1984) 'La demanda turística', *Situación* 1, pp.5–25

Molina del Pozo, C. and J. Pedernal Peces (1987) 'Una contribución al desarrollo de las regiones europeas: iniciativas de la Comunidad Europea en materia de turismo.' *Situación* 3, pp.78–88

Moreno, M. (1990) 'Adiós a los días de vino y rosas', Poderoso operador", Hoteleros por libre", El País 8 April Seccíon Negocios p.3

Morris, A. and G. Dickinson (1987) 'Tourist development in Spain: growth versus conservation on the Costa Brava', *Geography* 72, No.1, pp.16–25

Naylon, J. (1967) 'Tourism, Spain's most important industry', *Geography* 52, pp.23–40

Official Journal of the European Communities (1986) *Tourism policy.* Brussels

Official Journal of the European Communities (1988) *Council Regulation (EEC) No.2052/88, on the Structural Funds. No.L185/9–20,* 15 July Brussels

Osorio Páramo, F. and L. López Peláez (1988) 'Proyecto de Ley de Costas', *Urbanismo* 4, pp.16–19

Pearce, D. (1981) *Tourist development.* London: Longman

Pérez, E. and E. Torres Bernier (1990) 'Realidad y Perspectivas del sector turístico', *Papeles de Economía* 42, pp.292–305

Promotores de la Costa del Sol (1974) *Esquema de planificación del desarrollo de la Costa del Sol Occidental.* Málaga

Regional Studies Association (1988), *Newsletter* 155

Salmon, K. (1985) 'Spain: National Report No.103', *International Tourism Quarterly,* Vol.3, (Economist Intelligence Unit), pp.20–41

Salmon, K. (1989) 'Tourism, the public sector and regional development in Spain', *Journal of the Association for Contemporary Iberian Studies* 2, No.1, pp.32–43

Salvá Tomas, P. and M. Socias Fuster (1985) 'Las residencias secundarias y la agricultura a tiempo parcial', *El Campo* 100, pp.59–62

Secretaría General de Turismo (SGT) (1987) *Aprovechamiento turístico integrado de los Picos de Europa.* 5 vols. Madrid

Secretaria General de Turismo (SGT) (1989a) *Anuario de estadísticas de turismo, 1988.* Madrid

Secretaria General de Turismo (SGT) (1989b) *Concentración y asociacionismo empresarial en el sector turístico.* Madrid

Tamames, R. (18th ed. 1989) *Estructura económica de España.* Madrid: Alianza Editorial

Teixidor Roca, J. (1988) 'Proyecto Ley de Costas', *Horizonte Empresarial* 1,981, pp.30–34

Torres Bernier, E. (1979) 'El sector turístico en Andalucía: instrumentalización y efectos impulsores', *Estudios Regionales* 1, pp.377–442

Trigo Portela, J. (1988) 'El Turismo: variable fundamental de la economía Española', *Horizonte Empresarial* 1,981, pp.6–9

Truett, D. and L. Truett (1987) 'The response of tourism to international economic conditions: Greece, Mexico and Spain', *Journal of Developing Areas* 21, No.2, pp.177–90

Valenzuela Rubio, M. (1985) 'Everything under the sun', *Geographical Magazine,* LV11, May, pp.274–8

Williams, A. and G. Shaw (eds.) (1988) *Tourism and economic development: Western European experiences.* London: Pinter Publishers

♦ Appendix 1 ♦

Glossary of Spanish terms

Government organisations

ayuntamientos: municipal councils
Boletín Oficial del Estado, BOE: Official State Bulletin
Comunidades Autonomas, CCAA: administrative regions
Delegación Provincial: provincial office of a central government ministry
Diputación Provincial: a local authority operating at the provincial level
Dirección General del Patrimonio del Estado, DGPE: Directorate General of
State Assets
Instituto de Crédito Oficial, ICO: Official Credit Institute
Instituto Nacional de la Pequeña y Mediana Empresa Industrial, IMPI: National
Institute for Small and Medium-Sized Industrial Companies
Instituto Nacional de Empleo, INEM: National Institute of Employment
Instituto Nacional de Hidrocarburos, INH: National Hydrocarbons Institute
Instituto Nacional de Industria, INI: National Institute of Industry
Instituto Nacional de la Seguridad Social, INSS: National Social-Security
Agency
Instituto Nacional de Reforma y Desarrollo Agrario, IRYDA: National Institute
of Agrarian Reform and Development
Instituto Nacional para la Conservación de la Naturaleza, ICONA: National
Nature Conservation Institute
Ministerio de Agricultura, Pesca y Alimentación, MAPA: Ministry of
Agriculture, Fish and Food
Ministerio de Industria y Energía, MINE: Ministry of Industry and Energy
Ministerio de Obras Públicas y Urbanismo, MOPU: Ministry of Public Works
and Urbanisation
Ministerio de Trabajo y Seguridad Social, MTSS: Ministry of Labour and Social
Security
Ministerio de Transportes, Turismo y Comunicaciones, MTTC: Ministry of
Transport, Tourism and Communications
Partido Socialista Obrero Español, PSOE: Spanish Socialist Party
Red Nacional de los Ferrocarriles Españoles, RENFE: Spanish national railways

Agriculture

agraria: refers to agriculture, livestock, hunting and forestry
agrícola: Refers to non-livestock farming only
cajas rurales: rural savings banks
Cámara Oficial Sindical Agraria, COSA: Agricultural Chamber of Commerce, operating at both the provincial and municipal level
Catastro de la Riqueza Rustica: rural land catastral record office (estd 1906) maintaining records of land ownership and land-use for taxation purposes
Comisiones Obreras del Campo, COC: Andalucian communist-affiliated agricultural union
Confederación Nacional de Agricultores y Ganaderos, CNAG: National Farmers' Organisation
huerta: irrigated upland area
regadío: irrigated land
secano: land farmed without irrigation
superficie agrícola utilizada, SAU: utilised agricultural land, including cultivated land and pasture
tierras labradas: cultivated land including land in fallow
tierras no labradas: uncultivated land, including pasture, scrub, woodland
Unión de Federaciones Agrarias de España, UFADE: farmers' employers' organisation
vega: irrigated lowland area

Business

Acuerdo Económico y Social, AES: Economic and social accord
bienes de equipo: capital goods
caja de ahorros: savings bank
compañía del holding: holding company
cotizaciones: contributions
empresa: company
filial: subsidiary
fusión: merger
impuestos: taxes
Impuesto sobre el Valor Añadido, IVA: value added tax, VAT
Impuesto sobre la Persona Física, IPF: personal income tax
mercado de valores: stock market
pagarés de tesoro: treasury bills
patrimonio del estado: state assets
prestaciones: benefits
Pequeñas y Medianas Empresas, PYMES: Small and Medium-Sized Industries
recargos: surcharges
reconversión: rationalisation and renovation
sucursales: branches
saneamiento financiero: financial improvement
sociedades anónimas: limited liability companies

sociedades colectivas: partnerships
sociedad conjunta: joint company
tasas: charges
tributos: taxes

Employer and labour organisations

Comisiones Obreras, CCOO: Workers Council, a trade union
Confederación Española de Organizaciones Empresariales, CEOE: Spanish
    Employers' Federation
Confederación Nacional del Trabajo, CNT: National Workers' Federation, a
    trade union
Confederación de Trabajadores Independientes, CTI: Independent Workers'
    Federation, a trade union
Unión General de Trabajadores, UGT: General Workers' Trade Union

Economy

balanza de pagos: balance of payments
Formación Bruta de Capital Fijo, FBCF: gross fixed capital formation
franco a bordo, fob: free on board, fob
Indice de Paridades de Poder de Comprar, IPPC: index of purchasing-power
    parities
Indice de Precios al Consumo, IPC: retail price index, RPI
Presupuestos Generales del Estado: State Budget
Producto Interior Bruto, PIB: gross domestic product, GDP
Producto Nacional Bruto, PNB: gross national product, GNP
Sistema Monetario Europeo, SME: European Monetary System, EMS
tipos de cambio: exchange rates

Legislative terminology

anteproyecto de ley: preliminary draft law
legislación básica: comparable to framework laws
leyes de base: same rank as ordinary laws
leyes marco: same rank as ordinary laws
leyes ordinarias: the bulk of laws passed
leyes orgánicas: the highest-ranking laws below the Constitution; they can only be
    approved by the Cortes
ordenes: next-highest-ranking laws to *reales decretos*
proyectos de leyes: draft laws
reales decretos: highest-ranking laws emanating from national or regional
    government departments
reales decreto leyes: royal decree laws; temporary legislative provision that must be
    debated by the Congress within thirty days, if approved becomes an ordinary

law
reglamentos: standing orders
titulos: sections

Regional development

incentivos regionales: regional incentives
Gran Area de Expanción Industrial, GAEI: Large Area of Industrial Expansion, a former assisted area
Sociedad para el Desarrollo industrial, SODI: state-owned regional industrial development agency
Sociedad para la Promoción y Reconversión Económica de Andalucía, SOPREA: Andalucian Economic Development Agency
Zonas Industrializadas en Declive, ZID: Industrial Zones in Decline
Zonas de Promoción Económica, ZOPRE: Industrial Promotion Zones
Zonas Promocionables: Assisted Areas
Zonas de Urgente Reindustrialización, ZUR: Priority Reindustrialisation Zones

European terms

Banco Europeo de Inversiones, BEI: European Investment Bank, EIB
Comunidad Económica del Carbón y del Acero: European Coal and Steel Community, ECSC
Comunidad Económica Europea, CEE: European Economic Community, EEC
Fondo Europeo de Desarrollo Regional, FEDER: European Regional Development Fund, ERDF
Fondo Europeo de Orientación y de Garantía Agraria, FEOGA: European Agricultural Guidance and Guarantee Fund, EAGGF
FEOGA, Sección de Orientación: EAGGF Guidance Section
Fondo Social Europeo, FSE: European Social Fund, ESF
Montantes Compensatorios Monetarios, MCM: Monetary Compensation Amounts, MCA
Nuevo Instrumento Comunitario, NIC: New Community Instrument, NCI
Operaciones Integrades de Desarrollo, OID: Integrated Development Programmes, IDP
Pólitica Agraria Común, PAC: Common Agricultural Policy, CAP
Programa Integrado del Mediterráneo, PIM: Integrated Mediterranean Programme, IMP
Programas Nacionales de Intéres Comunitario, PNIC: National Programmes of Community Interest, NPCI
Renaval: European programme for the redevelopment of shipbuilding areas
Resider: European programme for the redevelopment of iron and steel areas
Star: European programme for science and technology in assisted regions
tipo de cambio verde: green exchange rate of the Common Agricultural Policy
Tratado de Roma: Treaty of Rome

Unión Monetaria Europea, UME: European monetary union, EMU
Valoren: European programme for alternative energy in assisted regions

◆ **Appendix 2** ◆

Research sources

General economy

Aduanas, Revista de Comercio Internacional y Estudios Fiscales: Esic Editorial, Madrid; monthly, academic/factual

Anuario del Mercado Español: Banco Español de Credito, Madrid; annually, detailed statistical and geographical analysis

Anuario El País: El País, Madrid: annually, journalistic/statistics

Boletín Económico de ICE: Secretaría del Estado de Comercio, Ministerio de Economía y Hacienda, Madrid; weekly

Boletín de Estudios Económicos: Universidad Comercial de Duestro, Bilbao; monthly, academic

Boletín Oficial del Estado: Madrid; daily, record of the state

Coyuntura Económica: Confederación Española de Cajas de Ahorros, Madrid; bi-monthly, factual

Cuadernos de Ciencias Económicas y Empresariales: Facultad de Ciencias Económicas y Empresariales, Universidad de Málaga; bi-annually, academic

Cuadernos de Economía: Centro de Estudios Económicos y Sociales, Barcelona; tri-annually, academic

Cuadernos Económicos del ICE: Ministerio de Economía y Hacienda, Madrid; quarterly, academic

Estudios de Historia Económica: Banco de España, Madrid, académic

Estudios Económicos, Revista del Instituto del Estudios Económicos: Madrid; quarterly, academic

Guía Fiscal: C. Albiñana, Dunbar Vida y Pensiones; annually, tax guide

Información Comercial Española: Secretaría General de Comercio, Ministerio de Economía y Hacienda, Madrid; monthly, analysis of the contemporary economy

Investigaciones Económicas: Fundación del Instituto Nacional de Industria, Madrid; Ministerio de Industria y Energía, quarterly, academic

Moneda y Crédito: Editorial Moneda y Crédito, Madrid; monthly, academic/ analysis

OECD Economic Surveys (Spain): Organisation for Economic Co-operation and Development, Paris, academic

Papeles de Economía Española: Fundación Fondo para la Investigación

Económica y Social, Confederación Española de Cajas de Ahorros, Madrid; quarterly, analysis of contemporary topics

Pensamiento Iberoamericano: Instituto de Cooperación Iberoamericana, Madrid; bi-annually, academic

Presupuestos Generales del Estado: Ministerio de Economía y Hacienda, Madrid; annually, factual/statistical

Revista de Economía: Madrid; quarterly, academic

Revista Española de Investigaciones Sociológicas: Centro de Investigaciones Sociológicas, Madrid; quarterly, academic

Revista de Historia Económica: Centro de Estudios Constitucionales, Madrid, academic

Revista del Instituto de Estudios Económicos: Instituto de Estudios Económicos, Madrid; quarterly, academic

Revista Española de Investigaciones Sociológicas: Centro de Investigaciones Sociológicas, Madrid, academic

Situación: Banco Bilbao Vizcaya, Madrid; factual/academic

Statistical series

Banco de España:
a   *Boletín Económico*: monthly
b   *Boletín Estadístico*: monthly
c   *Informe Anual*: annually
d   *Informe Anual Apéndice Estadístico*: annually
    Instituto Nacional de Estadística:
a   *Anuario Estadístico de España (edición manual)*: annually
b   *Anuario Estadístico de España*: annually
c   *Boletín de Estadística*: bi-monthly
d   *Boletín Trimestral de Coyuntura*: quarterly
e   *Contabilidad Nacional de España Anuario de Estadísticas Laborales*: annually
f   *Encuesta Industrial*: annually
g   *Encuesta de la Población Activa*: quarterly, employment statistics
h   *Estadística de Sociedades Mercantiles*:annually
i   *Estadísticas sobre las Actividades en I + D*: annually
j   *Indicadores de Coyuntura*: monthly, statistical
k   *Informe anual*: annually
l   *Movimiento de la Población de España*: annually, statistical
    Ministerio de Economía y Hacienda:
a   *Estadística del Comercio Exterior de España*, Madrid: annually, statistical
b   *Informe de Coyuntura Económica*: monthly, economic statistics
c   *Síntesis Mensual de Indicadores Económicos*: monthly
    Ministerio de Trabajo y Seguridad Social:
a   *Boletín de Estadísticas Laborales*: monthly
b   *Anual de Estadísticas Laborales*: annually

Censuses

Instituto Nacional de Estadísticas:

a   *Censo Industrial de España, 1978*
b   *Censo de Locales de España, 1980*. 1982–6
c   *Censo de Población, 1981*: 1984–8
d   *El Padron, 1986*
e   *Censo de Viviendas, 1981*: 1984–8
f   *Censo Agrario de España, 1982*: 1985–8

Agriculture

Ministerio de Agricultura, Pesca y Alimentacion:
a   *Agricultura y Sociedad*: quarterly, academic
b   *Anuario de Estadística Agraria*: annually, statistics
c   *Boletín Mensual de Estadística*: monthly, statistics
d   *Indice Bibliográfico sobre Economía y Sociología Agraria de Revistas Españolas*: annually
e   *La Agricultura, la Pesca y la Alimentación Españolas en 1986*: annually, survey of MAPA activities
f   *Manual de Estadísticas Agrarias*: annually, statistics
g   *Revista de Estudios Agro-Sociales*: quarterly, academic
Agricultura, Revista Agropecuaria. Madrid: Editorial Agrícola Española SA; Monthly, trade journal
Aral, Semanario de Artículos Alimenticios y Bebidas: Tecnipublicaciones SA, Madrid; weekly, trade journal
El Campo: Banco Bilbao Vizcaya, Madrid; quarterly, factual/analytical/academic
Quaderns Agraris: Institucio Catalana d'Estudis Agraris, Barcelona; bi-annually, academic
Revista Galega de Estudios Agrarios: Servicio Central de Publicaciones, Xunta de Galicia, Santiago de Compostela; quarterly, academic
Agricultural Censuses: 1952, 1962, 1972, 1982 and 1989
Encuesta sobre la Estructura de las Explotaciones Agrícolas, 1987: Madrid: Instituto Nacional de Estadística, 1989

Minerals, mining and energy

Ministerio de Industria y Energía:
a   *Boletín Mensual de Coyuntura Energética*: Secretaria General de la Energía y Recursos Minerales; monthly
b   *Estadística de la Industría de Energía Eléctrica*: Subdirección General de Estudios y Promoción Industrial; annually
c   *Estadística Minera de España*. Madrid: Subdirección General de Estudios y Promoción Industrial; annually
d   *Industrias del Cemento, de la Cal y Yeso: Memoria anual*: annually
e   *Informe Anual sobre la Industria Española*: annually
    Instituto Geológico y Minero de España:
a   *Boletín del IGM*
b   *Revista Minera*

Boletín de la Industría Siderúrgica Española: Unesid, Madrid; quarterly
Memoria, Aserpetrol (Asociación de Empresas Refinadoras de Petróleo):
  Aserpetrol, Madrid
Memoria, Campsa (Delegación del Gobierno en Campsa): Campsa, Madrid
Memoria, Repsol: Repsol, Madrid
Memoria, Unesa (Unidad Eléctrica): Unesa, Madrid

Industry

Ministerio de Industria y Energía:
a   *Boletín Estadístico*: monthly
b   *Boletín Mensual de Coyuntura Energética*: monthly
c   *Coyuntura Industrial*: annually
d   *Economía Industrial*: bi-monthly, detailed factual
e   *Estadísticas de Carbones*: annually
f   *Estadística de Energía Eléctrica*: annually
g   *Estadística de la Industría de Energía Eléctrica*: annually
h   *Estadística Minera de España*: annually
i   *Estadística del Cemento*: annually
j   *Estadística de Prospección y Producción de Hidrocarburos*: annually
k   *Información Anual sobre Nuevas Industrias y Ampliaciones*: annually
l   *Informe Anual sobre la Industria Española*: annually
m   *La Industria Química en España*: annually
La Industria Siderúrgica Española: Unesid, Madrid; annually
Información Siderúrgica: Unesid, Madrid; monthly

Annuals

Agenda financiera: Banco Bilbao Vizcaya, Madrid; basic data on companies
  quoted on the Stock Exchange
Anuario financiero y de empresas de España: Grafinter; information on selected
  companies
Censo Oficial de Exportadores: Instituto Nacional de Comercio Exterior, Madrid;
  information on main exporting companies
Dicodi, Directorio de Sociedades, Consejos y Directivos: Grupo INCRESA, Madrid;
  basic information on more than 20,000 companies
Duns 15000: Principales empresas españolas: Dun and Bradstreet International;
  basic company information
Empresas extranjeras en las ciudades españolas: EDINSA, Madrid; basic company
  information
Kompass España: basic company information

Services

Banking and commerce
Ahorro: Revista Mensual de la Confederación de Cajas de Ahorros, Madrid:

monthly
Informe Anual: Banco de España, Madrid: annually
Banca Española, Revista del sistema financiero y mundo empresarial: Bank
  Marketing Association, Madrid; monthly, trade journal
Boletín Informativo: Banco Central, Madrid; monthly
Ministerio de Economía y Hacienda:
a   *Memoría del Crédito Oficial*: annually
b   *Hacienda Pública Española*: Instituto de Estudios Fiscales, Madrid
c   statistics on insurance kept by the Dirección General de Seguros

Construction

Informe Anual Sobre la Construcción: Asociación de Empresas Constructoras de
  ámbito nacional (SEOPAN), Madrid; annual review of construction industry
  activity

Tourism

Ministerio de Transportes, Turismo y Comunicaciones (MTTC), Secretaria
  General de Turismo, Madrid:
a   *Anuario de Estadísticas de Turismo*: annually
b   *Coyuntura Turística*: quarterly
c   *Movimiento Turísticos*: monthly
d   *Estudios Turísticos*: quarterly
e   *Revista del MTTC*: bi-monthly, essentially transport issues
  Instituto Nacional de Estadística (INE), Madrid:
a   *Movimiento de Viajeros en Establecimientos Turísticos*: monthly and quarterly
b   *Movimiento de Viajeros en Establecimientos Turísticos, resumen anual*: annually
c   *Encuesta sobre Viajes de Vacaciones, 1983*: 1987
*Patronato Provincial de la Costa del Sol: El Turismo en la Provincia de Málaga:
  Datos Estadísticos*: Diputación de la Provincia de Málaga, Málaga: annually
Editur: Ediciones Turísticas SA, Barcelona: weekly
Revista del Ministerio de Obras Públicas y Urbanismo: Madrid: monthly

General Business Magazines

Actualidad Económica: S.A.R.P.E., Madrid; weekly, journalistic. Includes an
  annual special edition listing the 100 largest companies in the world and the
  1,500 largest Spanish companies (by sales).
Dinero: Servicio de Publicaciones Económicas SA, Madrid; weekly, journalistic.
  Includes an annual special edition listing the 500 largest private companies in
  Spain.
Economía y Finanzas: Revista de Economía, Industria, Bolsa y Finanzas:
  Ediciones Periódicas Especializadas SL, Madrid; monthly, journalistic.
  Includes an annual special edition listing the 200 largest companies in Spain
  divided into twenty sectors.

El Economista: Editorial Defide SA, Madrid; weekly news sheet.
Fomento de la Producción: Ramón Baratech Sales, Barcelona; bi-monthly, journalistic. Includes an annual special edition listing the 2,000 largest Spanish companies (including their distribution).
Mercado: Semanario de Economía y Negocios: Estructura Grupo de Estudios Económicos SA, Barcelona; weekly, journalistic. Includes a special edition listing basic information on the 500 largest Spanish companies.

Business Newspapers

Cinco Dias: Madrid: Estructura, Grupo de Estudios Económicos, SA.
El País: El País, Madrid; (especially the Sunday edition)
Expansión: Madrid

◆ Appendix 3 ◆

Select bibliography

Casares, J. (ed.) (1987) *La economía de la distribución comercial*. Barcelona: Editorial Ariel SA

Díaz Alvarez, J. (1988) *Geografía del Turismo*. Madrid: Editorial Síntesis

Donaghy, P. and M. Newton (1987) *Spain: a guide to political and economic institutions*. Cambridge: CUP

Donges, J. (1974) *La industrialización en España*. Barcelona: Oikos-Tau

García Delgado, J. (ed.) (1988) *España: Tomo II, Economía*. Madrid: Espasa-Calpe SA

Giner, S. (ed.) (1990) *España: Tomo I, Sociedad y política*. Madrid: Espasa-Calpe SA

Harrison, J. (1985) *The Spanish economy in the twentieth century*. London: Croom Helm

Hooper, J. (1987) *The Spaniards: a portrait of the new Spain*. Harmondsworth: Penguin

Laxe, F. (1988) *La economía del sector pesquero*. Madrid: Espasa-Calpe SA

Lieberman, S. (1982) *The contemporary Spanish economy*. London: George Allen and Unwin

Maravall, F. (ed.) (1987) *Economía y política industrial en España*. Madrid: Ediciones Pirámide, SA

Marchena Gómez, M. (1987) *Territorio y Turismo en Andalucía*. Sevilla: Junta de Andalucía

Martínez Serrano, J. (*et al.*) (1982) *Economía española: 1960–1980*. Madrid: H. Blume Ediciones

Mochón, F. (*et al.*) (1988) *Economía Española 1964–1987*. Madrid: McGraw-Hill

Nadal, J., A. Carreras and C. Sudria (eds.) (1987) *La economía española en el siglo XX: una perspectiva histórica*. Barcelona: Editorial Ariel SA

Pablo Fusi, J. (ed.) (1990) *España: Tomo V, Autonomías*. Madrid: Espasa-Calpe SA

Segura, J. *et al.* (1989) *La industría española en la crisis 1978/1984*. Madrid: Alianza Editorial

Tamames, R. (1986) *The Spanish economy*. London: C. Hurst and Company

Tamames, R. (18th ed. 1989) *Introducción a la economía española*. Madrid: Alianza Editorial

Tamames, R. (19th ed. 1990) *Estructura económica de España*. Madrid: Alianza Editorial

Terán, M. and L. Sole Sabaris *et al.* (2nd ed. 1986) *Geografía general de España.* Barcelona: Editorial Ariel SA

Torrero, A. (1982) *Tendencias del sistema financiero español.* Madrid: H. Blume Ediciones

Torrero, A. (1989) *Estudios sobre el sistema financiero.* Madrid: Espasa-Calpe SA

Papeles de Economía Española. Madrid: Confederación Española de Cajas de Ahorros

No.14 (1983) *Energía*

No.16 (1983) *La nueva agricultura española*

No.29 (1986) *Economía minera española*

No.32 (1987) *El sistema financiero: situación actual*

No.38 (1989) *La empresa pública en España*

No.42 (1990) *España: una economía de servicios*

No.43 (1990) *Transformación financiera en España*

No.44 (1990) Economía de las Comunidades Autónomas: País Vasco

Index